The Western Landscape in Cormac McCarthy and Wallace Stegner

Routledge Transnational Perspectives on American Literature

EDITED BY SUSAN CASTILLO, *King's College London*

The Western Landscape in Cormac McCarthy and Wallace Stegner

Myths of the Frontier

Megan Riley McGilchrist

Routledge
Taylor & Francis Group

NEW YORK AND LONDON

First published 2010
by Routledge
270 Madison Avenue, New York, NY 10016

Simultaneously published in the UK
by Routledge
2 Park Square, Milton Park, Abingdon, Oxon OX14 4RN

Routledge is an imprint of the Taylor & Francis Group, an informa business

© 2010 Taylor & Francis

Typeset in Sabon by EvS Communication Networx, Inc.
Printed and bound in the United States of America on acid-free paper by IBT Global.

Library of Congress Cataloging in Publication Data

McGilchrist, Megan Riley, 1955–
    The western landscape in Cormac McCarthy and Wallace Stegne: myths of the frontier / by Megan Riley McGilchrist.
        p. cm. — (Routledge transnational perspectives on American literature; no. 12)
    Includes bibliographical references and index.
    1. McCarthy, Cormac, 1933– —Criticism and interpretation.   2. Stegner, Wallace Earle, 1909–1993—Criticism and interpretation.   3. Landscape in literature.   4. West (U.S.)—In literature.   I. Title.
    PS3563.C337Z77 2010
    813'.54—dc22
    2009022157

ISBN10: 0-415-80611-9 (hbk)

ISBN13: 978-0-415-80611-4 (hbk)

For Lucy, James, and Kitty

Contents

Acknowledgments

The author and publisher gratefully acknowledge permission for use of the following material:

Excerpts from *Exploding the Western: Myths of Empire on the Postmodern Frontier* by Sara L. Spurgeon, published by Texas A & M University Press, Copyright Sara Spurgeon, 2005.

Excerpts from "When You Wake," by Dianne Luce, published in *Sacred Violence*, edited by Rick Wallach and Wade Hall, published by Texas Western Press, 1995.

Excerpts from Susan J. Tyburski's essay "Wallace Stegner's Vision of Wilderness" are reprinted with permission of *Western American Literature*, where the essay was first published, Vol. 18, No. 2 (1983).

Excerpts from *The Late Modernism of Cormac McCarthy*, by David Holloway, published by Greenwood Press, Copyright David Holloway, 2002.

Excerpts from Nina Baym, "Melodramas of Beset Manhood: How Theories of American Fiction Exclude Women Authors," *American Quarterly*, Vol. 33, No. 2 (1981): 133, 135. Copyright Johns Hopkins University Press. Reprinted with permission of the Johns Hopkins University Press

Portions of Chapter 3 were first published as "The Adversarial Feminine in McCarthy's Western Landscapes," by Megan Riley McGilchrist, in *Cormac McCarthy: Uncharted Territories/Territoires Inconnus*, Textes coordonné par Christine Chollier, Presse Universitaires de Reims, Publications du Centre de recherche surl'imaginaire, l'identité et l'interprétation dans les littératures de langue anglaise, 2003. Reprinted by permission.

Advice and encouragement during the process of writing this book has been given by friends and family too numerous to mention. I owe them all a huge debt of thanks and affection. However, I would like to particularly acknowledge Dr David Holloway of the University of Derby, for his scholarly guidance and support.

I would also like to thank my children, Lucy, James, and Kitty McGilchrist, who have lived through this process with me, from

x *Acknowledgments*

beginning to end. Without their faith in me, their constant encouragement, and their confidence that this project would one day be completed, it certainly would not have been. They have lived with a mother far too occupied with questions of literature and landscape for far too long, and I only hope that the numerous trips that we have made to look at western landscapes have somewhat mitigated this fact. This has been in a very real sense their project as well as mine, and it is to them that this book is dedicated with all love.

Introduction

A Changing Landscape

In the second half of the twentieth century, the United States went through its most traumatic upheavals since the American Civil War. America's assumed role as the protector of the free world against what was perceived as inexorably encroaching Communist domination was, after the Second World War, a belief almost as deeply felt as the doctrine of Manifest Destiny had been a century before, and for many of the same reasons. The dream of the endless frontier of the nineteenth century had been transformed into the concept of worldwide propagation of "the American way" with remarkably little ideological difficulty. However, just as there were always those who questioned the tenets of Manifest Destiny, so too there were those who questioned the idea that American global hegemony was unquestionably benign. Crucially, it was the period of the Vietnam War, the 1960s and early 1970s, the culmination of the Cold War, which woke up large numbers of ordinary Americans to the reality that American policy was not always right, or heroic, or very much good for anyone who was not a white American, and that in fact it never had been. Accepted history, always questioned within the academy, was re-examined on all fronts. Along with the widespread civil unrest caused by the war, the civil rights movement precipitated an extensive reappraisal of the legacy of slavery, and created a new awareness of racial inequalities throughout American history. Additionally the women's movement gained momentum during this period, calling into question many accepted views of American domestic life. It was a turbulent period indeed, and on either side of it may be placed the two authors I am examining in this book, Wallace Stegner and Cormac McCarthy.

My purpose is to examine Wallace Stegner's works and the western works of Cormac McCarthy in terms of their approaches to western American landscape and nature. Stegner and McCarthy at first glance may not seem an obvious pairing. Stegner's fiction concentrates on character development, self-awareness, personal loss, and the search for sanctuary in a world seen as hostile, both physically and metaphorically. The action of his novels happens mainly in domestic settings, and relationships between men and women are the cornerstone of all his major fictional works. His questioning of the myth of the frontier is based upon both personal experience and environmental concerns, which are paramount in his works. His concern with the lives of women in the West marks him as a precursor to later feminist thinking.

In his western novels, on the other hand, McCarthy describes an almost totally male world in which it appears that women are absent or objectified to the point of misogyny, exemplifying an exclusively masculine ethos. The action of McCarthy's western novels is continuously mobile: domestic settings are transitory, and are often destroyed or repudiated. Characters seem never to grow, but simply continue in a self-destructive cycle of violence, repetition and loss.

Yet however different their works, I believe that Stegner and McCarthy have similar concerns with regard to the western American landscape, and a similar concern with the social, political, and human ramifications of the myth of the frontier. I believe the subtext in both authors is a deep questioning of widely accepted western mythic imagery, and a re-imagining, particularly in McCarthy, of these images and myths. While a feminist view of western imagery and iconography is clearly not stated overtly in McCarthy, the fact that much of the action of the novels of *The Border Trilogy* is based upon an assumption of female betrayal opens the door to a feminist interpretation of these works in terms of nature and landscape.

My premise in this study of these two authors is that they provide a hinge between ways of thinking before and after the cultural watershed of the 1960s and early 1970s in terms of their treatment of landscape, nature, and the myth of the frontier. The 1960s, as Ronald Lora pointed out, began as an optimistic decade, with a new, handsome, apparently idealistic young president and his beautiful, glamorous wife: Camelot. As the decade continued, however, everything began to change and assume new forms: the handsome president was murdered. Martin Luther King, the spokesman for non-violent civil rights, was himself killed. Malcolm X, the spokesman for radical civil rights, was also murdered. Violence exploded in the streets of American cities. Middle Americans

> feared that the center would not hold as the second half of the decade brought a floodtide of change with major social explosions over race, violence, youth, drugs, differing life styles, and the war in Indochina.[1]

These changes radically altered Americans' concept of their place in the world. The Vietnam War in particular contributed largely to the formation of a new American identity. John Hellman speaks of Vietnam as the "death-agony of the American idea of itself," causing a re-evaluation of America's role and motives in the international community.[2] This new world, in which America knew neither what it was nor, crucially, what it had been, is the period during which McCarthy wrote his western novels—novels which are set during the era of Manifest Destiny (*Blood Meridian*[3]); just prior to the Second World War (*The Crossing*[4]); and during the Cold War (*All the Pretty Horses*[5] and *Cities of the Plain*[6]). I suggest that all four novels are deeply informed by the post-Vietnam world, looking at the past through the lens of a present from which all illusion has been stripped.

Stegner, on the other hand, writes from a vantage point which is firmly placed before the revolution in thought of the 1960s and early 1970s. Although chronologically Stegner wrote during and well beyond this era, his perspective was not significantly altered by it, and remained fixed in what might be described as realism influenced by late Transcendentalism. Stegner's perspective, far from being outmoded or dated, as many of his contemporaries now seem to be, rather epitomizes the best of liberal western American thought before the watershed of the 1960s.

Therefore, by examining Stegner and McCarthy as I have suggested, as a "hinge," I am questioning the notion that between pre- and post-1960s representations of the West there is an unbridgeable chasm. I believe that Stegner and McCarthy reveal an evolution in thought about the West, which allows us to reconsider some of the values posited by an earlier way of thinking in light of the developments of post-Vietnam era analyses.

Stegner comes from a literary tradition which is based in nineteenth-century thought and assumptions, influenced by the Transcendentalist thinkers. This is coupled with a deeply felt environmental awareness which questions the views of landscape and nature largely accepted during his own early life. That is, Stegner casts a critical glance at attitudes toward the landscape which were culturally accepted by a significant cohort of American policy makers and by westerners in general during his lifetime. Because historically many westerners had viewed the western landscape as a consumable commodity, Stegner's activism in aid of environmental preservation, which began in earnest during the late 1950s, was especially important. His environmental awareness also took Stegner toward an articulation of a spiritual dimension of nature, like the Transcendentalists, which focuses upon the transformative power of nature and landscape. In addition, his view of landscape and nature has a feminine dimension in both his own approach to landscape, and to women's issues in regard to landscape. His refusal to sideline women's issues in an era before feminism had an audible voice in western studies marks him as an important precursor to the New Western History and ecofeminist thought.

McCarthy views western landscape from what may be described in some respects as a postmodern point of view, seeing it as a liminal space in which desires are both created and acted upon. McCarthy's western landscapes begin from the centre of the myths of the West itself, pastiching the traditional western novel in *The Border Trilogy*, and critiquing commonly accepted western history in *Blood Meridian*, to draw the reader's intellectual eye beyond the surfaces to the meaning within. McCarthy's environmental concerns are initially revealed in the sense of betrayal and loss felt by the characters in *The Border Trilogy* with regard to ownership of landscape, later compounded by an awareness of their placelessness, and the futility of their actions. This betrayal is linked to the idea of the betrayal by women in the novels, and the betrayals which women cause male characters to enact toward their comrades. I suggest that in this way, women represent the western landscape in McCarthy's *Border Trilogy*. This unspoken dimension in McCarthy's work is, however, distinct from feminine aspects of Stegner's work. By contrast with Stegner's works, women's roles are seen as adversarial to those of men in McCarthy's western novels. While desired, women also represent the containment of men that was abhorred in the traditional western ethos. This perception of women at odds with masculine desire is not so vividly depicted in Stegner's work, for the reason that Stegner's understanding of women in the West is based on less mythic, more empirical grounds than McCarthy's. Stegner's women are real people with all the complexities of real people. McCarthy's women, on the other hand, are less characters than useful representations, representing either betrayal or victimization, or in some very few cases, such as the character Betty in *Cities of the Plain*, the maternal. While McCarthy does have certain sympathies toward women, I suggest that in the novels their function is mainly to characterize the betrayal, either willed or as a result of forces beyond their control, which is equated with his western protagonists' sense of loss and abandonment in the western landscape. In McCarthy's 2005 novel, *No Country for Old Men*,[7] this portrayal of women is rather different, a point which I will discuss briefly, examining some aspects of the novel, particularly in relation to *Blood Meridian*.

The placelessness and futility felt by McCarthy's young cowboys is related to the economic disenfranchisement felt by those engaged in many traditional occupations which waned in importance in the wake of post-World War II industrialization and globalization. Additionally, McCarthy's characters' belief in the tenets of the frontier ethos, representing an idealized vision of American history, are revealed as both hollow in content and productive of further depredations on both people and landscapes.

*   *   *   *

Stegner gives us a sense that nature and landscape possess a positive agency of their own, whereas McCarthy's landscapes, though desired in *The Border Trilogy*, often remain malign, inexplicable, finally empty of both meaning and purpose, indicative of a force which acts against the desires of his protagonists. In this study, I propose to examine this difference and its significance in the larger picture of the American West. In doing this I am suggesting that the West, through its connection with the frontiering ethos, has a larger meaning in the understanding of America itself. While not going as far as Stegner's own somewhat contentious suggestion that the West is the "most American" part of the country—a suggestion which too easily opens the door to gender and racially based stereotypes—I argue that in its continued reliance upon received mythic imagery, and its easy placement within cultural archetypes which accompanied exploration and settlement, the West occupied a singular place in the American imagination which allowed its history to assume an iconic status.

Establishing the link between these two very different authors across the ideological divide of the 1960s and early 1970s is my primary purpose in this book. I am not suggesting that these authors have a narrative equivalence, rather that in their different treatments of landscape, nature, and the myth of the frontier—which will be discussed and defined thoroughly in my first chapter—they reveal the sea-change which overtook American thought both in and out of the academy during the turbulent years of the 1960s and 1970s. Stegner himself was critical of much late twentieth-century fiction[8] and might have found McCarthy's works on one level despairing and nihilistic. I hesitate to attribute opinions to living authors, but my feeling is that Stegner's overt articulation of old-fashioned morality might irritate McCarthy by its lack of opacity and perceived lack of subtlety, as well might the tacit assumption of a moral high ground in some of Stegner's works. (Although it must be noted that in his latest works McCarthy too has adopted the voice of old-fashioned morality as his own, particularly in *No Country for Old Men*.) Stegner's respect for women and female values is also a point of perceived contention between the works of the two authors. This perceived contention is suggested by the arguments of McCarthy's apparent misogyny posited by Nell Sullivan and others. This is a view which I will challenge with the suggestion that what appears misogynistic in McCarthy is in fact allegorical, his female characters functioning as representations within the novels.

I propose to look first at the mythic image of western American landscape and discuss how this representation conflicted with the actual history, as we are beginning to understand it, of the West. I will look at McCarthy's and Stegner's images of the West as both mythic and historically identifiable space. The West has always suffered from an excess of mythologizing. This excessive mythologizing has made western imagery, if not historically true, exceedingly familiar to us, its iconic ubiquity resisting challenges. By his critiquing of this familiar imagery of the West, McCarthy forces us to look behind these natural-seeming signs to look at the limited messages which they impart. Having become the objects of what Barthes calls "mythical speech," western images have attained a status which conflicts with the actual meaning of the West in terms of practical matters such as land usage, gender relations, race relations, labor relations, and development.

Stegner looks at western issues from an empirical point of view, based on experience and close observation of the western landscape. Of course, it may be argued that Stegner's views were colored by his own historical placement, gender, life experience, and personal inclinations. But all commentators are influenced by their own concerns. My point is that Stegner's perspective is *relatively* balanced and free of unexamined prejudice. Stegner, being a threshold writer, in my view, takes us from the older, myth-based perceptions of the West to the borders of postmodern perception of western history exemplified in McCarthy's works. While the conflict between myth and reality in the West has been discussed, it has not been discussed in relation to landscape and environment in the works of these authors seen as a pairing, and I believe the value of this examination will lie in the correspondences and contradictions revealed between the two writers, and the subsequent revelation of continuity, and the discussion of discontinuities, between what initially appear to be two very different views of western landscape and the natural world.

I will also examine the issue of the many manifestations of feminine landscape as they pertain to the American West in the works of Stegner and McCarthy. By "feminine landscape" I am referring to several aspects of landscape. In Stegner's works, the concern with the lives of actual women in the West is primary. His works are suffused with respect for the work done by women, and sacrifices made, and a real understanding of the difficulties of domestic life in a newly settled region. Stegner's observations are, as I have said, empirical, based on his life as a pioneer child, among other experiences. The second strand in any discussion of feminine landscape in the works of Stegner is the fact that he himself had an attitude which might be broadly characterized as "feminine," that is, protective and nurturing, with regard to the often abused western landscape. In addition, and perhaps most contentiously, Stegner's relationship to nature, characterized by epiphanic moments, which I will discuss, brings one very close thematically to the experiences of religious mystics in relation to God, which are often characterized as feminine in relation to a male Godhead. Although it would be impossible for any westerner not to see nature and landscape in adversarial terms, as well, I believe that the western landscape in Stegner's works is finally seen in its feminine manifestation as the source of being.

Stegner and McCarthy may not seem an obvious pairing on these aspects of the study of western American landscape. McCarthy's landscapes are feminine in the same sense as the women in his *Border Trilogy*: faithless, damaged, hopelessly desired, ultimately degraded. I believe this attitude toward the landscape may be elucidated by Annette Kolodny's description of the American land as female being another version of what is probably America's oldest and most cherished fantasy: a daily reality of harmony between men and nature based on an experience of the land as essentially feminine—that is, not simply the land as mother, but the land as woman, the total female principle of gratification...[9]

The *failure* of this image of landscape in its feminine manifestations is what frustrates and embitters McCarthy's boy protagonists, particularly John Grady Cole, always searching for that which seems to be rightfully his yet which is inexplicably denied. Therefore while some critics, most notably Nell Sullivan,[10] have suggested basic misogyny in McCarthy's writings, I argue that while landscapes represent the female, the women in his works also represent the landscape. In this interpretation, McCarthy expresses a concern for the landscape which is a more radically expressed articulation of Stegner's environmentalism, and which again links the authors in ways which are not immediately evident, but which resonate through both authors' works.

The land as female is a point which bears further discussion, particularly in reference to the critique of this concept which may be read in *The Border Trilogy*. As Simone de Beauvoir stated, "Man finds again in woman bright stars and dreamy moon, the light of the sun, the shade of grottoes."[11] That is to say, man finds in woman a reflection of what he has had, or wishes to have had, in nature. Nature therefore becomes the more significant partner, a point often commented upon with regard to early American literature. A harsher view of this phenomenon is commented upon by feminist critics Collard and Contrucci:

> In patriarchy, Nature, animals and women are objectified, hunted, invaded, colonized, owned, consumed and forced to yield and to produce (or not). This violation of the integrity of wild, spontaneous being is rape. It is motivated by a fear and rejection of Life and it allows the oppressor the illusion of control, of power, of being alive. As with women as a class, Nature and animals have been kept in a state of inferiority and powerlessness in order to enable men as a class to believe and act upon their 'natural' superiority/ dominance.[12]

While I do not propose to take my argument as far as Collard and Contrucci take theirs, there is certainly evidence for this kind of desire for dominance in *The Border Trilogy* and in the character of the Judge in *Blood Meridian*. One only has to remember John Grady's vaguely obscene speech to the stallion in *All the Pretty Horses* to see an aspect of this,[13] or to consider the Judge cataloguing aspects of the natural world and aspects of ancient history before destroying them.[14]

However, returning to the concept of the land as female in McCarthy's works, a final comment from Gillian Rose is apposite:

> Woman becomes Nature, and Nature Woman, and both can thus be burdened with men's meaning and invite interpretation by masculinist discourse...feminine figures can stand as symbols of places.[15]

Because woman has become nature, she has also become land, and in McCarthy's trilogy it is the perceived failure of the land and the natural world which so troubles McCarthy's protagonists, Billy and John Grady.

Running through these broader themes is the historical fact of America's involvement in the Vietnam War and the political and social shifts which were caused by the war, as well as the larger social changes which occurred during the 1960s and 1970s. I argue that the war is an essential element in the understanding of these authors, both by its presumed absence in Stegner, and by its veiled inclusion in McCarthy's *Blood Meridian*, prequel to *The Border Trilogy*, as well as the sense in which it informs much of the action of *The Border Trilogy*. The Vietnam War was in many ways the fulfillment of an aspect of the American frontier ethos, characterized by Richard Slotkin as an act of "regeneration through violence," a premise discussed in his eponymous study. I will argue that the war, and the Vietnam era in general, changed American life, and particularly life in the myth-bound West in ways that are still being revealed.

The importance of this argument lies in the fact that politically, much of American life and government policy is still dominated by the myth of the frontier. The re-examination of this myth, its sources and its effects, in my view, cannot be done often enough. Stegner and McCarthy re-examine the myth from either side of the watershed of the 1960s and the Vietnam War. In so doing, the two authors provide a link between more traditional views of the West as the home of heroism and hope, and the extreme postmodern perception of the West as hollow simulacrum of reality, as suggested by Baudrillard.[16] Neither view, in my opinion, tells the whole story, but an examination of the link between the two provided by the Stegner–McCarthy hinge provides us with a new way of looking at the West, and the possibility of a fuller understanding of the conflicted nature of the western environment, and the West's complex history.

The examination of the feminine in the work of both writers has two functions. First, I will show that the more traditional world view which Stegner comes from has the possibility of being regarded as more feminist, that is in terms of the belief that women have been marginalized by society, than might have been previously assumed. Although he might be thought to represent a class of "traditional" western men, men for whom the accepted verities of gender relations were not called into question, Stegner's view of women's roles in the West is in fact unusually perceptive and may be read in terms in which the desires and perspectives of women are privileged over their assumed inferior status in relation to western men. His respect for women and valuing of their achievements and contributions to western life are understated yet profound. Secondly, by my examination of McCarthy's treatment of landscape as female, and his use of females as metaphors for landscape, I hope to refute the idea of McCarthy's misogyny as well as to reveal McCarthy's perception of landscape as an independent, equivalent entity, characterized by the concept of "optical democracy." I suggest that this concept, which in broad strokes suggests the equivalence of all things, may be further extrapolated to suggest a mindset—of which Judge Holden in *Blood Meridian* clearly expresses the opposite—suggesting that all things, including the landscape, deserve equal respect. I believe this environmental aspect of McCarthy's work is therefore continuous with Stegner's own environmentalism, while approaching it from a more oblique angle.

I have chosen Stegner and McCarthy because they are, in my view, two of the most perceptive writers of their respective eras in terms of their critiques of the treatment of western landscape, McCarthy in fictional terms, Stegner through fiction, biography, history, and essay. In summary, Stegner's perspective is "feminine" in the sense of protective and nurturing towards that landscape, as well as "masculine" in the traditional sense of male protectiveness towards the female. Additionally Stegner's awareness of a numinous quality in much western landscape gives his critique a further dimension linking it with transcendental thought of the nineteenth century. McCarthy on the other hand sees landscape as adversarial, equating it with his characters' attitudes toward the disappointing and inscrutable feminine.

Both authors are concerned with the ongoing crises of modernity and their effects upon individual lives and upon the physical world around us. In the works of both writers, the western landscape is a primary character. Both writers also question the myth of the frontier—those received verities which have attained mythic status in our understanding of the West: endless land, hardy men, passive women, the rightness of American possession of "virgin land" despite previous occupation, grandeur, hope. Aspects of the myth of the frontier are appealing, there is no doubt. Its imaginative pull is nearly irresistible. Yet there is no reason why we may not revel in the grandeur of the West, and praise the accomplishments of its undoubtedly heroic settlers while abhorring the results of unchecked frontier expansion on landscapes and individuals in the past and in the present time. McCarthy and Stegner offer us ways to do these things, yet from such different perspectives that we may be able to re-examine previous conclusions. Read alone, each author gives us a new perspective. Looked at together, I suggest, we are able to understand the

West from an unvisited perspective, reconsidering previous critiques and re-examining current ones.

In my first chapter, I will examine, broadly, some of the western issues which apply to the topic of this book. I will look at the development of the myth of the frontier, the myth's relation to environmental issues, and its relation to gender issues in the West. I will also consider the relationship of the myth of the frontier to the Vietnam War.

In the second chapter, I will examine Stegner's relationship to the myth of the frontier, his environmentalism, and his position on women's issues in the western landscape. Stegner's view of landscape's spiritual dimension and the transformative power of wilderness will also be examined in this chapter.

The third chapter will examine McCarthy's very thorough critique of the myth of the frontier and the meaning of living in a mythless world. The commodification of landscape and nature are large issues in McCarthy's works, and this topic will also be discussed. Finally, landscape as female and female as landscape will be examined in McCarthy's western corpus.

The fourth and final chapter will draw together the discussion of Stegner and McCarthy, their critiques of the myth of the frontier, the environment, and gender issues. I will examine how their respective positions on either side of the Vietnam/1960s divide inform both authors' works, and inform our interpretation of the history and myth of the western landscape.

1   Myth, Environment, Gender

The Background to the Myth of the Frontier

In this book I am concerned with how western myths affected behavior in regard to the western landscape, and particularly how this is represented in the works of Wallace Stegner and Cormac McCarthy. By this I am suggesting that mythic, often idealistic images of the frontier in particular and the West in general led to beliefs in the inexhaustible beneficence of a landscape which was available to those tough enough to endure its privations, and ruthless enough to take what they wanted. These images were often unrealistic, unsuitable, and dangerous in terms of the development and protection of the western landscape. Water issues are a case in point, in which the idea of endless resources has led to a dangerous "use and use up" mentality which has resulted in unsustainable development in arid western landscapes.[1] Stegner was particularly concerned with water issues in the West, a point which comes up in both his fiction and his non-fiction. In McCarthy's works his cowboys are driven off their ranches by oil exploration in one case and the government's desire to use the land, presumably for nuclear testing, in another. In these cases, the landscape is regarded as expendable.

Until relatively recent years, the mythic character of the West was a given. By "mythic" I am here referring to ideas and images which were present in the national consciousness as early as settlement began and which had particular reference to the West. Foremost among these ideas is the myth of the empty frontier—"virgin land"—the Promised Land, usually only available to white males. But the land was never empty in the sense that the non-native settlers imagined, and had been home to nomadic tribes for millennia. The misunderstanding was willful. As Manuel Broncano states in his essay, "Landscapes of the Magical,"

> From the beginning, America has been subject to utter misrepresentation, both in the European mind and in the minds of all those adventurers who came to the shores of the New World and then pushed farther and farther into the wilderness in search of a chimera of success and regeneration.[2]

This misrepresentation was made explicit in the myth of the frontier and the cultural and ideological practices which accompanied it. The myth of the frontier had three distinct strands. First was the idea of a Promised Land. This was a concept which fitted in with Judeo-Christian archetypes, which most settlers had in their cultural background—part of the reason why it was so readily accepted. The second western myth which forms an integral part of the myth of the frontier is that of the heroic lone man in the wilderness, regenerating himself through violence. This myth derives from Joseph Campbell's formulation of the mono-myth, which involves the rite of passage, separation–initiation–return of a young, male hero.[3] In the West both these myths found expression in the image of the cowboy on the open range. For example, Owen Wister's *The Virginian*[4] offers an example of the western synthesis of the two streams of mythmaking—the heroic cowboy on an open frontier. In addition, John Hellman states that heroic American mythic and folkloric characters embody

> self-reliance, democratic idealism, homespun practicality, adaptability, ingenuity, humor, and generosity making up the national character associated with its frontier ethic.[5]

This suggests that the myth of the frontier carried along with it not only the weight of aspiration for the Promised Land and the more atavistic monomyth described by Campbell, but also a good dose of outright self-aggrandizing: a heady mixture. As Sara Spurgeon comments,

> Part of the traditional American myth of the frontier holds that the frontier experience created a land of freedom-loving individuals dedicated to bringing democracy, not imperial conquest, to the rest of the world. Thus part of this myth is a narrative that must carefully ignore or disguise American imperialism abroad, as well as the reality of invasion, conquest, and colonization that made possible the European settlement of the Americas.[6]

This third element, that of the innate goodness, even chivalrousness, of the adherents of the myth is perhaps the most problematic aspect of it, requiring a veiling, if not rewriting, of history in order to validate the actions of settlers, colonizers, and actual outlaws. This veiling necessitated the creation of an adversarial "other" against whom the actions of those individuals previously mentioned might be performed. This "other" is present as the Indian in frontier literature as early as Cooper, and has recurred in every conflict in every generation: Mexicans, Filipinos, Cubans, Panamanians, Japanese, Koreans, Vietnamese, Iraqis, Afghans, Iranians. It is notable that during the Second World War, Germans, though they were military enemies, were not regarded with such fear and loathing as the more alien-seeming Japanese. Japanese Americans were interned in the United States. German Americans were not. Apparently the true "other" had to be, like the Indians, a different racial type. Additionally, the myth paradoxically survived into an era when the United States became more and more multinational. Sara Spurgeon argues this point:

> I would argue that one reason this myth has survived and flourished over the years is that it works equally well in a postmodern context. Since the frontier itself can be seen as a set of symbols that constitute an explanation of history, its significance as mythic space is more important than any actual geographical location. The transfer of symbol from its place of origin to a state of unfixed, floating signifier marked the birth of American international imperialism which began in earnest in the administration of Theodore Roosevelt.[7]

During Roosevelt's administration, all enemies were "indianized," a state of affairs which lasted well beyond his presidency. Roosevelt's presidency also saw the first beginnings of American imperialism with movement outward to Hawaii and Alaska. Roosevelt sought to extend American influence by any means, fair or foul. His most notable triumph was in wresting Panama away from Columbia so that the US could build the Panama Canal.

Significantly, Roosevelt had spent a formative two years in the West, working as a cowboy. A soldier and hunter, in sympathy with Kipling's idea that darker races were "the white man's burden," his views were openly imperialistic, based on a premise of white, male superiority. In addition, an expanding American economy was seeking more foreign markets for its goods, and a colonial empire outside the US, a new "frontier," would provide this.[8] Spurgeon's remarks highlight the connection between the myth of the frontier and American forays *beyond* the vanished frontier—imperialism, in fact. The concept of the frontier became a reality all its own, a floating signifier, as Spurgeon suggests, impalpable, but capable of provoking action.

Another serious consideration to be briefly noted in the discussion of American myth-making and thus our understanding of the West is the fact that American mythology was formulated in the age of the printing press. Therefore, as soon as events occurred, they could be written down, printed and circulated, creating the real possibility that living people, such as Daniel Boone, could become legendary within their own lifetimes. With a print-mythology in place, the process, "by which the nation came to be imagined, and once imagined, modeled, adapted and transformed,"[9] as Benedict Anderson describes it, had begun. Anderson further argues that national groups feel great attachment to "the inventions of their imaginations," and that in many cases they are willing to die for these inventions.[10] He also argues that these inventions are often the result of print capitalism,[11] that is, are created by their own artistic representations, which is frequently the case in the history of America, and particularly western America. Supporting the same idea, Henry Nash Smith argued that the formulaic "dime novels," produced in the nineteenth century, whose ostensible subjects were true western adventure, were a sort of sub-literary artifact which nonetheless had the effect of becoming an "objectified mass dream,"[12] further obscuring the reality of the West and replacing it with an extremely durable fantasy. This fantasy was projected upon a landscape in which the West then became a canvas for heroic action—an object of desire and fantasy on an epic scale.

This fantasy had a value, however. Ernest Renan has written that the soul of a nation lies in the "possession in common of a rich legacy of memories," and "the desire to live together, the will to perpetuate the value of the heritage that one has received in undivided form."[13] If we accept these premises, then the importance of the acceptance of a national mythology, however recently coined and however problematic, is understandable. Renan's premise suggests that the myth of the West, mingled as it was with a perceived historical memory, was, along with the overwhelming national desire to create a new country, essential for the young nation's survival and growth. Additionally, for the western pioneer and settler, social cohesion meant survival in an often hostile and dangerous landscape, as Stegner points out. If belief in the frontier myth helped to create cohesion, it was then vitally important in the social structure of the frontier. On this point Neil Campbell has written,

> Out of migration and movement comes a new rooted identity as the focus for the epic narrative that gave coherence and authority to the westward urge of nation-building and provided America with its own creation myth...The need for a national origin story occluded the recognition of the true nature of the historical processes being played out across the region and sought to reduce these to a managed set of images and stories that would become the West's official history.[14]

This suggests that although myth had its dangers, it did, as I have suggested, fulfill an important cultural role. Mythic images became embedded in western consciousness. Remaining largely unquestioned due to their essential importance in structuring society, they became totemic in significance, and hence remained largely unquestioned until the frontier era was over, and beyond. This suggests that as mythic imagery formed western identity, western identity became fixed within that very imagery. Hollywood, taking over where the dime novels left off, gave this mythic imagery iconic status, creating an alternate reality which took over from real events, and became the accepted "history" of the West. (Had America not moved so quickly from frontier mythology to nuclear armed modernity, the damage caused by the myth of the frontier might well have been mitigated, and events might have placed frontier history in its proper place, rather than setting it up as a continuing model for national accomplishment.)

This alternate reality has made the West a place which means different things to different groups. It is virtually impossible to reach a consensus of what the West is. Neil Campbell has further noted,

> The West-as-text is multilayered, "an agglomerative space" (Barthes, *S/Z*, 1975: p. 7) where "everything signifies ceaselessly and several times, but without being delegated to a great final ensemble, to an ultimate structure" (*S/Z*, p. 12)...The "ultimate structure" or metanarrative, in terms of the West, has been a series of dominant stories or myths told over time and endowed with massive cultural power, such as the Promised Land, Manifest Destiny, Turner's frontier thesis, each of which sought to encompass and define the West.[15]

This alternate reality and the lack of "an ultimate structure" in the West may be seen as its greatest strength and also as its greatest weakness, making the West, "analytically slippery," as Krista Comer describes the landscape.[16] This contradiction is in many ways true for the country as a whole. It is placed in a nationwide context by Leo Marx:

> A most striking fact about the New World was its baffling hospitality to radically opposed interpretations. If America seemed to promise everything that men always had wanted, it also threatened to obliterate much of what they had already achieved.[17]

Marx's comment suggests that America as a whole, and I suggest the West in particular, always existed in an uneasy alliance of opposed desires, interpretations, and practices. These oppositions are often obvious binary ones: male as opposed to female; conservationist as opposed to exploiter of the landscape; myth-driven idealist as opposed to pragmatist. Yet the interpretations of all oppositional forces often cross and recross in the shifting reality of the West, obliging the reader to reconsider ideological positions on landscape, gender, history, environment, and myth.

The myth of the frontier also had serious effects upon the western landscape, settlement, and development. The idea that the landscape was free for the taking was especially problematic considering the fact that much of the land in question was already occupied by native people. In his essay "Frontier Violence in the Garden of America," Reginald Dyck writes,

Most searchers for a new life in the garden of America had to take the peaceable kingdom by violence—against the Indians, the land, each other, and themselves. Western writers have presented the violent actions of their characters within the contexts of two apparently contradictory myths: the myth of the garden, which attempts to hide the American legacy of violence, and the myth of the frontier, which celebrates it.[18]

This suggests several points. First, if what Dyck refers to as the myth of the garden—which I interpret as the idea of "virgin land" in an untouched continent—attempts to hide the violence in the history of America, it recognizes the shame inherent in what the first Puritan settlers referred to as "our errand in the wilderness,"[19] as Henry Nash Smith commented. The garden mythmakers therefore at some level recognize the implication that the garden cannot exist without prior violence, hence the sanitizing of that violence into Joseph Campbell's hunter-monomyth. The monomyth, by its implied antiquity and subconscious references to Christian and pre-Christian heroic avatars, gives a kind of credence to the heroic nationalism which then expressed itself in pioneering and warfare. This, I suggest, gave by association validity to a "war" against the landscape, which meant using it, and using it up. This landscape was, ironically, a desired landscape, desired for its possibilities, its beauty, its strangeness, its newness. It was desired beyond realistic expectations, and additionally was understood as female, which further layers the complexity of understanding both the desire for and the misuse of the western American landscape. Understanding this desire is vital to an understanding of the perception of landscape in the works of Wallace Stegner and Cormac McCarthy.

Frontier Anxiety

The westward movement was tied to the hope of acquisition of land; it was also driven by the charged vision of Manifest Destiny. The frontier ethos of conquest and endless expansion rumbled on in the collective unconscious of the nation long after the frontier was declared "closed" by the census of 1890. "For nearly three centuries the dominant fact in American life has been expansion,"[20] wrote Frederick Jackson Turner at the beginning of the twentieth century. Although his views have been largely dismissed, it is tempting to discuss the frontier in terms of the simple binaries of process versus place, with Turner representing the myth-dominated, "process" camp. However apparently outdated Turner may be, there are elements of his position which having once been denigrated by the New Historians,[21] have been more recently reconsidered and re-evaluated positively. As Clyde Milner has argued, "The American

West is an idea that became a place…The idea developed from distinctly European origins into an American nationalistic conception."[22] That is, the West, in which the frontier was located, and which, as a definition, moved relentlessly from the eastern seaboard to the Pacific, was rooted in ideas which became, as Limerick suggests, "a creation myth."[23] Turner's emphasis on the importance of the frontier in the creation of national identity also suggests its importance in the creation of the *ideal* of that identity, an element of the myth of the frontier. Western identity, therefore, rooted in the frontier, for many became the model of *all* American identity, thus the deep anxiety felt when the frontier appeared to be finished. It is belief in this definition of identity which particularly motivates Stegner's Bo Mason, in *The Big Rock Candy Mountain*,[24] and McCarthy's John Grady Cole.

As the frontier expanded and moved westward, so too did the systematic exploitation of the landscape. Clear-cutting of ancient forests, strip mining, reckless damming projects, in the later frontier period; earlier, the hunting to extinction of the American buffalo and other species were symptomatic of the "use and use up" mentality of many of the westering immigrants. However, criticism of the dominant political ideology with regard to the commodifying and exploiting of western landscape was always heard in environmental circles, and as early as the mid-nineteenth century John Wesley Powell's vehement political opposition to the large-scale settlement of the arid lands of the public domain in the years following the Civil War, and John Muir's ardent preservationism of the Sierra Nevada a few years later were cases in point. In 1864, George P. Marsh wrote warning Americans they were destroying their environment with "progress."[25] Yet despite these early warnings, Rachel Carson was still ringing the alarm bells in 1962 with the publication of *Silent Spring*,[26] detailing the effect of widely used and governmentally encouraged pesticides on farmland. (Of course Carson and Marsh were not referring only to the West, but the country as a whole.) Thus events such as Stegner's campaign to save Dinosaur National Monument from government developers—effected through the publication of *This Is Dinosaur*, which he edited[27] and distributed to all members of Congress on the eve of the vote to flood the national monument in 1955—while not entirely unheard of, were the exception rather than the rule.

In this book, among other topics, I will consider environmental issues as they impacted upon the western American landscape as discussed in the works of the authors I have chosen. I will discuss these issues, for the most part, in terms of the literature I am examining, choosing Calliope rather than Clio, to paraphrase Forrest Robinson,[28] to guide my study. This is not simply because I am a student of literature rather than history, but because, as Robinson has so convincingly argued,

Like history, novels are grounded in social reality; but thanks to their imaginative liberty, they often illuminate the past in ways that strictly factual accounts cannot. Stegner acknowledges in *Wolf Willow*, for example, that he has "occasionally warped fact a little in order to reach for the fictional or poetic truth" that he ranks "a little above history" (*Wolf Willow*, p. 307). The volume achieves the middle ground, in other words, precisely because it acknowledges that history and literature overlap, and because it exploits their merging in the attempt to arrive at the imaginative truth.[29]

This imaginative truth is one which not only draws its inspiration from the myth of the frontier, but which also critiques that very myth by the evidence of its effects on characters' lives. Robinson's essay points to the fact that neither fact nor fiction tells the whole story in terms of the West, but both are essential to our understanding of the West, its people, and landscape.

*   *   *   *

While neither McCarthy nor Stegner might be described as belonging solely to the ecocritical tradition, by which I mean "the study of the relationship between literature and the physical environment,"[30] certain aspects of the ecocritical perspective may be useful in the study of both. A feminist ecocritical perspective, that is, an examination of the link between the oppression of women and the domination of the natural world, will be considered in my analysis of McCarthy's western works. As Glotfelty has stated, "Most ecocritical work shares a common motivation: the troubling awareness that we have reached the age of environmental limits, a time when human actions are damaging our planet's basic life support systems."[31] This awareness is evident in Stegner's works. His environmental concerns begin in the western past and are manifested throughout all his works. McCarthy's western novels have more to do with the passing away of a perceived, imaginary past, and a spiritually and physically degraded present. Both authors' works may be looked at usefully, though not exclusively, through the ecocritical eye. Both also belong to recognizable critical traditions: Stegner belongs to a line of writers for whom the actual physical environment of America was a source of inspiration as well as personal reinvention. Stegner's role in conservation movements marked him as a somewhat unlikely new radical in the tradition of Thoreau and John Muir. This was a tradition re-invoked in the 1960s and 1970s by campus activists, hippies, and radicals of many descriptions. A sympathetic government under John Kennedy began the process of protective environmental legislation in America during the same period. And, as Donald Worster states,

By the late sixties that call for regulating the polluters began to have a significant effect on the political process...

This discovery of nature's vulnerability came as so great a shock that for many Britons and Americans, the only appropriate response was talk of a revolution.[32]

Environmentalism therefore joined the political vanguard which included those who opposed the war in Vietnam, race activists, feminists, and other protesters. But for much of the western landscape it was a case of too little, too late.

I have stated that the environmental aspects of Stegner's fictions critique various attitudes towards the western landscape which manifested themselves, historically, in any number of schemes of development of unsuitable lands: of misappropriation of water rights, unregulated mining and forestry industries, land grabbing, and displacement of native peoples: what the historian Patricia Nelson Limerick has described as "the legacy of conquest."

The legacy of conquest of the western landscape and its people and creatures is a subject which has only gained recognition in recent years. As Limerick maintains,

> To most twentieth century Americans, the legacy of slavery was serious business, while the legacy of conquest was not...
>
> Conquest took another route into the national memory. In the popular imagination, the reality of conquest dissolved into stereotypes of noble savages and noble pioneers struggling quaintly in the wilderness.[33]

This legacy was largely created by the myth of the frontier. As Limerick has stated, the legacy of conquest was for many years subject to historical misinterpretations. This attitude to history, particularly western history and its effect on the western landscape, has made the western landscape one of the least understood and most damaged in America. In the larger scale of things, environmental depredations are worldwide, of course, but in the fragile western environment, they have had particularly profound effects which are in part a result of the quasi-mythic status of the western landscape itself, which has made interpretations of it at best difficult.

Western studies have moved on a good deal since Limerick wrote her words in 1987, and her amusingly arch comments have received their own share of opprobrium. To her credit, Limerick has modified some of her early, sweeping judgments on western history and historians. In commenting on her earlier stance, Forrest Robinson writes,

> But are Westerners the fatuous optimists, hopelessly inured to "Happy Face History," that the revisionists describe?...The tragic perspective on Western experience is hardly new. It is not new to the

historical record, nor, as I have indicated more than once, is it new to the literary record.[34]

Limerick's assumption of an acceptance of a version of western history is based on her own assumption that myth-driven idealistic imagery was all that anyone—prior to the New Historians—was aware of in western history. Clearly this is not true, and critiques of the myth and its effects were in evidence very early on. As Robinson argues, Stegner prefigured the New Historians by several decades. However, one can go back as far as Mark Twain, even Cooper, as Robinson points out, and find a questioning of the frontier ethos and its effects. Some of Limerick's points and positions are clearly apposite, and there is much to praise in her work, but there are omissions. Returning to Limerick's premise of a legacy of conquest in the West which includes the conquest of the natural environment, Harold Fromm notes,

> In the early days, man had no power over Nature and turned, instead, to his mind and its gods for consolation. Meanwhile, his mind produces a technology that enables his body to be as strong as the gods...Then it appears that there is no Nature and that man has produced virtually everything out of his own ingenuity...By now man is scarcely aware that he is eating animals and producing wastes or that the animals come from somewhere and the wastes are headed somewhere. This "somewhere" turns out to be...a finite world whose basic components cannot be created or destroyed...As more and more of these basic materials are rendered unusable by man, it becomes apparent that man has failed to see that...the roots of his being are in the earth.[35]

Fromm's argument goes on to state that modern man is surprised when, after generations of polluting and wasting, nature *turns against him* by returning the compliment with poisoned water, cancer-causing food, thinning ozone, and oil-slicked seas. Our sense of invulnerability to the natural world has made us believe we are its masters. This sense of mastery in the West caused huge environmental mistakes: damming of rivers; building cities in desert landscapes; emptying of underground aquifers; not to mention the disposal of hazardous radioactive waste which has made large areas of the western landscape poisonous no-entry zones which will remain so forever. The legacy of conquest of the western landscape has become a legacy of environmental disasters which still persists, indeed worsens.

Our cavalier attitude toward western nature culminates in twentieth-century environmental disaster scenarios such as the "Junkyard of Dreams," memorably described by Mike Davis in *City of Quartz*[36] and

Ecology of Fear[37]—the "Los Angeles of the next millennium...[seen] from the ruins of its alternative future."[38] In these books Davis describes a culture demanding water from deserts, growing like a cancer in a fragile environment which will eventually fail to support it, a description which fits much of the arid Southwest of America today.

Yet despite all the evidence against it, the frontier mythology of inexhaustible bounty lives on. The desire for the landscape to be what one imagines it might be overwhelms reality. My point is that in the history of the New World, the imaginatively "desired" landscape often took precedence over the reality of what the landscape could offer and sustain. This issue is paramount in the works of both of my chosen authors, and indeed in the works of many western writers. There is a tension in both Stegner and McCarthy's works created by the awareness of the conflict between the reality of a degraded environment and the imaginative perception of a Promised Land.

There is a long line of traditional literature which illustrates the profound nostalgia that affected notions of the West and western landscape, and illustrated the sense of loss that was felt almost as soon as events had passed. Though this nostalgia was not exclusively related to the environment, it was related to the sense of the loss of an open frontier of land. As the frontier moved westward, its impending absence was already mourned. Owen Wister's *The Virginian*, published in 1902, laments a brief period of doomed frontier bliss, echoing eastern frontier anxiety. The novel describes a period of dream-like frontier beatitude, a period which lasted, according to Wister, from just 1874 to 1890. What we feel in this novel is the nostalgia for a moment which has inevitably passed, and the attendant sense of loss which is the controlling emotion of the protagonist in Wister's world, as it is one of the main controlling forces in *All the Pretty Horses* and *The Crossing*. As well as East–West tension, *The Virginian* illustrates the nostalgia which is so prevalent in classic western fiction. The fact that the novel is written as retrospective heightens this sense of loss and sets the action in a golden age, never to be retrieved.

Frontier anxiety was an issue early on in western settlement. Even Thoreau expresses concern at the encroaching machines in his garden. In his study, *The End of American Exceptionalism*, David Wrobel states,

> As early as the 1870s, observers were expressing concern that much of the country's land had been settled or bartered away to railroad corporations and foreign syndicates. By the 1880s, a significant number of intellectuals had begun to question the nation's stability. Some began to respond to the gloomy state of affairs by seeking legislation to stem the tide of immigration...They argued that America's changing status rendered it incapable of housing and transforming the world's unfortunates.[39]

That is to say, less than sixty years after Lewis and Clark published their news, the New World was already, in many people's minds, finished. The seeds of this anxiety are clear in literature as far back as Cooper: Natty Bumppo is utterly unable to stay in the settlements or to form familial attachments; he flees to the woods as though afraid they will disappear, as indeed they were already doing. In more current literature, A.B. Guthrie's trappers in *The Big Sky*[40] lament the end of the frontier they helped to destroy when westward traveling wagons begin to use their trails. Equally McMurtry's mountain men in *Buffalo Girls*[41] regret the near extinction of the beaver for which they themselves have been responsible. This anxiety over the land being *used up* motivated early explorations, but poor use of the land made certain that, in the short term at least, the frontier would march inexorably westward as land was rendered infertile, filled up with a burgeoning birth population, and crowded by increased immigration. The pull of the "vacant continent" remained strong. Failure was simply a catalyst for reinvention somewhere further west. Steinbeck's short story "The Leader of the People" echoes sentiments similar to Wister's in the character of the grandfather whose brief moment of glory has been as a young man leading a wagon train across the plains. His life has been a disappointment since this one pivotal moment of existence: "We carried life out here and set it down the way those ants carry eggs...The westering was as big as God...Then we came down to the sea and it was done."[42]

Although they are not violent hunter characters such as Guthrie's Boone Caudill in *The Big Sky*, both the narrator in *The Virginian* and the grandfather in Steinbeck's story suggest a level of frontier anxiety, the idea of the frontier being used up, which supports Boone Caudill's notion that "it's all sp'iled." Steinbeck, Guthrie, and even Wister, are expressing a retrospective frontier anxiety, and it is clear that the ambivalence many nineteenth-century Americans felt towards the expansion of the country into what had been regarded as pristine wilderness, was genuine.

*   *   *   *

Western expansion, the "legacy of conquest," had little concern for preservation of the wilderness. It was rather "frontier anxiety," the fear that the seemingly endless frontier could be used up, that fueled much of the popular feeling that the wilderness ought in some way to be preserved. Significantly, frontier anxiety caused a backlash against immigration, one of the founding principles of American identity, objectifying in *the "other"*—this time the non-Anglo-Saxon immigrant rather than the native population—the source of the problems besetting the already wasteful nation. Increasingly, during this period, artistic representation of landscape began to express nostalgia for a lost Eden, a pure world which also had the advantage of being an economic goldmine, a goldmine which seemed threatened by both immigration and misuse of land and resources.[43] This is one of Stegner's major themes in his essays, as

I will discuss. The concept of a lost world is also a major element in McCarthy's *All the Pretty Horses*, and will also be discussed in the following chapters.

The Myth of the Frontier and the Vietnam War

In this book I suggest that the era of the Vietnam War—the 1960s and early 1970s—had a catalytic effect on Americans' perception of themselves and their history. The relevance of this much discussed premise to the authors I am considering lies in the fact that Stegner is an observer of the West from a pre-Vietnam, pre-1960s standpoint. Although he wrote throughout the period, and beyond, I have suggested that his perspective was based in an understanding of the West which was rooted in the cultural premises which existed prior to the upheavals of the 1960s. McCarthy, on the other hand, wrote his western novels in a time which had radically re-evaluated the past and its myths, in large part because of the effects of the Vietnam War and the cultural transformation wrought by the 1960s and early 1970s. Both authors deal with perceptions of the West which were significantly altered by the events of the war and the attendant cultural changes in America. In addition, the ostensible rationale for the war itself drew upon many tenets of the myth of the frontier.

The 1960s saw a re-evaluation of what had been fixed cultural givens in America, and indeed around the western world. The rise of feminism also shifted the cultural and political ground hugely, as did the disillusionment experienced by many of those who had previously believed in the essential benevolence of America's enterprises. The civil rights movement brought to the boil racial issues which had lain dormant since the end of the Civil War. In addition the continuing consequences of America's presence in Vietnam, and the later perception that the war had been *lost*, by a country which valued *winning* at all costs, led inevitably to a questioning of the very nature of America itself. While for my purposes the issue of Vietnam is essential, incorporating many elements of frontier ideology which are relevant to an analysis of the treatment of the western landscape, the issues revealed by the women's movement, environmentalism, and the civil rights movement, among several other less high-profile but nonetheless significant movements, also had huge effects on American culture which contributed to a climate of disillusion and uncertainty among all sections of society, and demanded a reappraisal of previously accepted cultural orthodoxies as well. As Jean François Revel wrote in 1971,

> The "hot" issues in America's insurrection against itself, numerous as they are, form a cohesive and coherent whole within which no one issue can be separated from the others. These issues are as follows: a radically new approach to moral values; the black revolt; the feminist

attack on masculine domination; the rejection by young people of exclusively economic and technical social goals; the general adoption of non-coercive methods in education; the acceptance of the guilt for poverty; the growing demand for equality; the rejection of authoritarian culture in favor of a critical and diversified culture that is basically new, rather than adopted from the old cultural stockpile; the rejection of the spread of American power abroad and of foreign policy; and a determination that the natural environment is more important than commercial profit.[44]

What Revel suggests here is that a wholesale re-imagining of the American self was taking place in the 1960s and early 1970s. While one might, nearly forty years on, regard the hope of change in many of these issues as naively idealistic, Revel's remarks capture the tone of the times. All these issues had existed as points of contention, if not conflict, but the combination of general discontent combined with the angry opposition of a generation of young men outraged at being made cannon fodder for yet another proxy battle in America's seemingly endless Cold War with the Soviet Union and China, tipped the scales, and grumbling acquiescence became open revolt among a vocal minority of young Americans. Crucially this minority was generally located in the educated and affluent Northeast, Wisconsin and the Great Lakes region, northern California, and the Pacific Northwest, areas which have long had a liberal political tradition. The Northeast, particularly, as the heartland of Yankee abolitionism in the nineteenth century, had a long history of dissent, as well as being the home of the Transcendentalist movement in literature. This regional character of dissent explains why so many more southerners and midwesterners, as well as a disproportionately large number of young men from minority groups, served and died in Vietnam than did the affluent, university-educated (who benefited from student deferments) from either coast. In this climate of dissent a snowball effect brought civil rights, feminism, Vietnam, the environment, and many other issues, together in a heady atmosphere of empowerment, self-belief, optimism, and hope which had as its defining goal ending the war in Vietnam, largely regarded by its opponents as illegal, immoral, and unwinnable. During the conflict, Frances Fitzgerald wrote,

> In going into Vietnam the United States was not only transposing itself into a different epoch of history; it was entering a world qualitatively different from its own...
> ...The impulse to escape, the drive to conquest and expansion was never contradicted in America as it was in Europe by physical boundaries or by the persistence of strong traditions.[45]

That is, in Vietnam, America not only came to terms with a war it almost certainly could not win, but also came face to face with a culture which did not share any of its values. The Vietnamese had lived for centuries within the village structure in which the accumulation of wealth was regarded as antisocial. They also regarded the land as sacred. Therefore America's capitalist, frontier ethos was doubly repugnant. Although it is doubtless that many Americans, policy makers, ordinary citizens, and soldiers, believed in the rightness of America's actions in Southeast Asia, regarding Vietnam as a similar conflict to the ostensibly less problematic Korean War of a decade previously, America was seen by its opponents and its own dissenting young as a nation of invaders, and indeed, invaders from a nation which regarded land simply as property. In addition, the experience of Vietnam questioned the frontier ethos of conquest and endless expansion—an ethos which, though outwardly finished, still rumbled on in the collective unconscious of the nation.

While the precepts of the Cold War posited the perceived adversaries of the ever-aggressive Soviet Union and Communist China, bent, it was said, on world domination, little acknowledgment was made of a similarly aggressive, economic and cultural imperialism practiced by the United States throughout the twentieth century. With the end of a physical frontier, America's frontiers had become economic ones. Although the census of 1890 had declared the frontier "closed," for many Americans the ideal of the frontier was deeply felt and lived on. "For nearly three centuries the dominant fact in American life has been expansion,"[46] Frederick Jackson Turner had written. It was a habit of mind which proved hard to break, and from the time of Teddy Roosevelt onward, this frontiering-by-proxy had been transferred to foreign shores, the pivotal one of which was Vietnam.

John Hellman suggests that the Special Forces, known as Green Berets, were used as an image of the American frontiersman and part of the psychological background to the war was the fact that soldiers in the Vietnam War sought to emulate their fathers, whose most recent war was World War II.[47] This is certainly reinforced by such films as Michael Cimino's *The Deerhunter*,[48] which portrays an American hunter-hero, in the central figure of Michael, significantly a Green Beret, regenerating himself both through the violence of the war and also through a close connection with nature. Hellman states, "Michael, like the western hero, is a man of extraordinary virtues and resources that are dangerous unless properly channeled into a role protective of the community."[49] That is to say, the hunter-hero of the myth of the frontier is himself potentially his opposite—the stranger, the phantom hitch-hiker, the isolate, Ishmael, even McCarthy's vile Anton Chigurh in *No Country for Old Men*. (The suggestion is made that Chigurh was once a member of the military, and his familiarity with Carson Wells, a former Green

Berets colonel who is hired to assassinate him, reinforces this supposition.) This also echoes Stegner's assertion that his father, depicted as Bo Mason, was the sort of man who once might have had an honorable role in American life, but that the country has left the frontier era too far behind for that sort of man, like Cimino's Michael, and McCarthy's young cowboys, to have a role.

The Vietnam conflict was overlaid with mythic as well as psychological significance. Hellman states, "What indeed distinguished the Green Beret from earlier versions of the western hero was the sheer ease with which he encompassed savagery and civilization."[50] The fact that the Green Berets were supported by President Kennedy who himself was falsely portrayed as both a war hero and a new frontiersman, a term he gave himself, added further significance to their role in the war and made the mythic overlay of the war even more potent. Kennedy was himself heir to the political rhetoric of the 1950s, that somnambulistic era so revered by Ronald Reagan a generation later. John Roper states,

> The political rhetoric of the 1950's thus would emphasize American exceptionalism—the idea that the United States was unbound by any laws, sociological, psychological or physical that might determine the fate of others. Moreover, to confound Marx's interpretation of the dynamics of history, America's own past was studied to endorse the nation's sense of itself as different...This mythologised version of the nation's past would be conveniently mined for political rhetoric, not least by John Kennedy, who famously would exploit the seam connecting contemporary America and its historical experience of the frontier.[51]

The imagined past was therefore drawn upon to justify the all-too-real present. Television assisted in this project. Children of the 1950s and 1960s were brought up with largely fanciful heroic portrayals of the West on television and in films. The average age of the American soldiers in the war was between seventeen and twenty-five, and the majority were poor and under-educated. These were young men who grew up with the imagery of the West before them at every turn. So it was not surprising that for these Americans, as well as many at home, the war in Vietnam received much of its ideological justification from the idea of the "Old West," and the myth of the frontier. This was a group of people formed by the mythos of the heroic American past as interpreted by that harbinger of its ever-more sedentary future, the ever-present, ever-on television. As Philip Beidler so persuasively states, these were ones who had been reared on

> Golden-age TV: cartoons, commercials, cowboys, comedians and caped crusaders, all coming together at quantum-level intensity in

a single frantic continuum of noise, color and light—child-world dreams of aggression and escape mixed up with moralistic fantasies of heroism...a composite high-melodrama and low comedy video-tape of the American soul.[52]

Therefore, in Vietnam, American soldiers were likely to be motivated by a fatal combination of idealism and fantasy—often further fueled by hallucinogenic drugs which were readily available. The fact that the war itself was constantly scrutinized by both left and right, its motivations and parameters the subject of constant confusion and uncertainty, added to this chaotic brew, creating a climate of bizarre unreality, captured by much of the literature and film dealing with the war. Michael Herr's canonical Vietnam work, *Dispatches*, illustrates this point:

"Come on," the captain said, "we'll take you out to play Cowboys and Indians"...We played all morning until someone on the point got something—a "scout," they thought, and then they didn't know. They couldn't even tell for sure whether he was from a friendly tribe or not, no markings on his arrows because his quiver was empty.[53]

Herr's commentary is chilling, a cross between *Swallows and Amazons* and *Lord of the Flies*, drawing on images of childhood and innocence, coupled with a strange lack of reality. The implication of depraved innocence in this quotation reveals something about both Vietnam and the myth of the frontier: there were those who enjoyed the fighting, regarding it as a game. This disturbing sense of *playfulness* suggests a postmodern slant to much Vietnam literature. This separates the Vietnam experience from all previous American wars, and renders it, in my view, not less but more significant even than a conventionally observed war, carrying with it not only physical but also spiritual annihilation inherent in the frequent postmodern view of reality with its arch flippancy regarding real events which have impacted upon living people. I am thinking of Baudrillard's contention that the first Gulf War did not happen, which while it was obviously a statement about language and perception, aimed to provoke discussion, still denigrated the suffering of those involved in that conflict. Equally, the view of Vietnam as a bad trip or a bizarre existential experience negates the damage done by the war to the Americans and the Vietnamese. As Philip Melling states,

Vietnam offers the postmodernist critic an image of Western disfigurement; it provides him with a symbol of "the abounding contradictions of postwar American society." Critics have become fascinated with Vietnam as a place redolent with the modes of modern experience—innovation, ingenuity, what Jerome Klinkowitz terms "military postmodernism"—at the expense of its moral or social contexts...What American experience in Vietnam reveals, says the postmodernist, is a level of sophistication and enterprise that is far more intriguing and relevant to the world in which we live than the primitive ideology of a third world country, or the social catastrophe that Vietnam has experienced in recent times.[54]

Melling's argument points to the conclusion that to extrapolate from such grotesque human suffering as has occurred in Vietnam the raw materials of another cultural theory is morally repulsive. The moral vacuity of such positions highlights the disengagement with reality in regard to Vietnam which is in part a result of its myth-based rationale, and also suggests that postmodernism as an approach to the business of life, as opposed to art, is potentially frivolous to the point of reprehensibility.

*　*　*　*

Because the myth of the frontier was used to make some sense out of this strangest of wars, the literature shows us that it was validated for many of the participants and indeed, one suspects, for many of the Washington-based perpetrators. In addition, the chaotic nature of the fighting in Vietnam made the war seem like an extended horror movie, or a drug trip, as has been depicted in many of the films and books about it. The distinction between the real and the surreal was always in question for many of the soldiers. It was not at all clear who was right and who was wrong and for what reason the war was being fought.

Recently Michael Lind has argued that the Vietnam War was a "necessary war," "neither a mistake nor a betrayal nor a crime...a military defeat."[55] Lind bases his arguments upon the valid contention that the regimes propping up the government of Ho Chi Minh, Soviet Russia, and Mao's China, were brutal, totalitarian regimes which were intent upon the domination of Indochina. Lind's argument has the effect of minimizing the sufferings of the Vietnamese people, positing the war as an academic object, rather than a very real conflict which affected individuals, rather than nations. I suggest that Lind's arguments, valid as they may well be, serve the same function of distancing us from the reality of the war as do the postmodern critiques and the myth-based rationales.

Eventually mythic models lost their almost magical power to mask reality as the numbers of young American dead steadily increased, and yet they were still invoked as a rationale for fighting. When national disgust with the war in Vietnam reached critical mass, the myths which had fueled yet another "errand in the wilderness"[56] also felt the presence of an unusually critical gaze. Commenting upon the effect of the Vietnam War upon national consciousness, Barcley Owens states, quoting Karnow,

The late sixties forced many Americans...to reject old myths and frankly reassess the brutal facts of nationalism. The climbing death toll and the planeloads of body bags bore awful "witness to the end of America's absolute confidence in its moral exclusivity, its military invincibility, its manifest destiny...With the young men who died in Vietnam died the dream of an American century."[57]

But the dream died hard, and has recently had a ghastly resurrection in the rhetoric employed to justify military forays into Afghanistan and Iraq. Although different from the doctrine of Manifest Destiny, the ideas of American exclusivity and political dominance, along with a cavalier attitude towards the United Nations in recent events, bear alarming similarities to the earlier doctrine. The attitude that America is somehow the arbiter of what is and is not "civilized," and an underlying belief in the inevitable rightness of the American cause and way of life have been revealed as absolutely alive and well, in some quarters, particularly since the World Trade Center disaster. However, like in Vietnam, there is clearly a cynical *éminence grise*, perhaps many of them, behind recent American foreign policy, with little regard for what idealism may still lie among the ashes of the myth of the frontier smoldering at Ground Zero.

Undoubtedly, the myths which were employed as a rationale at some level during the Vietnam War did not go entirely unquestioned. The dangers inherent in the continuing significance of the frontier myths in American thinking are clearly shown by John Clark Pratt in his essay, "The Lost Frontier: American myth in the literature of the Vietnam War." In his essay Pratt identifies the mythological structure, particularly the "Cowboy and Indians" motifs which not only appeared in much of Vietnam War literature, but which also in the actual war, motivated action. But Pratt, quoting Hellman in this extract, also comments that,

> Some of the novels' protagonists "uneasily sense that they themselves are the enemy of the population that they have ostensibly come to save, successors not to their own mythic forebears but rather to the Europeans against whom their forebears defined themselves." The result "is the destruction, not of America, but of the myth which gave it life and in which Americans once believed."[58]

This suggests that though the frontier myths do have continuing vitality, their essential corruptive power in society was largely recognized in the aftermath of Vietnam, along with an attendant sense of loss at their demise. The history of Vietnam has been well documented and the concurrent loss of national innocence and sense of direction is evident in many Vietnam films. Francis Ford Coppola's *Apocalypse Now*,[59] for example, recognizes the "heart of darkness" inherent in American frontier myths, with its Conradian theme. Invoking Conrad also suggests the post-colonial aspects of the Vietnam War, and the literature surrounding it, and suggests that the myths used to justify the Vietnam War are in some ways global in their ramifications, suggesting further that the desire for global hegemony was not simply a prerogative of the Soviets and the Chinese, but also of their American adversaries.

Along with the idea of corruption present in Vietnam literature is the concurrent theme of bemused innocence. Such popular films as *Born on the Fourth of July*[60] and *The Deerhunter*, already mentioned, present the American innocent, adrift in a strange and uninterpretable landscape which finally corrupts or kills him. This motif is arguably present in the character of the Kid in McCarthy's *Blood Meridian*, and certainly evident in John Grady Cole and Billy Parham in *The Border Trilogy*, and in the character Llewelyn Moss in *No Country for Old Men*. Moss is also, significantly, a hunter and a Vietnam veteran.

In further reference to the frontier myth, Pratt comments, "Basically, the literature of the Vietnam War is filled with American characters who enter Vietnam as traditional frontier huntsmen, then become men trying merely to survive in a wilderness they do not understand."[61] This reference back to the tenets of the myth of the frontier in regard to Vietnam suggests that the myth fails in Vietnam, though it is invoked. Rather than regeneration, the adherents of the myth barely achieve survival, and return like devotees of some fallen religion, with nowhere to go, psychically, philosophically, or morally.

A final point is the fact that in Vietnam, the American hunter-hero lost his connection with the natural world. The landscape of Vietnam, according to Hellman, has been represented in literature as one which "has a tendency to resolve itself into the dreamlike terrain of Hawthorne, Poe, and Melville."[62] That is, it is terrain in which nature has lost any semblance of beneficence and become a "howling wilderness" which may not be overcome by the hunter-hero. "In Vietnam the asylum of nature has become an invading hell,"[63] Hellman tells us. And yet the soldiers who entered into the strange world of Vietnam often did so for a variety of reasons, as Michael Herr suggests in *Dispatches*. Hellman further notes, "Herr's portrait...suggests his own underlying motivation in seeking the war, [was] a desire to escape the spiritual decay of an affluent, bureaucratic, inauthentic society."[64] That is, the perceived "primitive" society of Vietnam, complete with a war to equate with the "howling wilderness" of early American literature, provided an alternative both physically and psychically to the debased, unheroic, modern time. Like Cooper's heroes' desire to reach "the primitive core of the psyche,"[65] this quest for authenticity is central to much of Vietnam literature, and to the disillusionment felt by many of the returning soldiers, foundering in an inauthentic world which does not value or desire their experience. McCarthy's Vietnam veteran, Llewelyn Moss, is a case in point.

The horrors of the Vietnam War and the resulting crisis of national identity show most clearly the failure of the frontier myth in American society. The idea of applying heroic nationalism based on mythic archetypes to events in the modern world suggests metaphors of apocalypse. "The ceremony of innocence is drowned,"[66] as Yeats said of another war, and we are left like Billy Parham at the conclusion of *The Crossing*, bereft of context, sitting in the road with our cowboy hats next to us, holding our heads in our hands, weeping.

* * * *

If the sense of American identity, or the perception of it, was based in the frontier myth, then the clear falsity of the myth was shown in Vietnam, and suggested an indictment of that national identity on a very basic level. I would like to argue that as a result of this large-scale questioning of the myth, a loss of faith was experienced among members of society who would in ordinary circumstances never have become radicalized. Indeed, this cohort of society did not become radicalized, as did the campuses and some of the urban population, but rather *retreated* into the myths of American history, and the archetypal models of the frontier and the West, taking the myth backwards into the realm of nostalgia. The proliferation of World War II dramas and cowboy programs on American television during the 1960s and early 1970s are evidence of this tendency to look backwards, and indeed look backwards towards an imaginary past. In *Gunfighter Nation*, Richard Slotkin notes:

> Tropes and symbols derived from Western movies had become one of the more important interpretive grids through which Americans tried to understand and control their unprecedented and dismaying experiences in Vietnam. The infusion of large numbers of American ground troops between 1965 and 1968 brought to the scene a generation for whom the imagery of western movies and television programs (no less than rock'n'roll) provided a ready-made set of metaphors that seemed quite appropriate to the war in which they found themselves.[67]

It may be argued that this "ready-made set of metaphors" was cynically manipulated by the politicians safely ensconced in their jungle-free zones. Certainly Kennedy's first inauguration address in which he described himself as "a new frontiersman" nods in that direction. In 1965 President Johnson said that the Vietnam War was "a war of unparalleled brutality. Simple farmers are the targets of assassination and kidnapping. Women and children are strangled in the night because their men are loyal to their government. And helpless villages are ravaged by sneak attacks."[68] This is the sort of hyperbolic prose that might have come from a captivity narrative, or a dime novel. The easy binaries of evil Communists and stalwart farmers—a very thinly veiled appeal to the American heartland—is lacking in the slightest subtlety. But the parallels with cowboy and Indian motifs are clear. Popular culture employed these mythic motifs in an effort to understand Vietnam as well. For many, the only possible answer to the cultural confusion, loss of faith, and loss of face, of the Vietnam debacle—and the final perception that it was a war in which America was defeated by an enemy easily equated with the traditional dark-skinned "other" of American myth— was to plunge into a kind of cultural and historical nostalgia, a nostalgia based upon a past which was perceived as simpler, more in touch with "traditional" American values. The existence of this more "traditional" other place is the subject of the rehistoricizations of both Stegner and McCarthy, as well as those of the New Historians, Worster, Limerick, Cronon, et al. However, for a substantial proportion of the population, this mythic American past became an ideal, a longed for space of simplicity and understandable moral values: a desired landscape, in fact. The war in Vietnam was sometimes simplistically interpreted through tropes of western myth and frontier history rather than the interpretive grid that might have been provided by the bamboo cages in which both sides kept prisoners. When the war was discredited, and revelations such as the horror of the Mylai massacre in March 1968 became public, the western tropes were reversed: Americans became the savage Indians of frontier history and an intolerable moral dilemma was created. Of course, the visibility of the Vietnam War on national television made this dilemma all the more pressing. The antagonism with which the returning veterans were met by the American public revealed not only a sense of national failure, but also a widespread anger and disgust, which for want of a more accessible target was often directed at the veterans. This state of affairs lasted, more or less, until the Reagan presidency with its reductive and simplistic reinvocation of traditional American values and the sentimental assertion that it was "morning again in America." The dark night of the American soul was Vietnam, but that night was past, Reagan's rhetoric implied, and Americans could once again get on with the business of making themselves prosperous and expanding new frontiers. For Reagan, as for many Americans, the lessons of the war were not learned. It was an aberration, a historical anomaly in an otherwise perfect history. As John Roper states,

> American history, for Reagan, was a narrative of unparalleled success, based upon selective interpretations which avoided difficult and controversial issues. For him, the historical drama of the nation's past was based upon vignettes of heroes and heroic incidents, all of which confirmed ideas of exceptionalism, destiny, and the unrelenting optimism of the American dream.[69]

Employing the rhetoric of the frontier was not simply a trope for Reagan, but a reinvocation of Kennedy's rhetoric which in the early 1960s still held meaning, real or imaginary, for both the politicians and a large part of the community. The resonance of the frontier as an image had enabled Kennedy to embark on a struggle against the perceived threat of worldwide Communism. American politicians had a vested interest in the battle with Communism because of its threat to capitalist economic systems. In fairness, there was also a deeply felt and genuine fear of the specter of Communist world domination, and the well-documented horrors of Stalinism were undoubtedly things of which to be afraid. The "godless" Soviet Union was perceived by a "god-fearing" America as its nemesis, to be feared, and fought if necessary. The perceived plight of Vietnam gave the politicians an excuse to do so, while the public was mollified with images of the long-suffering Vietnamese welcoming their "liberators," just as the World Trade disaster, I suggest, gave the Bush government the purported grounds to mount a long-desired attack upon the uncooperative oil-rich states of the Middle East. Similarly, like the earlier fear of Communism which motivated action, there is now the fear, whipped up by politicians and the media, of international terrorism. So one shibboleth replaces another.

Unlike any other conflict in American history, Vietnam was uncomfortably close to home: right in the living room. Live television reports meant that Americans saw the war in all its lurid, vivid color. When Americans witnessed the summary execution of a suspected Viet Cong guerrilla on national TV, there was no way to modify or glorify events. Nor was there a way in which the sight of children burned when American planes napalmed their villages could be made to fit into any heroic paradigm. When reports of unseen atrocities did filter back, they were worse than the television: murder, torture, the appalling atrocity of Mylai. All wars are ugly. Vietnam was particularly ugly and the ugliness could not be whitewashed, no matter what efforts were made. American idealism—Manifest Destiny in the twentieth century—could be seen as cultural imperialism, with a subtext of racism. During the war, Vietnamese were "gooks," less than human. Even if the war had actually been the idealistic project marketed to the American people, its methods were too brutally cynical for a large, vocal minority of the American public to tolerate. (The fight against the perceived threat of Communism retained its credibility for some time after the conclusion of the war, until the former "iron" and "bamboo curtain" countries toppled their own Communist regimes.) The acknowledgement of what was actually happening in Vietnam, its historical roots and ideological foundations corrupt, led gradually to the realization that those same ideological tenets, those of Manifest Destiny, and the idea that the country belonged by divine right to those who took it, *had always been corrupt*. The racial subtext was nothing new. Indians, blacks, and Mexicans had been among the less-than-human victims of the previous centuries. A radical re-thinking of some of the rhetoric of American identity was necessary. The suggestion that there was a "unified identity" in what has always been a manifestly multicultural society was clearly a product of heroic frontier mythology.

The napalm glow of burning villages cast a new light on American frontier history and required a new evaluation of events which had long been regarded as largely heroic, undoubtedly iconic, and historically *closed*. In employing frontier mythology to partially justify the Vietnam War, its proponents cannot have known that with the war's failure, the tenets upon which it had been based would themselves be scrutinized as never before. With the failure of the Vietnam War, Americans experienced a monumental loss of faith. America had been perceived to be on the side of justice, even the most hardened cynic would agree, in the Second World War. Its rhetoric was that of the strong protecting the weak, as shown by the Truman Doctrine. And yet the rhetoric suddenly seemed empty, the history questionable. This loss of faith was precipitated by the Vietnam War as well as several other factors. These other factors included the expansion of capitalist commodification into all areas of life, a new awareness of racism, rampant poverty in an affluent society, and fears that the environment, so long regarded as an endless, exploitable resource, was being systematically destroyed by negligence and design. The consequent questioning of America's motives and goals led to—among other things—a reappraisal of western history. Donald Worster discussing the post-war, militarized West, wrote,

> Around the year 1970 (the year when Dee Brown published...*Bury My Heart at Wounded Knee*...) that untold side of the western past began to find its tellers...What was missing was a frank, hard look at the violent imperialistic process by which the West was wrested from its original owners and the violence by which it had been secured from the continuing claims of minorities, women, and the forces of nature...It was time for historians to call such violence and imperialism by their true names.[70]

This is not to suggest that the Vietnam War and its aftermath were totally responsible for this reappraisal of history, but as I have argued, Vietnam acted as a catalyst, along with the cultural changes which happened in its wake, for the new discussion of the nature of the West. This new approach to western history has privileged the accounts of non-white peoples and women in a way which the old frontier story did not. The renewed examination of what is often considered early imperialistic expansion from the era of Roosevelt onwards was also one of the results of the break with the past caused by the re-evaluations necessitated by the psychic upheavals precipitated by the Vietnam War. As Charles Reich wrote in 1970,

> The war did what almost nothing else could have: it forced a major break in consciousness. The breaches in consciousness caused by the consumer–worker contradiction or the rigidity–repression syndrome

were significant, but they were slow acting and might have taken indefinite time. It might have been years before marijuana and riots catalyzed disillusionment. The war did that with extraordinary rapidity. It rent the fabric of consciousness so drastically as to make repair almost impossible. And it made a gap in belief so large that through it people could begin to question the other myths of the Corporate State.[71]

In short, the effects of the 1960s and early 1970s transformed the vision of those who had previously seen America and the American West through a haze of myth and symbol.

I believe that the Vietnam War and its aftermath were also crucial to the overall reshaping of American identity. As Chatfield and Debenedetti note:

> The opposition to this war was also linked to the liberalization of popular culture. Wars tend to breed cultural conformity and conservative politics, but the Vietnam War was different. In varying measure, the antiwar movement aligned the organized disaffection of blacks, women, and students. It also competed with these groups and others, such as environmentalists...
>
> These social demands and cultural trends were part of what Ronald Lora, in *America in the Sixties*, has aptly called "a revolt against traditional cultural authorities." They included challenges to the conventional wisdom about religion, scientific objectivity, national security, the sources of poverty, the infinite durability of the environment, and adult, white, and male dominance.[72]

That is to say, the effect of the Vietnam War and its aftermath was to call into question many previously ironclad assumptions about American life and history, including race relations, gender relations, and the treatment of the environment.

The more cynical, wary, post-Vietnam sensibility which developed as a result of both the Vietnam War and the cultural chaos which accompanied and followed it has thoroughly permeated academic criticism, but the significance of the discussion goes far beyond the academy. In his essay, "Marxism and Ecocriticism," Lance Newman suggests that,

> The research priorities that now dominate most culture departments developed in response to a quite specific and deeply significant set of historical events; namely, the worldwide revolutionary movements of the late 1960s and the related struggles against racial and sexual oppression. While there is no limit to the potential triviality and backwardness of professional responses to the questions raised by those events, the questions themselves remain vital. To

dismiss questions of class, race, and gender as "mere humanism" is not merely an act of towering self-absorption, it also ignores the fact that they bear directly on the question of "how to save the earth." For the same forces that generate exploitation and oppression, generate ecological damage.[73]

That is, events of the 1960s created a climate in which social structures and founding myths of nationhood are questioned and re-evaluated in the light of the multiple forms of dissent and commentary. Thus we have, in the modern world, a bewildering variety of approaches to experience which reinforce the idea that all representations of experience are, at best, partial, at worst, misleading. And yet, as Newman reminds us, the answers to these academic questions are vital for the future of civilization and culture, and the planet itself. While Newman does not specifically mention Vietnam, one of the "revolutionary movements" he mentions was the movement against the war in Vietnam.

The national backlash to the disaster of Vietnam, therefore, also repudiated the dominance of this specifically western heroic type, precipitating to some extent the re-imagining and re-framing of the perceived national identity which in turn contributed to the emergence of non-white cultural spokesmen in literature, culture and the arts. Certainly there has been a flowering, post-Vietnam, of cultural diversity in American life. This is also related to the fact that the revolutionary spirit which engulfed the country during the war led to a certain freeing-up of other cultural mores. Chomsky comments,

> Anybody who's my age or even a little bit younger must also realize that it's a very different country today—and a much more civilized one. Just look at the issue of rights of indigenous peoples...There have been very important changes in the culture.[74]

This suggests that the climate of discontent that the Vietnam War provoked was actually a positive thing. Rather than simply destabilizing society, as it appeared to do during the 1960s and 1970s, it would appear to have created a society in which much more dissent is possible, or at least was until the World Trade Center attacks of 2001. The American government during the younger Bush administration seemed intent upon creating a society once again terrified of the "other," and scare stories proliferated. Like the Puritans who founded the United States, the recent powers of the country, equally Puritan in their avowed values, feared the mysterious dark-skinned heathens who threatened their way of life, and tapped into atavistic fears of much of the myth-ridden populace.

Yet it still must be allowed that during the 1970s a wholesale re-imagining of culture took place, at least within the academy. Some of this had to do with the advent of postmodernism as an approach to literature and the arts. This re-imagining has led to further diversity in all realms of culture. In addition, large-scale immigration from third and second world countries has also had a huge effect upon the previously WASP status quo. Although, as Frederic Jameson archly notes,

> Driven out of the Third World by our own counter-insurgencies, and lured out of the Second by our media propaganda, the would-be immigrants (whether spiritual or material), not understanding how little they are wanted here, pursue a delirious vision of transubstantiation in which it is the world of the products which is desired, like a landscape.[75]

Yet whatever the cause, the very fact of such large numbers of new immigrants has had yet another destabilizing effect on the traditional imagery of the American heroic type.

The other side of this destabilization is the reaction it has provoked in the governing elite. Far from welcoming changes in national identity, Chomsky argues that the governing powers have, in their sense of embattlement, become more intransigent, more likely to make war clandestinely, and therefore without public scrutiny, more likely to choose soft targets, such as Afghanistan, which have the will but not the power to fight back. And in this climate of oppression, the image of the western heroic man, battered, destabilized, deemed guilty of a thousand crimes against humanity, is re-invoked, again and again, as a symbol of America's rightness, goodness, honorableness, and manliness: a paradox without remedy.

Not only does the myth of the frontier and the doctrine of Manifest Destiny allow for foreign incursions and destruction, it also allows for, and always has allowed for, a similar treatment of the western landscape, under the guise of progress.

*   *   *   *

Now that the power base in American politics has shifted to the ever-expanding West, it is alarming to see that the myth-driven among the western population have combined with cynically opportunistic establishment elements. The frontier is now purely economic, but those engineering its conquest employ the failed rhetoric of western expansionism. America, yet again, exhaustedly returns to the days of the original frontier: its enemies are suitably dark-skinned and foreign enough to be equated with the "other" of the primeval forests of seventeenth-century New England. The landscape may still be "conquered" by the intrepid SUV drivers and dirt-bikers who tear up whatever is left of unspoiled green spaces.

By examining the traditional American romance of the flight to the wilderness in search of self in the light of the Vietnam War, we find that rather than finding coordinates of identity in the search, those coordinates are irrevocably lost in the process. In a post-Vietnam world, innocent pastoral romance is no longer possible, if it ever was. The guilty knowledge of the weird Magical Mystery Tour, as Michael Herr so aptly called Vietnam,[76] made true innocence regarding the nation itself a thing of the past. The metanarrative of American benevolence was successfully challenged by Vietnam commentators such as Frances Fitzgerald, who, in 1972, wrote:

> Those who have seen combat must find a reason for that killing; they must put it in some relation to their normal experience and to their role as citizens...In 1971 the soldiers had before them the knowledge that President Johnson had deceived them about the war... They had before them the spectacle of a new President, Richard M. Nixon, who with one hand engaged in peaceful negotiations with the Soviet Union and the People's Republic of China and with the other condemned thousands of Americans and Indochinese to die for the principle of anti-Communism. To those who had for so long believed that the United States was different, that it possessed fundamental innocence, generosity, and disinterestedness, these facts were shocking.[77]

This guilty knowledge required, if it was assimilated and understood, a rehistoricization of previous, similar episodes in American history, particularly since aspects of the myth of the frontier had been invoked in aid of the Vietnam debacle. In this sense the myth is a sign which points to no reality but itself. It was invoked as a rationale, but in fact the very invoking of it pointed to the dead falsity of its original premises. We reach a point beyond innocence in a world in which we look towards a past we feel *is* innocent, only to find it irretrievably corrupt. This world is based upon a myth whose referents are flawed, hollow, applicable to nothing but themselves. Seen on a national scale, this approach to life is even more reprehensible. In the past it gave us the massacres of the Native Americans, black slavery, the appropriation of Hawaii, the war with Mexico, all in the name of "rights," conveniently clothed in the language of heroic nationalism, and aided by the fact that for most Americans, the events described were happening very far away. In our lifetime, this approach has given us Vietnam, Cambodia, El Salvador, Iraq, and a host of other conflicts, as well as the larger specter of American global hegemony, a reaction to which recent events in the Middle East are a horrifying response. Shortly after the World Trade Center disaster and its predictably aggressive aftermath, Lewis Lapham wrote,

> Words pressed into the service of propaganda lose the name and form of meaning...Human beings adjust their interpretations of reality in order to recognize the mass murder of other human beings as glorious adventure and noble enterprise...Let war become too much of a

felt experience, as close at hand as the putrid smell of rotting flesh or the presence of a newly headless corpse seated in a nearby chair, and most people forget to sing patriotic songs.[78]

The rotting flesh and headless corpses of *Blood Meridian* attest to Cormac McCarthy's concurrence with Lapham on this issue. The explosion of America's deeply held myths is, as Slotkin so forcibly concluded in *Regeneration Through Violence*, a matter of the utmost urgency, for as Lapham states, "Once placed within the context of a mythical reality, even the most fantastic notions of omnipotence acquire the semblance of everyday sense."[79]

And that is where the gravest danger lies.

Feminine Landscapes

In addition to examining the works of Stegner and McCarthy in the light of the myth of the frontier, and environmental issues, a third lens which I will look through is gender, by which I mean the western landscape seen as feminine in the works studied. Additionally, I will look at Stegner and McCarthy's attitudes towards actual women in the West in their works. While this area of my study will not be exhaustive, I hope to cast a light upon both authors and their positions on women's roles in the West, and to the gendering of the western landscape. The American continent seen as female in relation to a dominant male presence is a cultural given, and one which, it may be argued, is particularly present in McCarthy's *Border Trilogy*. That this particular feminine aspect of McCarthy's ever-disappointing, ever-unfaithful landscapes is in keeping with what has been persuasively argued is his misogyny towards living women is a point with which I will take issue. The feminine aspects of Stegner's view of the landscape have more to do with Stegner's view of the role of the actual women living in the landscape, as well as his own sense of being a guardian or "steward" of nature, a role which suggests a masculine and protective attitude toward nature seen as feminine. This is largely problematized by Stegner's often repeated assertion that growing up in Canada he felt that he was a "target" of a hostile natural world, and while there is little which might be called friendly or feminine about the wild, raw, and brutally cold landscape of Saskatchewan in winter, yet Stegner finds beauty in it, and a deep sense of its numinosity, which I will discuss further.

The landscape as feminine is a concept which has deep roots in the American psyche and which has particular relevance to the West. Annette Kolodny has written of "the persistent pervasiveness of the male configurations" which saw the ever-westering American frontier in terms of available female landscape. In the words of Captain John Smith it was a landscape "her treasures hauing yet neuer beene opened, nor her originalls wasted, consumed, nor abused."[80] This was a landscape both virginal and maternal, Kolodny argues, which inspired fantasies of erotic discovery and possession, and a vision of "filial receptiveness" as Crevecouer's new man is "received in the broad lap of our great Alma Mater."[81] The inevitable conflict implied by the ravishing of a landscape both erotic and maternal was only ameliorated by the continued projection of the fantasy on landscapes further west, but the problems produced by such a vision continue, and the subtext created, of female as commodity, is disturbing.

Gendering landscape obviously is not new in human history, but what is unusual in American history is the use of such opposition of genders in order to articulate a national identity, based upon the myth of the frontier. The landscape as female falls victim to male enterprise. The American Adam lives in a throwaway paradise from which Eve is excluded, while the paradise, viewed as female itself, is trashed. A landscape perceived as feminine is viewed, particularly in the westering enterprise, as something to be acquired, used and abandoned. In 1981, Nina Baym wrote,

> Of course, nature has been feminine and maternal from time immemorial, and Henry Nash Smith's *Virgin Land* picks up a timeless archetype in its title. The basic nature of the image leads one to forget about its potential for imbuing any story in which it is used with sexual meanings, and the gender implications of a female landscape have only recently begun to be studied. Recently, Annette Kolodny has studied the traditional canon from this approach. She theorizes that the hero, fleeing a society that has been imagined as feminine, then imposes on nature some ideas of women which, no longer subject to the correcting influence of real-life experience, become more and more fantastic. The fantasies are infantile, concerned with power, mastery, and total gratification: the all-nurturing mother, the all-passive bride. Whether one accepts all the Freudian or Jungian implications of her argument, one cannot deny the way in which heroes of American myth turn to nature as sweetheart and nurture, anticipating the satisfaction of all desires through her and including among these the desires for mastery and power.[82]

I have quoted Baym at length because her premises are central to my argument, particularly in reference to McCarthy's western works. As society fails McCarthy's characters, landscape is burdened by expectations it cannot fulfill. Yet however useful Baym's argument, feminist scholarship has moved on a good way since she wrote her groundbreaking words in 1981. Recently Krista Comer's concept of the "dominant geocultural imaginary" has suggested that western landscapes are gendered male and racialized white, and that public space is therefore ideologically male, suggesting not only female marginalization, but a reversal of the previously held notions of a female, receptive landscape. I suggest that these two positions do not actually contradict one another, but rather that Comer's position goes beyond Baym's in the sense that it is going beyond the idea of settlement—a concept which has relevance to both Stegner and McCarthy—to a discussion of intellectual appreciation, something not inevitably relevant to settlers. Comer writes, "To whom other belongs a visual ideology of the panoramic? As feminists across the disciplines have repeatedly demonstrated, public space is by definition male, off limits to women."[83]

In addition the idea of landscape being "off limits" to women may be interpreted as being due to the fact that the landscape itself is female, in the male view, and therefore the human female represents an unwelcome competitive element with the female landscape. Susan Armitage has referred to the literary West as "Hisland,"[84] suggesting that women's presence was neither needed nor particularly welcome in western narratives. Arguments such as Armitage's have been echoed by Jane Tompkins, Annette Kolodny, Peggy Pascoe, and others. In McCarthy studies, specifically, Nell Sullivan has argued along similar lines. The obviation of the human female seems to be part and parcel of the western myth.

In the larger picture beyond western studies, the Australian ecofeminist philosopher Val Plumwood links arguments about the denigration of the female in general to denigration of nature with which the female is associated, and the attendant risks to both humanity and the planet as a whole. This sidestep in the argument opens the larger question of whether the denigration and/or obviation of the female is a sign of a deeper male hostility to the feminine which, when enacted upon landscape viewed as female, leads perilously close to the abyss of ecological disaster. Plumwood states, "The question of a woman–nature connection cannot just be set aside, but must remain a central issue for feminism. The connection still constitutes the dynamic behind much of the treatment of both women and nature in contemporary society."[85] Plumwood's remarks are apposite for my study of McCarthy, particularly. Women are the focus of complex issues of both domination and predation in McCarthy's novels; so too is nature both benign and desired, and alternately, vicious and lost. In their attitudes toward the natural landscapes, McCarthy's cowboys in *The Border Trilogy* equate the natural world with the female and behave accordingly.

This equation of the natural world with the female has the corollary of the land viewed as passive, denied agency of its own, as the living female is traditionally denied access to the imaginative world of American literature. As Judith Fetterley writes,

> The woman reader's relation to American literature is made even more problematic by the fact that our literature is frequently dedicated to defining what is peculiarly American about experience and

identity. Given the pervasive male bias of this literature, it is not surprising that in it the experience of being American is equated with the experience of being male. In Fitzgerald's *The Great Gatsby*, the background for the experience of disillusionment and betrayal revealed in the novel is the discovery of America, and Daisy's failure of Gatsby is symbolic of the failure of America to live up to the expectations in the imaginations of the men who "discovered" it. America is female; to be American is male; and the quintessential American experience is betrayal by woman.[86]

This suggests that not only is the land viewed as female, it is also paradoxically unable to fulfill the grand desires of men who imagine it to be inexhaustible and capable of endless bounty. This is certainly the case in *The Border Trilogy*, in which unreliable females—as perceived by the young cowboys—mirror a landscape which, owing to no intrinsic cause, is rendered faithless, degraded, and unavailable.

Ecofeminism addresses this problem with its configuration of a vital connection between the oppression of women and the denigration of nature, and more specifically suggests a model for reading texts which may usefully be addressed using the ecocritical frame. Colleen Mack-Canty writes,

> In one of the earlier ecofeminist anthologies, *Reweaving the World*... the editors [Diamond and Orenstein]...discern three important, and sometimes intersecting, philosophic strands in ecofeminism. One strand emphasizes that social justice cannot be achieved apart from the well-being of the Earth. Human life is dependent on the Earth; our fates are intertwined. Another strand in ecofeminism is spiritual, emphasizing that the Earth is sacred unto itself. A third strand emphasizes a strong recognition of the necessity of sustainability—a need to learn the many ways we can walk the fine line between using the Earth as a resource while respecting the Earth's needs.
>
> One of the main endeavors of ecofeminism, in its efforts to reweave the nature/culture duality, is to understand the ideology that perpetuates the domination of women, other humans, and non-human nature. There are many approaches taken by ecofeminists who are engaged in analyzing how the subjugation of women, other suppressed people and nature are interconnected.[87]

Mack-Canty's remarks present a more adversarial approach to traditional metanarratives than I have previously suggested, and I do not wholeheartedly endorse all of her premises. I do not believe that all white men are interested only in the domination of women, non-white races, and nature, and I believe that cooperation between the sexes is more the norm than she suggests. However, there certainly exists subjugation of women alongside a reckless endangerment of the natural world. This is possibly most evident in some third world countries. There is, on the other hand, also a subjugation of men in the same areas, and a more plausible critique might be one which examined the capitalist motivations for such subjugations, as in Amazonia, where tribal people are driven off their lands and enslaved to work for the same people who have destroyed their ancient habitats; or the Indian subcontinent, where men, women, and children work twenty-hour days in factories which provide the affluent of the first world with cheap consumer products. There are, of course, many other examples. My point is simply that the ecofeminist frame runs the risk of reductionism if it does not include all victims of capitalist greed, not simply the female ones.

However, Mack-Canty's points about the sacred nature of the earth, the importance of its well-being and our respect for it, coupled with our own need to live on the earth and to use it, are apposite to this study, and are particularly useful with regard to Wallace Stegner, for whom these sentiments were central. Our treatment of the natural world, as we are aware, has reached a state of crisis, and the prescience which Stegner showed in addressing this issue as early as the 1950s is central to my argument about his continuing importance as a voice in environmental debate. While remaining silent on the subject of capitalism, Stegner would surely have agreed with Anne Fisher-Wirth's analysis of our culture as "a culture so ravenously materialistic, so obsessed with capital, that it is destroying the very grounds of our existence...No culture has ever been as environmentally destructive, on as large a scale, as our own."[88] Stegner's own environmental activism shows an early, intense awareness of this point, and it is a point he develops thematically in *A Shooting Star*,[89] and the Joe Allston stories, particularly, as well as in much of his non-fiction.

* * * *

The new world had a history of dramatic misrepresentations which fueled some of the worst abuses of the years of settlement, and which endure, transformed, and continue to feed the culturally imperialist consumer ethos which unfortunately often dominates American political life. In 1950, Henry Nash Smith wrote of "the pull of a vacant continent."[90] Historical revisions in the past half-century have laid to rest the idea that the continent was either "vacant" or "virgin" in the sense which the settlers might have wished, or Smith implied. But more recent scholarship has argued that our idea of what the original settlers of America either wanted or believed has been continually distorted by the mythology of exploration and the frontier—a mythology which was created almost as the actual events occurred upon which the legends were based. Crucial to these misrepresentations is the gendering of landscape. In *The Green Breast of the New World*, Louise Westling suggests a way of understanding this:

Gender is a field of imperialism central to more obvious political and historical forms of colonization. Attention to gender can do much to explain the puzzle of ambivalence in American literary responses to landscape and nature...desiring to unravel the strange combination of eroticism and misogyny that has accompanied men's attitudes toward landscape and nature for thousands of years. These attitudes are not at all empty tropes but instead part of a complex evolution from the most ancient human past in which an analogy seems to have been assumed between the body of woman and the fruitful body of the land.[91]

Gender, according to Westling, is the key to the particular puzzle of American attitudes to landscape. These attitudes encompass a range of behavior and feeling from the cloyingly sentimental to the reverential to the brutally exploitative. Seen as female, within the parameters of violent conquest and acquisition, the landscape is alternately cherished, used, protected, ravaged. The implications of what Kolodny refers to as "suppressed infantile desires unleashed in the promise of a primal garden"[92] are not specifically American, but on the American continent these desires were, up to a point, unchecked. Indeed, this position was politically validated by the doctrine of Manifest Destiny, with its implicit advocacy of empire-building aggression.

In the following chapters, I will discuss how Stegner and McCarthy, as heirs to this tradition of gendering landscape, critique the traditional frontier perception of the country west of the 100th meridian as female, and the distinction between their perspectives: Stegner as a liberal humanist of the realist school, McCarthy as a post-1960s, post-Vietnam observer of the new America of recent history. I will also examine the subject of the search for the pastoral sanctuary, particularly in reference to Stegner's women, and the inevitable failure of this search. Stegner's attitude of protectiveness toward the landscape, coupled with a respect for its power, posits both a more traditional attitude toward the female, as well as a deeply sympathetic respect for female values in both life and landscape.

Conclusion

In this chapter I have established the parameters of the following study. As I have suggested in my introduction, I believe the Stegner–McCarthy axis is a useful tool with which to examine the ramifications of the myth of the frontier upon the perception of western American landscape. Resting either side of the divide created by the Vietnam War in historical and ideological terms, the comparison of Stegner and McCarthy offers a unique opportunity to look at western issues developmentally, through the works of two authors who, while on some levels very different, share similar concerns about western landscape and nature. Additionally, both Stegner and McCarthy are, in my view, exemplars of some of the best western writing, again in very different styles. And finally, both authors have a seriousness of purpose and an artistic integrity which gives gravity to their works, and which commands respect, and hugely repays analysis.

Stegner's world view is, despite often brutal realism, basically a hopeful, optimistic, vision of western America filled with humanity, clarity, and inspiration. His view is formed by both knowledge and experience of pioneer history, and an appreciation of the diverse and inspiring western landscapes, and an abiding belief in the dignity of the human spirit. One might almost suggest Stegner's vision was an *innocent* vision, were it not so deeply rooted in history and environmentalism, and were his characters not so richly complex. There is nothing naive about Stegner's writing. His critique of the West speaks from every page of his western novels and essays, yet he retains confidence in the West, referring to it as "the geography of hope." Stegner's position is one which was still possible for a liberal thinker to hold, prior to the cultural upheavals of the Vietnam era with the consequent loss of faith in America and all its projects. Although Stegner lived and wrote through that time, his outlook was formed in an earlier, more ideologically innocent era, an era in which America's projects were not always—at least in the popular imagination—immediately suspected of being motivated by venal, base, and exclusively economic concerns.

McCarthy's western vision could not contrast more with Stegner's. It is dark yet humorous, full of death and despair, but possessed of an odd exhilaration as well. The action of the western novels mainly takes place in bleak desert landscapes, doomed ranches, dark, godless prisons. Characters' motivations are rarely clear, and characters themselves are taciturn, seemingly lost in history, placeless, even nameless. The innocent suffer and often die. And yet there is a grandeur and dignity in McCarthy's novels which lifts the action and the characters to a plane rarely achieved in contemporary literature.

What then is the link between these writers, superficially so opposed? I suggest Stegner and McCarthy are linked primarily by the importance given to the natural world in their works and their concern with the western landscape and the meanings which that landscape is given. Additionally they both share the sense that nature is possessed of its own character, power, and agency, separate from the anthropocentric view of the world to which we, as successors to Western European culture, are heir. The natural world is not objectified by either author. Stegner's view, linked to Transcendentalism, anticipates later developments in thinking about landscape and nature such the ecocritical view, and feminist ecocritical perspective as articulated by Mack-Canty. McCarthy also, in his concept of "optical democracy," suggests an equivalence of all things in the natural world, both living and inert. However, I do not believe that this rather contentious possibility intends to minimize humanity, but rather to valorize the natural world. Both authors approach the borders of deep ecology in their attitudes toward nature (as does the strand of thought present in feminist ecocriticism previously mentioned in reference to Stegner), though neither actually crosses into that highly conflicted realm. However, this movement along the edge of what is considered an almost revolutionary approach to environmentalism marks Stegner, once again, as far ahead of his time. Additionally, deep ecology's openness toward Native American configurations, for example the naming of species as simply "four-legged, two-legged, and feathered," effectively de-centering man as the pinnacle of evolutionary process,[93] suggests that far from being totally out of touch with anything to do with Native Americans, as Elizabeth Cook-Lynn suggests, Stegner was in fact in touch, intuitively, with a spiritual dimension of Native American thought. When he refers to his childish self as a "sensuous little savage"[94] it suggests that by sheer connection with the land and nature, Stegner acquired habits of thought which gave him an innate understanding of the spiritualized view of nature which we commonly associate with some Native American cultures. It also suggests, as I will argue, that nature has agency of its own, and transformative power, a power of which Stegner is very much aware.

Both authors, I believe, would agree with the ecocritical principle stating that "We need to find new ways to talk about human freedom, worth, and purpose, without eclipsing, depreciating, and objectifying the non-human world."[95] In McCarthy this point is particularly apparent in *The Crossing*, and Billy's relationship with the natural world as seen through the first episode with the wolf. In Stegner's work it is in a reverence for the natural landscape—mountains, rivers, deserts, forests—that I suggest this particular ecocritical perspective is articulated.

*   *   *   *

McCarthy's vision is characterized by some critics as postmodern, by others as late modernist. Certainly Lyotard's description of postmodernism, "incredulity towards metanarratives," is an obvious aspect of both *The Border Trilogy* and *Blood Meridian*, the metanarrative in question being the idealized vision of western history often purveyed by western fiction and film. And yet much of *The Border Trilogy* looks back nostalgically toward a lost time from an oppositional perspective, which might indicate a more modernist bias in the works, or as Holloway has suggested, at least a repudiation of reactionary aspects of postmodernism.[96] Robert Jarrett has suggested that McCarthy's works are predominantly realistic and modernist pre-*Blood Meridian*, the first of the western novels, and postmodern after it.[97] In fact the novels defy classification as such, and in any case, as Holloway has noted, such terms of classification, "tend to obscure the heterogeneous, conflicted, or contradictory character of the broad tendencies they name."[98] This is not to say that one may not look at McCarthy in these critical terms, but simply that he often goes beyond, and between, the parameters of critical definition. His views are, in my view, deeply affected by the worldwide crises and upheavals of the 1960s and early 1970s, and the radical rethinking which followed events in that era.

Robert Jarrett describes McCarthy's novelistic landscape as "often a primary, if inhuman character, haunting the background of the novels as does fate in Greek tragedy."[99] In addition, Vereen Bell suggests that, in McCarthy,

> The landscape lends a panoramic grandeur to the spectacles of conflict, bloodlettings, and stoic endurance and causes the otherwise meaningless procession westward to seem like a dream of history. And yet it diminishes the events and the human participants in them. The farthest reach of this landscape is the stars, so the distance of the constellations in their void, their impersonal autonomy, becomes a sobering theme in itself.[100]

Dana Phillips has described McCarthy's style as "radically unanthropocentric,"[101] and in this agrees with Bell's suggestion that the landscape itself lends meaning to human activity, and in its diminishment of humanity creates the "optical democracy," of McCarthy's literary style in the western novels, which posits the equality of human and non-human objects. I would go further and suggest that for McCarthy's western protagonists, landscape and aspects of the natural world—Billy Parham's wolf, for example—create meaning, and without them, these characters would cease to function,[102] indeed, cease to exist as literary creations. McCarthy's western characters' existence is posited against the definitions provided by their own perception of the natural world. When the natural world seems to fail them in some way, these characters lose their place in that world.

Stegner's views, as I have stated, are rooted in an earlier period. He may be usefully described as a realist writing during the age of modernism, and the beginnings of postmodernism. Though he, too, lived through the Vietnam years, Stegner, until the end of his life, retained a basically hopeful, yet balanced outlook, not oblivious to the tumult of the 1960s and 1970s, but rather focused on other aspects of life. For example, his mature characters often spend a good deal of their time meditatively, in gardens, as did Stegner himself. Stegner's view came from a deep grounding in the nineteenth-century Transcendentalist writers, particularly Thoreau and John Muir, with their reverence for the natural world, their beliefs in the sacredness of all life, and their faith in the innate goodness of the human spirit. That spirit is mirrored, for Stegner, in the awe-inspiring western landscape, and in humanity's acceptance of the responsibility to preserve and protect it and the rest of the natural world. Like Thoreau, whom he resembles in many ways, Stegner's view of the world and nature are based on experience and instinct rather than any particular theory. Stegner *is*, despite himself, a product of the Enlightenment, and could never truly be described as a deep ecologist, yet his absolutely vital, visceral and spiritual connection with the natural world places him on the perimeter of the deep ecologists' camp.

Stegner's greatest work, *Angle of Repose*,[103] deals largely with the transformative power of nature. His environmental writing and his influential biography of John Wesley Powell reveal both the grandeur and fragility of the natural world, and its continuing importance in the national consciousness. Stegner constantly emphasizes the necessity of an attitude of what he refers to as *stewardship* of landscape and the natural world. His major works examine the relationship of humanity to the specifically western landscape, a landscape often exploited and misunderstood by a mobile population believing in Manifest Destiny and the endless availability of land, and by business and government interests, seeing in the West both a nearly infinite natural resource and a valuable power base. Stegner challenged the precepts of frontier philosophy, although he accepted the fact that development and settlement would not always necessarily equate with environmentalism, and that settlement was clearly necessary and inevitable. He writes from a point of comparative enlightenment within the dominant ideology of his era, and speaks as one who understands the limitations of man's influence on both the development and preservation of the natural world.

Although Stegner was chronologically within the Modernist era, he was not part of the modernist movement, focusing rather on realism tied to his environmentalist stand. Krista Comer describes him thus:

> He believed the modernist movement assaulted national identity in ways that were both unwestern and un-American...
>
> Stegner's realist project could also contribute to an overall advocacy of ecological awareness. A lifelong environmentalist, Stegner took advantage of the fact that westerners, given their long history of dialoguing with the federal government about land disputes, were closer than most Americans to national debates about environmental issues...Stegner aimed to wrestle control of the West away from the mythmakers and profit takers. His deployment of a realist historical narrative in the service of a liberal political vision anticipated the new western history by at least twenty years.[104]

That is to say, Stegner's project was at heart a political one: he aimed to make a difference, to dismantle the damaging myths; to point a finger at the exploiters, and to do this he used his own historical expertise to prove his points. In this anticipation of the New Western History, which has the same goals, Stegner establishes western literature and western studies as central, rather than peripheral, to American literature in the twentieth century. Stegner's relationship with the New Western History is a point to which I will return.

Until late in his life and career, Stegner retained the view of the West as "the geography of hope."[105] It was only in the 1990s, shortly before his death, that Stegner "relented," according to Comer, "chastened by a lifetime of witnessing boom and bust economic cycles"[106] and admitted that the West was for some people, anything *but* the geography of hope.[107] Stegner's critique therefore comes full circle in certain ways. While he always cast a wary glance at the frontier myths, until late in his career he retained a certain optimism and hopefulness regarding the West as a whole. Despite the fact that he did revise his views somewhat, his earlier views are not negated by the somewhat fuller critique which he posited in his final years.

*   *   *   *

While Stegner critiqued the fabulous, often untrue imagery of the West through historical engagement in his novels, biographies, and historical works, McCarthy's approach is different. He works towards an undercutting of traditional western mythology, clearly identified in his western works as the epic of the lone man in the wilderness; the idea of an endless frontier; and free and available land—in fact a Promised Land. He engages with these myths in order to both identify and subvert their corrosive effect upon American thinking and life. McCarthy accomplishes this through the employment of the archetypal western figure, the lone cowboy on an open range. His young cowboys are both victims and purveyors of the myths which control them. As recent history has clearly shown, the image of the gun-slinging cowboy, rewritten as an American soldier, moving from place to place freely, is all too alive and well. The acceptance of a mythic structure in American life is a danger which McCarthy's western novels clearly reveal in all of its ramifications and consequences.

Both Stegner and McCarthy through their works aim for the transcendent knowledge which is, or ought to be, the goal of art. Both writers believe in codes of behavior which motivate their characters. And I believe both writers are motivated by the desire to reveal that which, in much of American life and literature, remains hidden, a true understanding of the complex, conflicted history, and present life of the country whose culture now, for good or ill, dominates the world. Writing either side of the cultural watershed of the 1960s and early 1970s, these authors give us a unique perspective into how approaches to western nature and landscape have been altered by the cultural revolution of the second half of the twentieth century.

2   Stegner's West

An Overview

In my introductory chapter, I have suggested that the American frontier functioned as a sort of Holy Grail: a metaphorical goal surrounded
by mythology which dictated action while undermining it at the same
time. The great significance given to the frontier has specific causes,
among which is the comparative uniqueness of American mythology, its
symbolism codified, indeed stratified, within a print culture. That is to
say, in early American history, fact often became legend, with the attendant distortions of legend, almost as it happened. In addition, I have
argued that the actual facts of some of America's most basic historical
myths gained power in part from the fact that they fit into an already
extant myth structure present in the contemporary consciousness of the
population.

Re-historicization of the American past has long begun, but the myth
structure created by the frontier and its archetypal characters has sunk
deep into the national psyche, and the controlling power of this myth
structure is both crippling and dangerous in its continuing ability to
influence contemporary thought and action. Yet within the canon of
classic American literature, there has always been a tradition of examining and challenging myths, and that tradition has been continuous
in western American writing. However, the marginalization of western
writing by the dominant critical establishment has had the result that
some of the most powerful voices in the discussion of the development
of American thought, and in the critique of the myth, have remained
relatively unheard, shelved with the limiting label of "regional writers."
I suggest that it is only by de-marginalizing the literature of the West,
so that western voices may be heard without prejudice, that a coherent
critique of the myth of the frontier may be accomplished.

It is in the specifically western idiom of discussion of the western
landscape that the reconceptualization of the myth of the frontier—and
thus one of the basic tenets of the American sense of self—is achieved. I
believe that, by failing to consider those writers in whose work landscape

functions as a primary element in the narrative, the powerful codifiers of the canon have thrown away one of the keys to understanding significant aspects of American culture.

The myth of the frontier is a major theme in several of Stegner's novels, a subtext in others. It is one of his major themes in the non-fiction and biographical works. In this chapter my aim is to examine Stegner's critique of the myth of the frontier in these works and discuss the ramifications of this critique in terms of one of Stegner's larger projects, that of dismantling the damaging aspects of western mythology while retaining an appreciation for the West's grandeur, both physically and imaginatively. I will also discuss Stegner's environmentalism and his treatment of the feminine, both as principle and person, in landscape and in the western project as a whole. I will also argue that Stegner's search for sanctuary within the landscape undercuts the historical image of the "Wild West" and some of its more damaging implications.

In Stegner's works, there is an opposition between humanity and landscape in the sense that man is seen to struggle against landscape, while still possessing an appreciation of it, within the occupations of farming, mining, surveying, gardening, ranching, and so forth. Stegner's characters live on intimate terms with landscape and are very much caretakers of the landscapes they inhabit. Stegner's characters use the land, but honor it. This is evident throughout his canon, but particularly in the long novels, *The Big Rock Candy Mountain* and *Angle of Repose*, both of which may be described as western novels.

Stegner is not a western writer in the sense of traditional western writers such as Owen Wister or Zane Grey, that is, writers who generally fulfill the expectations of a reading public accustomed to certain familiar character types and plot structure. Stegner does not glorify the romantic aspects of the frontier as many of these more traditional writers have done. Rather, he reveals problematic aspects of the West, through, among other things, an emphasis on its geography and landscape, and the issues associated with its development. In this Stegner rightfully belongs with such writers as A.B. Guthrie and Aldo Leopold, Ivan Doig, Edward Abbey and Wendell Berry, Mary Austin and Willa Cather. These are writers for whom, like Stegner, the land remains an essential element in their narratives. While Leopold, Cather, and Berry are not specifically western writers, landscape itself, and human connectedness to nature, is essential in their writings, and Cather, particularly, deals with the myth of the frontier's effect on immigrant farming people, a theme which we find most notably in Stegner's *The Big Rock Candy Mountain*.

Stegner's westerners' relationship to the landscape reveals the contradictions of the frontier ethos, while admitting its possibilities. That is, Stegner's characters are, on some level, aware of the fact that while they sometimes exploit the natural world, on another level they have no choice, or are in fact reluctant to pass up the opportunities offered by such exploitation. They are surviving in a hostile environment; like Thoreau, they are "driving life into a corner," but unlike Thoreau, theirs is not an eastern experiment, but a western fight for survival. Stegner's later novels, set in a contemporary twentieth century, reveal aspects of western mentality much more subtly, without recourse to obviously "western" themes at all, often concentrating mainly on environmental issues and character development.

Stegner clearly opposed those aspects of frontier mythology which encouraged belief in the inexhaustible wealth of the West, and the irrational belief, so tragically exemplified in the misguided axiom, "rain follows the plow," that success in the West was simply a matter of wanting it enough. Stegner believed that land, not man, set the limit on human activity in the West. I suggest that in the larger scheme of things, to understand the facts of frontier mythology's disastrous effects on landscape, was to understand the implicit dangers of its twin, the doctrine of Manifest Destiny, which posited the inevitable domination of the entire American continent by the Euro-American people of the United States. I have briefly discussed the "legacy of conquest" in the preceding chapter. This legacy was largely created by the myth of the frontier. It is one of Stegner's themes in *The Big Rock Candy Mountain*, and is also significant in *Angle of Repose*. The ramifications of the frontier legacy on the Western landscape are also the subject of many of Stegner's environmental essays and memoirs, and have bearing on the later "pastoral" novels in his canon.

In a paper delivered at the Second European Conference of the Cormac McCarthy Society in June 2000, Robert Jarrett stated,

> The critique of Bo Mason in *The Big Rock Candy Mountain* and *Recapitulation* is a repudiation of the West's legacy of conquest, its wealth by extraction, and its class and labor relations. The type of the quintessential nineteenth century westerner...is marooned within the twentieth century and burdened by his social roles...Equating his essential self with the Western landscape across which he roams, Bo identifies himself with the Turnerian myths of the West.[1]

This "essential self," posited by Jarrett, is in many ways attractive: independent, self-reliant, courageous; yet as a definition of character, these attributes alone are inadequate. The idea of a character's "essential self" is one to which Stegner returns in *Angle of Repose*. This relative simplification of what postmodern writers would consider the multiplicity of character again links Stegner with late nineteenth-century sensibility and its emphasis on wholeness rather than fragmentation of character. Jarrett's suggestion that Bo's identification with the landscape is also identification with the Turnerian myths of the West suggests a self-consciousness which

Bo does not possess. On the other hand, if, as Stegner has argued elsewhere (most notably in *Angle of Repose* and *Wolf Willow* and the nonfiction collected in *Where the Bluebird Sings to the Lemonade Springs*, and *The Sound of Mountain Water*), landscape itself has shaping power, then Bo's identification with landscape does in fact identify him with Turner's western myths in the sense that his life reflects the westward march which Turner profoundly believed in. The irony, of course, is that Bo's westward travels were travels for the most part into further levels of chaos, revealing the failure of the myth of the frontier combined with an aggressive belief in Manifest Destiny. Bo's intractable belief in the myth of the frontier and his own inevitable success illustrates one of the myth's most damaging features—the tenacity with which its adherents clung to it, despite all logic and evidence to the contrary. The West was clearly *not* a Promised Land, though there are certainly sublime, beautiful, and arable parts of it. There are also intractable deserts, perilous mountain ranges, and unnavigable rivers. What there is, in abundance, is space, and it is this space, equating with possibility, by which the continued belief in the myth of the frontier was driven.

For Stegner, landscape shaped identity in two ways. First, and most obviously, characters are shaped by the lives they are compelled to lead in often harsh and unforgiving environments. This aspect of the effects of landscape was particularly important for Stegner's understanding of and sympathy with the arduous and relentless lives that women often lived in the West. Secondly, characters are shaped, and identity is shaped, by an openness to the sublime power of landscape and nature. This is a point discussed with reference to other western landscapes by Jane Tompkins in *West of Everything*, but her comments may be applied to some of Stegner's settings as well. Tompkins writes of an environment which is

> inimical to human beings...But the negations of the physical setting...are also its siren song. Be brave, be strong enough to endure this and you will become like this—hard, austere, sublime. This code of asceticism founds our experience of Western stories.[2]

Sublimity in this sense is clearly *not* the same as beauty—attractiveness, or the picturesque—and while the sublime in nature may be beautiful, it is not necessarily so. The sublime in landscapes, particularly western American landscapes, is to do with their effect upon the viewer, which I suggest is something even beyond the "delightful horror" posited by nineteenth-century landscape painters in their interpretations of the sublime in landscape. The imaginative effect of landscape, the capacity to lift the mind to a level of contemplation bringing it closer to an understanding of the divine, transforms the viewer. Their capacity to thus transform character gives certain landscapes a sentience which I believe Stegner reveals in much of his writing, allowing for the transformation of characters through the agency of the landscape. Some characters, however, are *not* changed by association with the sublime, such as Bo Mason, who never develops anything but an adversarial relationship with landscape and nature. His desired landscapes are those he can use, solely. Any shaping of Bo is simply the wearing down of hope and aspiration in a world which does not give him the rewards he seeks. The character Susan Ward in *Angle of Repose*, on the other hand, is endowed with high sensitivity to the world around her, and is changed by that world. Yet the actual life she leads in the western landscape is one which is disappointing, indeed heartbreaking.

Landscape as an equation with the western self, Stegner argues through his depiction of Bo, is outmoded, doomed to failure, essentially tragic. Turner's frontier thesis was suspect even at the time it was written. It is only retrospectively that people like Bo Mason who have outlived the frontier era may be seen as viable personalities. Characters such as Bo are marooned, as Jarrett suggests, like time travelers, in the present, acting out fantasies of pioneering in a world which no longer has either the space or the tolerance for those activities. I suggest that this argument of the obsolescence of characters such as Bo lifts Stegner's work beyond that of many of his contemporaries who dealt with similar themes, for whom western experience was still a defining element of the perceived American character. Stegner's tragic awareness links him with thinkers far beyond his milieu, and gives him the status of a threshold writer, linking the pre and post Vietnam-era views of the West. These positions may be described as the ideologically innocent, idealistic, yet often rapacious view of the West held by generations who still believed in Manifest Destiny and the endless frontier; as opposed to the concept of the West as a locus for competing realities and identities, undermining the master narrative of the idealized western frontier, which had become suspect in the aftermath of the Vietnam War.

While *The Big Rock Candy Mountain* may be read partly as autobiography, it is clear that it may also be read paradigmatically as a statement of Stegner's attitude toward the destructive possibilities inherent in the perception of landscape as a Big Rock Candy Mountain: a limitless source of potential wealth and possibility. Bo's characterization, therefore, is posited on the premise that he and his sort of man represented an archaic, roving, western masculinity, initially important in pioneer settlement, but latterly set firmly in opposition to the civilizing, settling effects of women. Rooted communities and communal values are integral to Stegner's concept of "sanctuary," a concept which is central to his work. Therefore, while admiring frontier toughness and independence on the one hand, yet freed by his own childhood experience from any illusions about western life, Stegner is able to argue against the romantic illusions of western myth, while still admiring certain aspects of the western ethos.

Stegner therefore challenges the simplistic male-freedom versus female-homemaking synecdoche as a paradigm for western gender relations, while allowing its very limited validity, up to a point. In broad terms, it is true, male freedom and female homemaking were at odds in the West, and certainly appear to be so in classic western literature, such as *The Virginian*. However, the hybridity and contradictions of western life are always apparent in Stegner's works. As Neil Campbell has pointed out,

> The West formed by expansion, exploration, hunting and settlement trails, enforced and chosen displacements, and multiple contacts is a space that is best examined by seeing these diverse routes alongside and in dialogue with the alternative impulse to "rootedness."[3]

The "impulse to rootedness" is one which Stegner has characterized as female in his works, as opposed to the classic roving westerner of popular fiction and myth. This again places Stegner in the vanguard of western revisionists, and reveals both his ethos and his aim as political in the sense of providing an active critique of dominant western imagery and interpretations.

The lives of Stegner's westerners are based on real lives, but as Stegner himself emphasized, his stories are fiction, and as fiction it is fair to suggest the context of, particularly, *The Big Rock Candy Mountain*, and *Angle of Repose* also reflect the historical condition of the West itself during eras of pioneering and development. In both novels the pioneer ethos is pitted against the reality of the end of available free land and the perceived endless opportunities of resource rushes, and various forms of profiteering.

* * * *

In re-examining the myth of the frontier, Stegner focuses on the search for sanctuary, the ever-elusive "safe place." Stegner's women typically search for a home, among the vicissitudes of a transient western lifestyle, while the continuing quest for the chimerical "Big Rock Candy Mountain" is the driving force for Stegner's men. These usually gender-specific desires were, in early western literature, nearly always represented only by the masculine model. Stegner's re-evaluation of a world otherwise seen through the lens of male perception is a significant step towards the re-imagining of the West. Krista Comer suggests that he therefore posits the foreground for an entire tradition of reading western American literature:

> In the mid-1960's, Stegner's essays "History, Myth and the Western Writer" (1967) and "Born a Square" (1964) provided a critical blueprint for much later scholarship. And that critical blueprint, to a surprising extent, remains intact…Stegner read a range of western

narratives from 1880 to 1960...He broadly characterized them thus: they displayed a tendency towards realist narrative, a nostalgic tone, a belief in heroic virtue, a focus on the romantic frontier past rather than the urban present, a marked attention to western landscape, and a recurrent concern for gendered conflict, represented via what Stegner calls the "roving man" and "civilizing woman."[4]

That is to say, in the canon of western American literature, Stegner at one point set the parameters within which much of western American fiction was studied. As well as suggesting a critical blueprint, Stegner's own fiction, as well as his historical works, critiqued the accepted imagery of the pioneer and the frontier. While Stegner's novels certainly could be called realist, and gendered conflict is one of his main themes, he avoids the Scylla and Charybdis of nostalgia and romanticization of the frontier, and recognizes heroic virtue for what it is, often shown in female rather than male behavior, in contrast with the usual western fare. His attention to landscape also critiques the traditional model in that it does not focus on landscape as a testing ground for male strength, but rather sees it in its feminine manifestations, which I have mentioned and will further discuss in this chapter.

Western scholarship has moved on since Stegner was an almost lone, myth-denying voice, and recent developments have carried western studies well beyond the old western history, the New Western History, the critique of the New Western History, regionalism, ecocriticism, feminist ecocriticism, and no doubt other new isms which are yet to appear. But I argue that Stegner is still important, his critique of the West representing a *threshold* over which many other writers and critics crossed. While he may seem dated to some now, it is important to remember that among critics of the West, he was one of the first to articulate a critique of the myth of the frontier in specific terms.

I also argue that in Stegner's constant search for sanctuary, in his novels, historical works and essays, he iterates a female perspective and an understanding of the landscape as not simply an object of male power, but rather in its "feminine" manifestation, a source of its own power which ultimately defeats the traditional concept of Manifest Destiny as settlement and control. This sense of the natural world possessing agency of its own places Stegner from the 1950s onward far in the vanguard of ecocriticism, a theoretical standpoint which was not to find widespread expression until the mid-1990s.

I will begin my examination of Stegner's works with an analysis of *The Big Rock Candy Mountain* and *Angle of Repose*. I will examine how these two novels illustrate Stegner's view of the West, a view formed prior to the changes in American perspective which occurred as a result of the massive cultural upheavals catalyzed by the Vietnam War and other factors during the late 1960s and early 1970s. I will argue that

Stegner's is a revisionist sensibility formed by his particular historical circumstances, and by his attachment to certain values formed in the nineteenth century, principally Transcendentalism and the idea of the West as radically new. As John Daniel notes, "For sixty years, every morning till noon, he extended a carefully considered pathway out of the nineteenth century through the broad terrain of American life."[5] Stegner remained loyal—up to a point—to these nineteenth-century values, despite his own critique of them in various works. I will discuss Stegner's pastoral fiction, the non-fiction, and finally, I will address Stegner's environmentalism and his concept of landscape itself as a transcendent force. In addition, Stegner offers a perspective on the gendered dimension of landscape which I will address throughout the chapter.

Although Stegner was one of the most prolific and talented American writers of his time, much of his work has remained unknown outside the West. Jackson Benson describes him as "the greatest of our non-celebrity authors,"[6] and suggests various reasons for this. One of the problems which dogged Stegner's career was that, even after he won the Pulitzer Prize for *Angle of Repose* in 1971, he was always considered a regional writer by the East Coast literary establishment, and was not regarded in the same light as many of the mainstream (eastern) American authors of his era. He often compared his plight to that of Faulkner before Malcolm Cowley. In 1946, Malcolm Cowley had "rescued Faulkner through a reappraisal of his work and propelled him towards his current position as one of the premier writers of the twentieth century."[7] Benson goes on to assert that it was through this legitimization of Faulkner that southern writing has attained its rightful place in American letters, but that the same thing has not happened to western writing, which is still classed as regional, although significant inroads have been made since Benson made his comments in 1996. Additionally, Benson notes in a later study that Stegner is not a solely western writer in terms of settings:

> They range from the plains West at the turn of the century to the California West of post-World War II, but also the Midwest of the prewar and postwar periods, Vermont, Florida, Salt Lake City, Santa Barbara, Los Angeles, as well as several foreign locations...On this basis it would be hard to categorize Stegner as "regionalist" which is the term some critics have used to diminish him.[8]

Another reason why Stegner's voice was not heard was that he was, as he says himself in his essay, "Born a Square,"[9] often seen as an unfashionable traditionalist, a liberal, but not a radical. Criticism of this aspect of Stegner's work, I believe, is overstated. While he admired some traditional values, traditional values are certainly not the sum of what Stegner is about. Criticisms of him, such as those made by Elizabeth Cook-Lynn, focus on what Stegner did *not* do, among which failings are included his failure to include native American issues in his canon, rather than sticking with issues and a milieu with which he was familiar. Cook-Lynn criticizes Stegner and other non-Native American writers for referring to themselves as native to the North American soil:

> Un-self-consciously they write about the plains and the American Indian and their own experiences in an attempt to clarify their own identities. Yet in a moment of schizophrenia so appropriate to one who continually withdraws from reality, Stegner claims an affinity with Indians by calling himself "a sensuous little savage," not a child of Europe.[10]

There are many avenues to follow in taking issue with this limited appraisal, but one of the most obvious is the fact that Stegner has not claimed affinity with the Indians. It is Cook-Lynn who assumes that his use of "savage" implies a connection with Native Americans, showing that she herself has adopted the language of the perceived invaders. In fact the greater part of Cook-Lynn's contentious essay criticizes Stegner for relating to and loving the place he came from, denying that he may be "indigenous" to the place since his ancestors were not.

While the Native American camp certainly possesses the moral high ground in any discussion of their mistreatment, Cook-Lynn is holding Stegner responsible for wrongs he did not commit. As I have mentioned elsewhere, Stegner does not discuss the Native American side of American history because it was not part of his field of vision. Perhaps he did not feel that it was part of his remit to deal with a side of western life of which he admittedly was largely ignorant. Stegner's own concept of pioneering was largely based on early twentieth-century settlement, and was formulated principally by experience and study of Saskatchewan and Utah—both places which never had large indigenous populations, and which indeed are still among the most sparsely populated areas in North America. Stegner is not arguing for the rightness of the settlers who took the Black Hills in breach of treaties, nor is he suggesting that the forcible removal of the Miwok from their homes in the Sierra was just; he does not argue that Wounded Knee or the Trail of Tears were good things, to give examples of the more obviously wicked treatment of Native Americans. He simply doesn't engage with those themes, narratively. Native Americans, like African Americans, Mexicans, and other non-white groups are simply not on Stegner's radar. And while Cook-Lynn feels that this is a fault, given that Stegner writes about the American land, I would argue that while it may be a limitation, it is a limitation dictated by Stegner's historical placement. He may ignore the Native Americans, but he does not denigrate them, and Cook-Lynn's remark shows a desire to denigrate all non-Native American settlement:

Perhaps we can weep for all American who were and are *merely passing through*. But that does not mean we can excuse them for imagining and believing that American Indians, too, are or were, *merely passing through*, a mere phase of history to be disclaimed or forgotten or, worse yet, nostalgically lamented. To do so is to misunderstand indigenousness and to appropriate the American Indian imagination in the same way colonists appropriate the land and resources of the New World.[11]

The condescension of Cook-Lynn's assertion that settlers are those who only "passed through" suggests an attitude of moral superiority based upon possession, something for which the settlers themselves are rightly criticized. How then does one make a new country? When is one allowed to call a place one's own? Are not Native Americans themselves "new-comers" as well, in Cook-Lynn's terms, having come to the Americas from Asia? Are all non-native people forever considered outsiders?

No right-thinking person can do anything but lament the treatment of the Native Americans, but in choosing Stegner, a soft target for her attack, Cook-Lynn has chosen badly. Spiritually transcendentalist, concerned with the effects of landscape upon humanity, Stegner may not be plowing the same furrow as Native Americans, but he is plowing in the same field.

I see no failure in this: writers cannot do all things. What Stegner did do, he did very well, and his inclusion, particularly, of feminist issues in his approach to the western canon as a whole is laudable and, for his historical moment, unusual. While he considered himself a traditionalist, much of his writing goes beyond traditional boundaries and approaches universal themes, themes which are not always in vogue, it must be said, but which generally stand the test of time and the vagaries of succeeding waves of academic criticism.

Jackson Benson summarizes this aspect of Stegner's work:

> Can a middle-class white male who wrote not about victimization, but about the facing down of adversity, and who, through example both in his life and work, extols the old verities of love, friendship, sacrifice, compassion and forgiveness—can this writer find a place in the literature of the 1990s?[12]

Benson's remark is contentious, assuming as it does the moral high ground in opposition to what he possibly sees as a degraded age. I believe Stegner has indeed been overlooked, but not necessarily for Benson's reasons. His novels, particularly the later ones, contain the sort of discerning character studies which have always been popular among serious readers. I am thinking of the characterizations of Susan Burling Ward in *Angle of Repose*, Charity Lang in *Crossing to Safety*,[13] and Joe Allston in *All the Little Live Things*, particularly. The fact that his work was viewed as regional has categorized him in a way that may have excluded a large readership. That his fictional themes overlap with western themes can be seen as a strength when one considers that the traditions of classic American literature are expressed in his work.

My interest in Stegner is in his treatment of the western landscape and its effect on characters, and the search for sanctuary in that landscape. In the landscape argument, Stegner is firmly on the side of the wilderness surveyor and conservationist, John Wesley Powell, and the great naturalist, John Muir, among others. He is a profound realist with a deep and abiding love for a landscape which he understands and respects. He is one who has been formed by the landscape of his childhood. Walter Isle suggests that it is this formation, rather than transformation, which gives Stegner his particular power, but limits his continuing effectiveness in the discourse of the West:

> In general, Stegner's experience is past and was formative. He places his childhood experience in the context of his later historical understanding of the region and represents it in the recovery of personal memory, the recounting of the history of a place, and in his fiction.[14]

Isle contrasts Stegner with the Canadian writer Sharon Butala, who, living in the same landscape as Stegner's *Wolf Willow*—that of Stegner's boyhood—has, through her life and writing, transformed the experience into an almost mystical appreciation of the landscape of the short grass plains of southern Saskatchewan and northern Montana, as detailed in her book, *The Perfection of the Morning*.[15]

Isle's contention that Stegner's experience is somehow dated and ineffective might be allowed had Stegner himself not continually reassessed his own experience, and reframed his insights both in fiction and essay, throughout his career. An obvious progression is evident throughout Stegner's canon. This reassessment alone would have given Stegner's work continuing currency. Combined with the universality of many of his fictional themes, it suggests that Stegner's star, though perhaps not quite ascendant, still shines.

The Big Rock Candy Mountain and Recapitulation[16]

In the first few pages of his autobiographical novel, *The Big Rock Candy Mountain*, published in 1943, Stegner immediately challenges the romance of the myth of the frontier. Although Elsa Norgaard feels freer from her oppressive background with every mile further west she travels, every mile makes her sicker. The beginning of the novel is a

description of Elsa vomiting repeatedly in the filthy lavatory of a sti-
fling train. There is very little western romance in the scene. The story
is a familiar western one: fleeing a bad situation for a worse one. The
essential quality of hopefulness created by a large landscape, the perceived freedom from history, as well as the various free land schemes
that drew settlers west—all hallmarks of western experience—could
not outweigh the actual reality of *being* in a new, unsettled, wild, dangerous country.

The novel is based on Stegner's own life. Bo Mason, the father in the
novel, is George Stegner, Wallace's father. Bo clearly represents the old
way, born with what Stegner calls "the Western disease,"[17] the disease
of the Big Rock Candy Mountain, the optimism which kills realism, and
the profound knowledge that, "Just around the corner, there's a rainbow
in the sky," as the old song says. Being born with it, he had it in its worst
form: not visionary expectation, as Stegner terms it,[18] but the expectation of a free lunch; get-rich-quick schemes, which even though they
required hard work—what Bo was best at—also required a capacity for
smallness and meanness.

It is this aspect of the frontier myth, the smallness and meanness,
dishonesty and exploitation, paradoxically coupled with a simple faith
in hard work and an assumption of natural privilege, which Stegner
examines through the character of Bo Mason. The critique of Bo is fully
realized against the characterization of Elsa. We have in the novel's configuration of characters the classic western problem stated previously:
the roving man opposed to the ever-hopeful-of-making-a-home woman.
Jackson Benson suggests that Stegner

> came to see the conflict between his father and mother as a synec-
> doche for the Western clash between the forces of frontier toughness
> and independence on the one side and the forces of cooperation and
> community on the other.[19]

This synecdoche recurs throughout Stegner's work in the short fiction as well as the novels, but most particularly *The Big Rock Candy
Mountain* and *Angle of Repose*. Krista Comer's discussion of Stegner is
particularly useful in relation to his position on women in the West. She
states that

> most of western criticism regards Stegner...as "good on women's
> issues." In western literary history, as Stegner mapped it, gendered
> conflict recurred as a defining western theme. He imagined women...
> not as symbols of entrapment but as complex characters with legiti-
> mate motivations and understandable needs; he imagined men as
> both desirous of western adventure and domestic fulfillment.[20]

Therefore, in Stegner's world view, women do not fall into the familiar pattern of an older western fiction. We are not looking at the Virginian's Molly, who gives him improving books to read by the campfire, or Aunt Sally, "civilizing" Huck. The men in Stegner's specifically western stories (*The Big Rock Candy Mountain*, *Angle of Repose*, *Recapitulation*, *Remembering Laughter*, *Wolf Willow*, and various short stories) may have lit out for the territory, but their wives have come with them. Their women may want different things, but Stegner sees female desires as acceptable and not in such conflict as to define that irresolvable war between the sexes, resulting in what Annette Kolodny has described as the "pre-sexual"[21] American male who simply cannot cope with the feminine and so departs from society altogether. Stegner is therefore challenging both the male-freedom versus female-homemaking synecdoche suggested earlier, but, I would argue, also crucially equating it with the treatment of nature and the attitude towards settlement in the West.

This is a significant departure from figures such as Cooper's Hawkeye, men in the mould of the Boone character, unable either to marry or to live in settled communities. In Stegner's fiction one overcomes what Kolodny describes as "the persistent pervasiveness of the male configurations."[22] One does not sense that one is dealing with the West of the dime novel or the traditional "western" which adheres to mythical stereotypes. Stegner himself wrote:

> A Western is not a unique performance but a representative one. Its characters are not individuals but archetypes or stereotypes, and its themes are less interesting for their freshness or their truth to history than for their demonstration of a set of mythic patterns.[23]

Stegner recognizes that in many respects the archetypal western man's masculinity is, as Kolodny says of Hawkeye, "infantile; expressed in sternness and stoicism, not sex."[24] Of all Stegner's men Bo Mason has the most elements of this western type, coupled with a fecklessness and disregard for law which are also arguably characteristics of the traditional western hero.

If one agrees with Kolodny's critique with reference to Stegner's men, it may be argued that Stegner's awareness of the tragic collision of desires articulated in the characters of Bo and Elsa in *The Big Rock Candy Mountain*, and later similarly in *Angle of Repose*, was based on a deeper sympathy with the feminine than the masculine. Stegner articulated this sympathy in an article published in 1962, stating, "In a jumpy and insecure childhood where all masculine elements are painful or dangerous, sanctuary matters."[25] This suggests that for Stegner the masculine was generally associated with unpleasant sides of life on the frontier, and is not romanticized at all. This also points out the conflicted relationship

Stegner had with his own father, whose coarse masculinity alienated the sensitive young Stegner.

I suggest that Stegner's critique of Bo is also a critique of the archetype which allowed men like Bo Mason to function, after a fashion, in society, highlighting their inadequacy as national models. As Annette Kolodny wrote in 1975,

> Our continuing fascination with the lone male in the wilderness, our literary heritage of essentially adolescent, presexual, pastoral heroes, suggest that we have yet to come up with a satisfying model for mature masculinity on this continent; while the images of abuse that have come to dominate the pastoral vocabulary suggest that we have been no more successful in our response to the feminine qualities of nature than we have to the human feminine.[26]

While Bo Mason is in the mold of the lone male in the wilderness, Stegner's depiction of him reveals the flaws in it, and most importantly challenges the myth of the frontier to which the character of the lone male belongs. The challenge to this myth was not new, even in Stegner's time, but the fact that he coupled it with an appreciation of feminine values *was* new. Part of Stegner's challenge to the myth lay in the fact that he did appreciate feminine values and recognized that the feminine contribution to the West was not simply a side trip, but was in fact at the heart of the journey itself, no matter what the mythmakers thought. Stegner also believed in the importance of community, something quite foreign to the western man following the myth of the frontier to the wide open spaces imagined in the West. Stegner's further connection to environmentalism suggests links between feminine values and conservation which allow for a much fuller critique of accepted western values in gendered terms than the simple "roving man—nesting woman" scenario. I suggest this because the traditional feminine values of the creation and preservation of the home equate much more with an ethic of conservation and preservation than do the values of the western man, who, according to Stegner, is interested primarily in extracting profit from the land, and indeed often simply gaining wealth, as in mining and logging, then moving on. This link between an abiding interest in the environment and a feminine perspective also links Stegner to the tenets of feminist ecocriticism mentioned previously, though anticipating that movement by many years.

Stegner was deeply sympathetic with his own mother, and truly alive to the sufferings of women in a world which seemed to demand a peripatetic lifestyle antithetical to the desire for settlement which women, mainly, wanted. But men wanted what Comer refers to as "domestic fulfillment" as well. It was only in the myth of the frontier, that powerful, pervasive, persuasive undercurrent in American thinking, that "Go

West Young Man!" continued to echo as the siren song for generations. Comer writes,

> Stegner exceeds by every measure any other male rendering of the literary past. For this last reason, the Stegnerian spatial field *must* be counted as part of western feminist geographic imaginations. In a Stegnerian spatial field, women are historical subjects with integrity, legitimate needs and desires, agency.[27]

Comer's argument continues to suggest that because Stegner was not a feminist, that is, did not "hold the fundamental feminist conviction that women are oppressed,"[28] he did not rethink the entire history of the West to accommodate women's history, but in fact did become more aware of the destructive and self-centered nature of masculine narratives in a world which had been completely dominated by male images of western experience. Comer's argument is fair, but again, I suggest that Stegner's awareness of feminist issues in an age in which feminist language was not yet spoken, reveals a deep, instinctive and profound understanding of the issues which not only predates but also surpasses much later commentary owing to the absence of over-simplification of complex human issues which sometimes is seen in the more radical feminist arguments.

Melody Graulich, in her essay, "O Beautiful for Spacious Guys," summarizes aspects of this argument, but calls into question one of its main threads:

> At the heart of this "archetypal" American story is an opposition of values symbolized by gender conflict, the "inescapable" opposition summarized so neatly by Wallace Stegner: "male freedom and aspiration versus female domesticity, wilderness versus civilization, violence and danger versus the safe and tamed"...Few feminists would be so certain as is Stegner that these are the "legitimate inclinations of the sexes," that what Henry Nash Smith has called the myth's "drastic simplifications" represent fundamental female and male dreams.[29]

Graulich here suggests a simplification in Stegner's view of women, but I argue that in his treatment of female characters, particularly Susan Burling Ward in *Angle of Repose*, Stegner allows his women characters to develop and expand within a novelistic structure which critiques the myth of the frontier while at the same time allowing for the fact that historical characters lived in a world in which the currency of the myth would certainly have had an effect on their lives. Elsa Norgaard, by the tragedy of her own passivity in relation to her overbearing husband's endless quest for "the Big Rock Candy Mountain," illustrates the heartbreaking fate of a woman subject, partly through inescapable circumstance, to a wholly male-dominated lifestyle in the pioneer and post-pioneering eras. Graulich may object to the implicit simplification posited in Elsa's objection to Bo's dream chasing, but it nonetheless represents what was a lived reality for many western women, as Stegner knew from his own childhood experience.

Nevertheless, it is the characterization of Bo Mason in *The Big Rock Candy Mountain* which dominates the novel. Elsa is seen as patient and long-suffering, passive to the point of being an almost willing victim of Bo's fecklessness. The novel is truly Bo's novel, and his characterization is at the centre of the novel as the myth of the frontier with all its unspoken contradictions and disgraceful episodes was at the centre of American consciousness for so many years. Stegner recognized this himself and said in his essay, "Letter, Much Too Late," that he had allowed the figure of his father to dominate, as it had in life, because he felt that the kindness and goodness of his mother was almost unbelievable.[30] As his father was a creation of the myth of the frontier, so was Stegner's mother. Therefore, I suggest that it is possible to argue that the perception of western spaces seen through the referent of the myth of the frontier was distinct for women and men, and that that distinction was not fully recognized as other than an adversarial relation between the sexes until the reconfiguring of western history which, though approached by other writers, began in earnest with Stegner's early work.

Also evident in *The Big Rock Candy Mountain* is the search for the "safe place" which recurs throughout the novel, and which is so important in Stegner's understanding of the West. In the novel, as in the short story "Genesis," sanctuary is only ever achieved through the intervention of the female-identified principles of community and cooperation. This inability of the pioneer male landscape, and mindset, to accommodate the female has been much discussed by feminist critics. In 1987, the same year Patricia Nelson Limerick published the groundbreaking *Legacy of Conquest* and set in motion what was to become the New Western History, Susan Armitage wrote,

> There is a region of America that I have come to call Hisland. In a magnificent western landscape, under perpetually cloudless western skies, a cast of heroic characters engages in dramatic combat, sometimes with nature, sometimes with each other. Occupationally, these heroes are diverse...but they share one distinguishing characteristic—they are all men. It seems that all rational demography has ended at the Mississippi River: all the land west of it is occupied only by men.[31]

This exclusion of women from the imaginative space of the West has been commented upon by Kolodny, Comer, Graulich, Tompkins, and others. The critical assessment is ongoing, but like the New Western History, some of its origins must be attributed to the early critiques made by Stegner.

This obviation of the female, as identified by Armitage, in Elsa's case, bears parallels with the landscape as female. As Elsa is dominated by her overbearing husband, so too is the landscape dominated by the "boomers" of pioneer settlement, users and usurpers of the western landscape. (This point provides us with a thematic link with the treatment of women in McCarthy's works, which will be discussed in the next chapter.) This claim is crucial in my arguments and is based upon the assertion that there is in the concept of stewardship, as defined by Stegner, that which is quintessentially "feminine" in the sense of developing a relationship with the land, and caring for landscape, in opposition to the "masculine" sense of using the land in the archetypal "use-and-use-up," myth of the frontier pattern, which includes mining, trapping, deforesting, dam building, and so forth. In "Stegner and Stewardship," Ann Ronald further argues that Stegner's appreciation of the landscape partakes of a deep, organic sense of the land and landscape,[32] positing an additional spiritual dimension to his appreciation of nature and landscape, which further deepens Stegner's relationship with landscape.

*   *   *   *

Although *The Big Rock Candy Mountain* is autobiographical, it is not an autobiography. In his conversations with Richard Etulain, Stegner commented, "Some of the father–son stuff is of course pretty literal: I was exorcising my father. But a lot of the rest of it is invention, and I would have to insist on that."[33] And later, in reference to his own parents, Stegner states, "There was the wandering husband and the nesting woman…It's perfectly clear that if every writer is born to write one story, that's my story."[34]

Therefore while *The Big Rock Candy Mountain* may be read partly as autobiography, I suggest that it may also be read paradigmatically as a statement of Stegner's attitude toward the destructive possibilities inherent in the myth of the frontier, and particularly as they impacted upon western women. The myth of the frontier in its active characterization in Bo Mason is seen as antithetical to the search for sanctuary. A final irony in the story is the fact that Elsa says Bo was at his happiest when he was building their family homestead in Saskatchewan, the only home in which the family spent more than a few months. The myth has given Bo his durable optimism, but has taken away his chances for happiness as well, creating in him a need for constant movement and change. At the conclusion of the novel when Bo is finally succeeding, running a casino in Reno, he sells out and gives up for reasons which neither he nor his son are able to articulate, but presumably because believing in the frontier means always moving on.

Recapitulation, a return to the territory of *The Big Rock Candy Mountain*, was published more than three decades after the first book. It employs very different narrative techniques and a mixing of past and present. It is arguably a far weaker book. The novel suggests that the theme of the search for sanctuary continues as the protagonist, a much older Bruce Mason, now an ambassador, has returned to the home which was destroyed by the death of his brother and mother, and the later suicide of his father, in order to bury another deceased relative. The regret felt for a painful past and the nostalgia for what might have been give the novel a tone of melancholy similar to the Joe Allston books, *The Spectator Bird*[35] and *All the Little Live Things*. The theme of lost childhood and lost possibility recurs throughout the novel, but closure with an unhappy and troubling past seems avoided rather than achieved.

The fact that, in *Recapitulation*, Bruce has become an ambassador, a professional wanderer, without visible emotional ties, seems to suggest that the damage caused by the past can never be fully resolved. The dominant tone of the novel is nostalgia, and the action progresses through a series of flashbacks and dream imagery. Stegner has used this novel to fill in some of the blanks in *The Big Rock Candy Mountain*, and to reiterate many of the points made in the earlier work. In *The Big Rock Candy Mountain* and *Recapitulation*, Stegner is, in addition to telling his own story of a peripatetic frontier childhood, critiquing the historic imagery of a romantic pioneer past and the destructive capacity of the myth of the frontier. He continues this critique in his greatest novel, *Angle of Repose*.

Angle of Repose

In *Angle of Repose* there is a synthesis of many of the issues which had occupied Stegner in his earlier writings. The theme of the roving man opposed to the nesting woman is central, as is the marginality suffered by the West and westerners in the larger frame of American life and affairs. The loss of the "safe place" and the search for sanctuary coupled with the problem of protection of "all the little live things" looms large in the text. In "Ruminations on Stegner's Protective Impulse and the Art of Storytelling," Melody Graulich suggests that,

> Often in search of their own "safe places"…the characters Stegner most admires, or those with whom he most identifies, are commonly aspiring "protectors" who finally fail in a host of ways to protect those they love.[36]

In *The Big Rock Candy Mountain*, for example, Bruce tries to protect a sparrow which his father, in one of his unfathomable rages, shoots;

Elsa tries to protect her sons from Bo's anger; Bruce tries to protect Elsa from the knowledge of Bo's infidelities; and in one of the most harrowing scenes in the novel, Bruce tries to protect his lame colt from the fate which is gruesomely revealed to us as the family leaves Saskatchewan for the last time. All would-be protectors fail.

In *Angle of Repose*, the failures are even more dramatic. Oliver is unable to protect Susan from the vicissitudes of real life in the raw West; Susan brings up her children in a cocoon of civility and education, but a moment's fatal inattention results in her dearest child's death and the life-long alienation of her eldest. Good characters remain good, but significantly, they fail. Similarly, in the Joe Allston stories and *Crossing to Safety*, strong men watch as women they love are destroyed by forces they are helpless to stop. I suggest that this failure of the protective male in relation to a vulnerable female reflects not only Stegner's childhood experience, but also once again articulates an environmentalist's despair at the depredations visited upon the western landscape, viewed in this aspect as female. All these examples reflect Stegner's own life experience, brought up on the frontier by a woman who tried and failed to protect her son from a brutal husband: a son who tried to make life bearable for a mother who only wanted the wheels to stop turning as her husband dragged the family from one end of the country to the other, over and over again. It may also be suggested that it reflects the despair of an environmentalist who saw, among other environmental tragedies, the exquisite Glen Canyon flooded in order to create Lake Powell and provide water and power for much unsustainable southwestern development, and who deeply regretted the lack of harmony between man and the fragile western environment.

The idea of the romantic West is effectively undercut in Stegner's work, while the appreciation of the landscape remains, illustrating the real and durable appeal of the West, retained in the actual geography, rather than in the old story of the heroic man on a horse riding off into yet another sunset, carrying with him the baggage of unresolved mythic expectation.

In *New Ground*, A. Carl Bredahl suggests that westerners

> ultimately had to ask what the land would tolerate. What therefore developed in the place of the effort to impose and reshape was the perception of the need to realign assumptions about an individual's relation to the land. Much western writing is the story of that realignment.[37]

If one agrees with Bredahl, then the real western story is not man overcoming nature, which Bredahl describes as a literature of enclosure, typified in eastern narratives, but a literature of co-existence with large areas of unfamiliar space. Viewed in this light, Stegner's western narratives, particularly *Angle of Repose*, successfully challenge the earlier, eastern narratives of enclosure and suggest that the truly western idiom is the product of the act of cooperation with the landscape itself. In his western narratives, co-existence with the landscape is central. Bo Mason cannot co-exist with the landscape, western or otherwise, but seeks only to exploit it, sealing his own fate. Oliver Ward, on the other hand, in *Angle of Repose* eventually achieves an "angle of repose" in his relationship to the natural world, after a lifetime of fighting with a landscape which was ultimately too powerful for him. His wife's relationship with the landscape, however, was somewhat different. A brief look at the historical background is necessary here in order to further elucidate these relationships.

Susan Burling Ward, the central character of *Angle of Repose*, moved west with her husband Oliver in 1876. The Centennial year of the Republic was also the year of Custer's fatal battle with the Lakota Sioux in southern Montana. It was, according to Richard Slotkin, a year in which, "the United States...was in the midst of the worst economic depression in its history, and [was experiencing] a crisis of cultural morale as well."[38]

By 1876 the American industrial revolution had created, for the first time, an urban proletariat: Dreiser's factory girls and the exploited immigrants of Upton Sinclair's *The Jungle*.[39] The frontier was theoretically still open, but the aftermath of one of the bloodiest and most deeply divisive civil wars in history meant that no longer did Americans head westward on a wave of Jeffersonian optimism. The country had nearly destroyed itself. It had killed off much of a generation in the Civil War a little over a decade previously, and the wounds would be long healing. Moving west was now a movement away from the memory of war and the overcrowding of the cities.

In *The End of American Exceptionalism*, David Wrobel discusses the state of westward expansion in the years before the official "closing" of the frontier:

> Those who consulted the Census could gauge that the United States had more tenant farmers than any European country, that many farms were too heavily mortgaged to be profitable, that large holdings were becoming more common, and that there was no longer an extensive frontier of free land that might serve to reverse the process.[40]

Thomas Jefferson's dream of the nation of yeoman farmers had already become an impossibility. Stegner's Bo Mason is one of the refugees from that dream, endlessly trying and failing to achieve the idealized life once thought possible in the West. The frontier anxiety felt by those who felt that the free lands of the West were a necessary escape valve for the East with its ever-expanding population, much of it immigrant, was understandable. It was in this climate of anxiety that Susan Burling Ward left for the West less than a month after the Battle of the Little Big Horn. What Krista Comer calls "the dominant geocultural imaginary"[41] was clearly male, predominantly white, and was perceived by many of its adherents to be under attack.

The Battle of the Little Big Horn went from fact into mythology in less than the time it took to print a daily newspaper. Whitman's "Death Sonnet for Custer" was published barely a week after the news of the battle reached New York. In it the hagiography has already reached divine heights, with Custer, Christ-like, "yielding up" himself to the savage hordes of the "fatal environment." Like the Chanson de Roland, the battle became the benchmark for heroism, the romantic lost cause to top them all, and further fueled the anxiety, while reinforcing dominant national mythology, of the western white man, for whom, at the same time, all escape routes were gradually closing. It was in this same climate of loss that John Wesley Powell, an early exemplar of landscape steward- ship, and an important figure in Stegner's works, wrote his *Report on the Lands of the Arid Region*[42] in 1878. The response to Powell's report, however, was a simple and stark refusal to believe. While the facts of the Little Big Horn might not be evaded,—though a kind of evasion took place in the translating of facts into mythology—Powell's pains- taking monument of research and erudition on the possibilities for the lands of the plateau province was simply too unpalatable for the western boomers.

This was the historical background to the novel. I believe that what we are looking at behind the text of *Angle of Repose* is the historical situation of the frontier in the last quarter of the nineteenth century, seen in human terms. In addition, the structure of the novel with the twenti- eth-century narrator telling the story of his nineteenth-century ancestors suggests further comparisons. In response to Richard Etulain's question whether *Angle of Repose* was a comparison of the frontier and the new West, Stegner stated, "It's more than that. It's not only a comparison of the frontier and the New West; it's a comparison of West and East."[43] The comparison of West and East plays itself out in the relationship of Susan and Oliver, and *their* relationship to the land, as well as in Susan's gradual and painful transformation of character:

> Time hung unchanging, or with no more visible change than a slow reddening of poison oak leaves, an imperceptible darkening of the golden hills. It dripped like a slow percolation through limestone... every drop...left a little deposit of sensation, experience, feeling. In thirty or forty years the accumulated deposits would turn my cultivated, ladylike, lively, talkative, talented, innocently snobbish grandmother into a Western woman in spite of herself.[44]

Stegner here adds another possibility to the idea of the western landscape being a test of predominantly male strength, as Tompkins has suggested. Stegner's depiction of Susan's transformation in *Angle of Repose* suggests that the western landscape, despite its undoubted harshness, also possesses the capacity to cause an aesthetic transformation which has as much to do with artistic appreciation, the agency of the land itself, and spiritual openness, as it does with toughness and strength.

This process of acclimatization and acculturation is a theme which recurs throughout Stegner's work. He addresses some of the same issues in *Where the Bluebird Sings to the Lemonade Springs*, in which he speaks of the western landscape as the "geography of hope." He also describes "visionary expectation" and "transience"[45] as major influences on western life and character. The effects of these influences on the lives of Susan Ward, her husband, their children and friends are delineated throughout the novel. By the rather loose term "geography of hope," Stegner suggested that the West was "something unprecedented and unmatched in the world."[46] While Stegner modified this view, it remains a useful lens through which we may view his western landscapes. Stegner's western exceptionalism—for it cannot be called anything else—is directed toward the landscape in terms of natural features rather than inhabitants. Coupled with what I have suggested is Stegner's tacit belief in the numinous power of the natural world itself, this point further refutes Cook-Lynn's criticisms, suggesting that Stegner's understanding of the western land went inexpressibly deeper than anything to do with ownership. The significance of Stegner's reference to the West being an unspecified *something* unprecedented also emphasizes the inexpressible aspect of his understanding of landscape, that which I describe as spiritual. Stegner was alive to landscape in a way clearly reminiscent of the Transcendentalists, a point which will be discussed.

At this point I would like to address Susan Burling's relationship to "the geography of hope," and through that her relationship to landscape. It began early, back in New York when she took Oliver to Big Pond. Oliver was already the "other" in terms of the literary and artistic New York crowd with whom Susan associated. Although eastern himself, Oliver was not of Susan's world: "His character and his role were already Western, he had only that way of asserting himself against the literary gentility with which her house was associated in his mind."[47] Later on Lyman Ward, Susan's grandson, states that, "Exposure followed by sanctuary was somehow part of Grandmother's emotional need."[48] Perhaps that is why the geography of hope, as personified by her husband, was able to carry her away from her safe eastern world into a world which was definitely *not* safe, but which was made so, temporarily, by Oliver. Thus the episode at Big Pond when Susan hangs over the edge of the waterfall, held by Oliver, assumes such significance.

Susan's first exposure to the West is interesting. Her comments in a letter to her friend Augusta show that at first she is baffled by the sheer scope of the land she has come to. She writes of

> lonely little clusters of settlers' houses with the great monotonous waves of land stretching miles around them, that make my heart ache for the women who live there. They stand in the house door as the train whirls past, and I wonder if they feel the *hopelessness* of their exile?[49]

But upon her arrival at New Almaden, her reaction to the West has changed, as, of course, the landscape has changed:

> What she felt…was space, extension, bigness. Behind the house the mountain went up steeply to the ridge, along which now lay, as soft as a sleeping cat, a roll of fog or cloud. Below the house it fell just as steeply down spurs and canyons to tumbled hills as bright as a lion's hide. Below those was the valley's dust, a level obscurity, and rising out of it, miles away, was another long mountain as high as their own.[50]

And, "It took her breath to look east, it filled her heart to look west or south."[51] Susan is obviously alive to the sublimity of her surroundings, but in the early stages of the novel is in the process of reframing her response to the physical world. Nothing looks like anything from the familiar eastern world of "enclosure." Susan's response to the landscape is obviously mixed. Its newness doesn't fit the frame which her sheltered eastern upbringing has given her. Shortly after arriving in the West, she writes to Augusta,

> Don't you know how we lose the sense of our own individuality when there is nothing to reflect it back upon us? These people here have so little conception of our world that sometimes I feel myself as if I must have dreamed it.[52]

However, as Susan's individuality comes to be reflected back by a western rather than an eastern world, through the progress of the novel, her optimism regarding life in the West increases. She never quite "catches the western disease" as Oliver does, but nearly. An interesting coda to this point is in the description of the literary development of the real Mary Hallock Foote, the model for Susan, discussed by Janet Floyd.

> Lee Ann Johnson…[argues that] Foote's engagement with her new life makes it possible for her to practice the clear-sighted observation on which a realistic representation of the West rests. That is, the

further Foote moves toward the "local color" that Johnson characterizes as spontaneous realism, the more she is able to leave behind
the inadequate literary tools (and the resistance to the West) that she
brings with her to the West and its representation.[53]

This suggests that the experience of becoming western and allowing herself to adopt western perspectives was one of liberation for Mary Hallock Foote, and it does not seem too untenable a leap to suggest the same
for Stegner's Susan Ward.

Susan's cautious optimism, acquired by experience rather than intention, about the life possible in the West suffers a reverse in "On the
Bough," when she contemplates her husband's irrigation scheme:

> She saw in his face that he had contracted the incurable Western
> disease. He had set his cross-hairs on the snowpeak of a vision,
> and there he would go, triangulating his way across a bone-dry
> future, dragging her and the children with him, until they all died
> of thirst.[54]

It is here that the geography of hope comes into conflict with visionary expectation. Until this point in the novel, it has been Susan's visionary expectation—the dream of a house on the beach in Santa Cruz, the
possibility of Oliver working for the US Geological Survey, the chance
of a life in Mexico—which had come into conflict with Oliver's realism.
Now the roles are reversed and Susan is assuming the typically western
woman's role: the realist in a land of dreamers. Earlier, in the "Leadville" chapter, Stegner says that "our pioneer women were always more
realistic than our pioneer men."[55] However, until this point in the novel
it has seemed to be the other way around. Susan is becoming a western
woman as her husband assumes the truly western character that Stegner
himself knows so well—the boom-or-bust, go-for-broke visionary who
stakes it all on a throw of the dice, sufficient rainfall in an arid country,
or an irrigation scheme in a world where *all* irrigation cultures have
inevitably failed.

The geography of hope is coupled with visionary expectation and the
inevitable transience that at this point dominates Susan's life and thinking. She had been transient before, but the hopefulness of that early
transience is at this point in the novel replaced by the unhappy transience
that accompanies dream chasing, particularly dream chasing with ever-
diminishing returns, brief, heartbreaking moments of hope, and finally,
painful, disastrous resolution, accompanied in the novel by the corresponding breakdown of Susan and Oliver's marriage and the death of
their child Agnes.

In the chapter, "The Canyon," we are reminded again of what
Nancy Owen Nelson refers to in Stegner's work as the "metaphor for

the despoiled Eden that is inherent in much of his writing."[56] Susan has described life in the canyon as the life of a band of pilgrims. Despite the hardship, there is something pristine and beautiful about their life. With the death of Agnes, what was beautiful becomes horrible and deadly. A similar reversal happens in "Michoacán" when Oliver's unfavorable mine report spoils their idyllic visit to Mexico. After the report, Susan notices how badly the servants are treated in the hacienda where they are staying, and the basic inequalities of life, a hidden corruption in a world she had thought exotic and beautiful.

If, as Myra Jehlen rather contentiously suggests, "the American romance is the story of a *defeated*, a downed flight,"[57] then *Angle of Repose* is the American romance par excellence. The characters in the novel are defeated again and again, till the reader can hardly bear to hear of another of Oliver's plans, so certain are the failure and heart-break that will accompany it. Yet in the defeats there is an understanding acquired of what the land itself is saying. Melody Graulich states:

> Again and again Susan recognizes that beneath the surface of the "picturesque" and the landscape, the West has something new to say to her, perhaps through her, and that she cannot find the right perspective or vocabulary.[58]

Yet Susan does eventually find both perspective and vocabulary, and it is her efforts to find a perspective on the West which is at the heart of the book. Stegner said that he was trying to tell the story of a relationship between a man and a woman and their achievement of an "angle of repose" in their lives, but the novel is also a study of Susan's struggle to find an "angle of repose" with a world and a landscape which she initially rejected because it did not fit into the frame of reference which she held up to it, and which she later grew to accept and understand. I also suggest that Stegner himself is offering an "angle of repose" for the understanding of the myth of the frontier. In the realistic story of Susan and Oliver, the frontier ethos is examined, but not accepted. The symptoms of the "western disease" referred to in the novel are not the same as those McCarthy's young cowboys suffer in *The Border Trilogy*, but the illness is, and Stegner, even at his most optimistic, never allows us to forget that behind the myth of the frontier are the ruins of many western lives.

Another strand in the narrative of the novel is Stegner's overt articulation of the numinosity of places, related to transcendental thought. In "The Canyon," Susan is waiting for Oliver late one evening. She had crossed the rope bridge over the river and was waiting by the corral:

> A trance was on her eyes, she saw up, down, ahead, and to both sides without moving head or eyeballs. Before her, reaching to her

feet, was the pocked, silvered dust of the corral, across which the shadow of the opposite fence was drawn like a musical staff. High across the river her window glowed orange; straight ahead, and up, Arrow Rock jutted black beside the moon. All her right hand was a blackness of cliff. Upward the sky opened, a broad strip of silver gilt with the moon burning through it and stars like fading sparks flung down towards the world's rim.

She stared with eyes stretched to their widest, and as she stared, the firmament rolled one dizzying half turn, so that she was looking not up, but down, into a canyon filled with brightness, on whose bottom the moon lay among silver pebbles, a penny flung for luck into a cosmic Serpentine.[59]

Here Susan, leading a life like Thoreau's at Walden Pond, has become Emerson's "transparent eyeball," seeing all, assumed into the sublime aspect of the landscape. Nature moves through her: she is as much a part of it as an observer. It is in this aspect of Stegner's work that the unspoken understanding of nature and landscape, expressed through epiphanic moments such as this one, reveal an understanding of nature's inexpressible spiritual dimension. Susan has been moved by nature before. At this stage in the novel she has come a long way from the woman who rode out on the western train feeling nothing but despair at the sense of exile on the prairies, but in this quotation we see for the first time the true transformation of perception which has led to the transformation of character in Susan.

One cannot help but hear the echo of Fitzgerald's description of Jay Gatsby gazing at the "silver pepper of the stars" in this passage, and wonder if Susan too, is "come out to determine what share is [hers] of the local heavens."[60] She and Gatsby have few things in common, but longing for the impossible is something they do share. Gatsby longs for the past, Susan for a future which allows her to keep her past, not the new world her husband is looking for. In this intertextual passage Stegner reminds the reader of the undoubted appeal of the myth of the frontier, echoed in *The Great Gatsby*.

However, this is not the appeal of those things the myth promised: endless space, a Promised Land, the lone man, regenerating and creating himself through the vicissitudes of the West and its challenges, not at all. Susan's appreciation of the natural world is something more than just appreciation; it has nothing to do with opportunity or profit; it is a visceral, deeply felt *connection* with the world around her. Appropriately, moments like this are given some of Stegner's most limpid prose. This scene, like other epiphanic moments in Stegner's writing reflect his vital connection to the natural world and express an understanding of it which may only be described as spiritual.

* * * *

The structure of *Angle of Repose* is full of echoes and reflections. Susan and Oliver's life is reflected in the life of their grandson who narrates the story. The decline of the frontier is framed in the time frame of the novel: Susan goes west in 1876, the Centennial year, a few weeks after the Battle of the Little Big Horn, for Americans the most significant mythogenic event of the nineteenth century. Susan returns to the East, defeated, in 1890, the year the frontier was officially declared closed by the Bureau of the Census. These dates cannot be accidental.

The narrator, Lyman Ward, sat down at his typewriter just about the time American troops invaded Cambodia; the stop–start peace process in Vietnam was at stop. Some troops had been withdrawn, but the American war would stagger on until January 28, 1973. The South Vietnamese fought on until July 2, 1976, 100 years and a week after Custer's defeat, two weeks less than a century after Susan Ward headed west. These dates *are* accidental. Stegner's book was published in 1971, when it looked as if America would never pull itself out of the quicksand that the Vietnam War had become. Nonetheless, the resonance of these facts adds to the texture of the book looked at from the perspective of the year 2009.

Stegner wrote *Angle of Repose* during one of the most chaotic and divisive periods of American history. The Vietnam War tore the country apart more thoroughly than any event since the Civil War. The aftershocks of the crisis of confidence that accompanied the realization that, as a nation, America had failed, and not only had failed but had been on the wrong side of a movement of popular resistance, are still felt. I believe that one strand of what is behind the text in *Angle of Repose* is that America was never the same after the myth of the frontier was declared finished. As Susan has failed in her dream, so has the frontier. An unstated parallel with the Vietnam conflict is clear.

As in *The Spectator Bird*, the structure of *Angle of Repose* is that of a novel within a novel. The story of Lyman Ward, Susan and Oliver's grandson and the narrator of the novel, runs a close counterpoint to the story of Oliver and Susan. As Susan was faithless to Oliver when his failures became overwhelming, Lyman's wife was faithless to him. As Oliver turned to stone, metaphorically, Lyman turned to stone physically, paralyzed by bone disease. Lyman has tunnel vision, unable to turn his head from side to side; Oliver spent his life in mining tunnels. Lyman's inflexibility regarding his wife is expressed physically, Oliver's by a wall of silence. Neither man articulates the fact that he might have had a part in the disloyalty of a previously faithful wife, but Lyman comes closer to understanding than his grandfather. Oliver, however, returns to Susan. At the conclusion of the novel it is unclear whether Lyman will accept his wife's overtures of reconciliation, whether an historian fixated upon the past can achieve an angle of repose with an inadequate present. Stegner leaves us to make our own conclusions.

The Pastoral Novels

In what I have described as the pastoral novels, three of which might further be described as California novels, there is continued exploration of the theme of seeking sanctuary in the landscape, as well as an exploration of environmental topics. Written over a period of twenty-six years, these mature novels (for the purpose of this study I will not discuss at length the early minor fictional works) refine and develop themes which preoccupied Stegner throughout his writing life.

The California novels do not deal with the historical West of *The Big Rock Candy Mountain*, *Recapitulation*, and *Angle of Repose*, but with the contemporary life lived in California in the latter half of the twentieth century. *Crossing to Safety*, which is as much memoir as novel, moves from the Midwest to the East, and is set primarily in Vermont.

A Shooting Star

This novel does not represent a significant contribution to Stegner's canon; however, there are several of Stegner's signature themes within it. The heavy-handedness with which Stegner treated a narrative with which he was obviously uncomfortable is discussed in his conversations with Richard Etulain: "*A Shooting Star* wasn't a novel that I had my full heart in, but I was interested in doing it—to see what I could do with such a theme...I don't think that much of it. It was close enough to popular trash."[61]

Though Stegner's own estimation of the novel is clearly valid, the issues of sanctuary and environmentalism are significant, and it is those aspects of the novel which have relevance for my argument. The novel centers on the main character, Sabrina Castro, and her search for sanctuary and self-definition. This leads her to any number of contradictory places. The novel follows her through several affairs, the first of which begins at Monte Alban, outside Oaxaca, one of the most deeply sinister of ancient Toltec sites, a leveled mountaintop ringed with funerary pyramids, barren and disturbing. Stegner's choice of Monte Alban suggests that the first step of Sabrina's breakdown is in exposure of the most improbable kind. It is followed by her search for sanctuary in the family home, a sort of gilded island of ancestor worship and old money, utterly cut off from the real world and inhabited by Sabrina's autocratic mother and her Caliban-esque brother, Oliver Hutchens (strangely given the same unusual first name as Stegner's most appealing male character, Oliver Ward), crude, lustful and coarse, ridiculous except for the power which vast wealth has given him. The action of the novel continues into wilderness and concludes at the family home.

Oliver, with his huge, over-muscled body and limited imagination, represents everything Stegner abhors in a certain type of American man:

rampant and impatient as a boy frantic at being balked from doing something…His kind never anticipated consequences. His was the kind that left eroded gulches and cutover timberlands and man-made deserts and jerry-built tracts that would turn into slums in less than a generation.[62]

Stegner here challenges the heroic masculine literary tradition in this depiction of Oliver, dominantly, even violently male. A war hero, he despises all poorer, smarter, smaller, and weaker than himself. Women he sees as sexual objects only, and Stegner more than once describes him in animal terms, goatish, dog-like.

Significantly Oliver wishes to rape the landscape, turning 400 acres of private woodland into a "jerry-built" tract in opposition to Sabrina's wish to make the land into public space. Stegner's point here is that the boomers, mindlessly invoking a male paradigm of domination on to a feminized landscape, are challenged by the feminization of landscape represented by Sabrina's desire to turn the disputed acreage into a park. In Stegner's world, Sabrina wins, but the vehemence of Stegner's feelings toward the Oliver Hutchenses of the West are reflected again in his environmental essays, and earlier in his depiction of his father, who represents a similar, reckless, unthinking, using-and-using-up type, leaving behind landscapes whose water has been depleted or poisoned, stripped of timber or ancient prairie grasses, failing at one form of settlement or another, and moving on.

Through the device of making Oliver Hutchens a war hero, Stegner suggests that there was at one time something of value in him, in limited and very particular circumstances. Thus is reiterated the problem of frontier male virtues, and vices, which have survived into an age which no longer needs or respects them, and in which such values become agents of destruction. The virtues of the frontiersman in the post-frontier world find their only real expression in war of one kind or another, Stegner seems to be saying through the depiction of Oliver.

Sabrina significantly goes in search of wholeness into nature, and into the past. Her remark to Oliver shows both the purposelessness of her current life and the power of the myth of the frontier:

I was just thinking how lucky pioneer women were. I wish Burke had been driving a covered wagon when I met him, and I'd had to clear away the rattlesnakes to build a cabin, and wash clothes every Monday in a boiler set on a greasewood fire, and make soap out of ashes and bacon fat, and stand off Paiutes with a Sharps rifle.[63]

This is romance, yes, but romance with a clearly recognized cast of characters and an obvious purpose. This suggests that in the mythological West, one never needed to ask the big questions of existence. The answers were simple. It is that supposed simplicity for which Sabrina yearns. Sabrina is unable to embrace the appreciation of nature of Susan Ward—she cannot become the "transparent eyeball" because she does not have the spiritual awareness to do so. She is depicted as an utterly different type of character, sympathetic in some ways, but weak. She is, also, not living in the sublime western landscapes of Susan Ward, but rather in the tidy, domesticated landscapes of the affluent green suburbs—pretty, not grand.

And yet, despite all her failings, Stegner does not simply dismiss Sabrina as a parasitical member of a debased class. Circumstances have conspired to take responsibility away from her, and at the conclusion of the novel, responsibility is given back: a longed-for child will be born; Sabrina will gain a place in her mother's affections and look after her in her old age; responsibility will reform Sabrina and re-invent her as a woman of purpose. Personally I think Stegner's original conclusion— Sabrina's suicide—would have been more believable. But the ending we have is neat and the novel achieves closure. (Interestingly, this novel was Stegner's best seller, and his most translated work.) Stegner is here doing away with sanctuary as a goal, but not offering another option, only suggesting that there may be one. However, his point about the character of Sabrina is significant in the late fifties, early sixties world in which she is portrayed:

> What's happening to her is serious...attractive, intelligent, advantaged women who were educated beyond anything they were allowed to do in the world...in the 1950's a woman had nothing to rebel with except her body.[64]

Stegner's recognition of the intolerable position in which many educated women found themselves, by chance or intention, is, at the time of the writing of this novel, unusually perceptive, again pointing to Stegner's sympathy with a feminist point of view, much before feminism entered the political or critical arena.

A Shooting Star suggests some of the environmental themes which Stegner takes up again in the Joe Allston novels, themes of stewardship of the landscape, relating to protection and maintenance of nature, rather than the discussion of the sublime elements of western landscape found in such works as *Wolf Willow* and *Angle of Repose*. It also reiterates the themes of the American West versus East, and finally articulates a rare opposition to the search for sanctuary. The fact that Sabrina achieves sanctuary in what we have already been told at the beginning of the novel is a prison to her does not bode well for the protagonist. However weak the novel, it flags up important Stegnerian themes, and again points out an awareness of environmental issues at odds with frontier mythology transposed onto western landscapes.

The Joe Allston Stories

The Joe Allston stories, "A Field Guide to the Western Birds," *All the Little Live Things* (1967), and *The Spectator Bird* (1976)[65] are best described as California pastoral, that is, the pastoral, already nebulous as it has undoubtedly become by the late twentieth century, seen from a distinctively Californian perspective. California pastoral might be said to be different from other American pastoral in the sense that California itself was the goal of so much western migration and the imaginative landscape of the Promised Land was often transposed to Californian geography. In these Californian works, Stegner first uses the first-person narrative voice which he employs with notable success in *Angle of Repose* and *Crossing to Safety*. "A Field Guide," written in 1952, fifteen years before the next Joe Allston story,[66] belongs to Stegner's mature period, despite the chronological placement with his middle works. Joe Allston, based on Stegner's agent,[67] is a retired New York literary agent, grumpy, difficult and morose. Through Joe, Stegner examines, among other things, the search for sanctuary within the western environment.

All the Little Live Things

At the beginning of *All the Little Live Things*, Joe and his wife have retired from New York to the Bay Area of northern California, specifically to the peninsula south of San Francisco, the same general area as the setting of *A Shooting Star*. (Stegner himself lived in this area for many years during and after his spell at Stanford.) The inter-textual references to Shakespeare's *The Tempest* are obvious from the beginning of this novel, as are the deliberate correspondences with Stegner's own life. Joe, an unlikely Prospero, has fled many things: the city, the suicide of his shiftless son, and community life. He gardens relentlessly and much of his time is spent in killing creatures which invade his man-made Arcadia. Into his self-imposed exile come two significant characters, the first, Marian Catlin, an idealistic young woman who believes in preserving all the eponymous "little live things." She is horrified by Joe's systematic eradication of pests and chides him for attempting to grow non-native plants. She believes in letting natural things grow, including the cancer with which she is afflicted. She refuses chemotherapy because she is pregnant, thus creating a death-in-life metaphor which is the cornerstone of the action of the book. The second character to invade Arcadia is Jim Peck, a hippie who camps on Joe's land. Joe and his wife are taking a walk in their woods when Joe

> had a cold, visceral shock, a stoppage of the heart followed by a pounding pulse. For there, down in that quiet creek bottom where nobody but an occasional horseman ever passed, and where the only

wheeled tracks were those of the man who periodically serviced our
well pump, was this motorcycle sitting quietly, and on its seat this
person in orange helicopter coveralls bulging all over with zippered
pockets. The suit was unzipped clear to his navel, and his hairy chest
rose out of it and merged with a dark, dense beard. Caliban.[68]

Jim Peck, a character type repeated in the nameless figure of Shelley's
boyfriend in *Angle of Repose*, bears similarities to Kaminiski, the "glan-
dular genius" reviled but ultimately pitied in the early Joe Allston story,
"A Field Guide to the Western Birds." There is more of a problem for Joe
with Jim Peck than simple dislike. Representing all the forces of social
and moral disorder which Joe despises, he may be despised; however,
he reminds Joe of his own son, Curtis, with whom Joe was never really
able to make contact. In addition, Jim, too, is a seeker of sanctuary. Into
Joe's Arcadia he comes, seeking a home. He appeals to Joe's kindness,
and grudgingly receives permission to camp on his land. Throughout
the novel Joe grows increasingly irritated with Jim's cavalier opportun-
ism. In the end, Joe orders Jim off the property, ostensibly because of
the noise and mess he is making. In fact Jim's eviction corresponds with
Marion's physical deterioration, which, like Jim's encroachment, Joe has
watched spread inexorably: two cancers.

Joe is in fact very much like Stegner himself, according to Forrest
Robinson, who states,

> Stegner's mounting disenchantment with life in California is
> nowhere more clearly and vigorously expressed than in *All the Lit-
> tle Live Things* (1967), in which Joe Allston, looking very like his
> maker in age, family, residence, and outlook, casts a disapproving
> eye on the youth culture of the Vietnam era, with its gravitation
> to sex, drugs, and its contempt for all things adult and traditional.
> Joe's nemesis is a hippy named Jim Peck, a bad boy indeed, "the
> incarnated essence of disorder" (22), who lives in a tree-house on
> the Allston property. Peck is the fictional embodiment of much that
> disturbed Stegner in the youth culture of the 1960s and '70s—the
> brazen rejection of history, convention, civility, established leader-
> ship, and all else that contributed to the maintenance of fragile,
> precious human order.[69]

In addition, Robinson argues, Joe's relationships with both Curtis, his
dead son, and Jim Peck, are modeled on his own troubled relationship
with his only son, Page. Damaged by his own extremely difficult relationship with an overbearing and abusive father, Stegner by his own
admission was a less than attentive, though demanding, father, and his
son reacted as a teenager by being rebellious and taciturn. Resenting an

intrusion into a life in which order and self-discipline were paramount, both Joe, and Stegner, by all accounts, regard those who lack their own qualities as threats to a carefully cultivated order—like Joe's garden.

Joe is clearly an unreliable narrator. The reader never feels that Jim is as pernicious as Joe does. It is the accident of Jim's arrival corresponding with Joe's inability to protect Marion which casts him in the demonic role which he assumes in Joe's eyes. At the end of the novel when Joe, brutally, tells Jim that Marion is dying in the back of a car on a blocked road, he

> saw at once that he hadn't the slightest notion of Marian's condition. He thought she was pregnant. And in that moment I had a kind of a rush, a revelation, an understanding of how it is with the Pecks. They think it is simpler and less serious than it is. They don't know. They fool around. They haven't discovered how terrible is the thing that thuds in their chests and pulses in their arteries, they will never see ahead to the intersection where the crazy drunk will meet them.[70]

Joe's dark view of life has made him unable to see beyond the fact that to him the world is evil and full of pain, and that sanctuary is only a temporary reprieve from the sheer agony of life. Jim's careless, youthful thoughtlessness is like a slap in the face to Joe, who never forgets that,

> The peach trees behind me would shortly come out into bloom as rampant as these acacias, only to show with their very first leaves the swellings, the warpings, the obscene elephantiasis of their chronic disease.[71]

Joe, like Stegner himself, never forgets that he is a "target"[72] of an invariably hostile, or at least indifferent, natural world, representing the early American fear of the "howling wilderness." Marian, on the other hand, might be said to represent the positive impulse of the pastoral, finding regeneration in nature, yet being destroyed by a disease which she won't have treated, letting "nature" take its course. Her idealism contrasts with Joe's pessimism, revealing Stegner's own conflict between an ideal of allowing nature to remain untouched, and the sense that, even allowing for "stewardship," nature still needs to serve humanity. However, narratively, Marian represents Stegner's appreciation for nature's importance, beauty, and wonder in her championship of the eponymous "little live things." This is a conflict never resolved in Stegner's work, and one which may be understood in terms of his pioneer upbringing, after which it might be thought surprising that Stegner retained any idealism at all, having seen nature as the enemy, certainly in his father's terms. This conflict is an undercurrent in Stegner's canon, but might be said to find its fullest, most unchallenged manifestation in *Discovery!*,[73] an odd yet readable book about oil exploration, which I will discuss later in this chapter.

Forrest Robinson calls Joe a Manichean, but in fact his guilt and regret about almost everything in his life, and his vision of the relentlessness of the dark fate awaiting us reveal something else. At the critical juncture in the novel when Marian dies, Joe's desolation is absolute, despite his already admittedly dark view of the world:

> Her death merely confirms what Joe has known all along—that the world is arbitrary and unjust. Why then is Marian's loss such an intolerable insult to him? Why doesn't the positive pole of his Manicheanism—which might seek confirmation in the love Marian gave and received during her life—carry more weight, and yield more consolation? Why does the inevitable make him so angry? Why does he respond to the authority of evil and destruction with petulant bitterness rather than wise, stoical resignation?[74]

Robinson suggests that it was Stegner's identification of the character of Marian with his own mother, a suggestion also made by Jackson Benson, which made the despair of Joe so fierce and the expression of it so profoundly believable. The importance of this for this book is the fact that, as Robinson says,

> Stegner's parents served as a kind of template for their son's analysis of the American experience in the Far West. "You believed in all the beauties and strengths and human associations of place," he observes of his mother; "my father believed only in movement. You believed in a life of giving, he in a life of getting."[75]

I suggest that this template extends to Stegner's view of the treatment of the natural world, and informs his protective attitude toward it. Stewardship is a concept Stegner's mother would have understood immediately. Stegner's father would have wondered what the profit was in it.

All the Little Live Things thus functions on various levels. In addition to being one of Stegner's most personal novels, it is also perhaps the most deeply rooted in environmental advocacy, more usually found in his non-fiction. Stegner's environmental concerns here focus on thoughtless development of green lands—not sublime landscapes, but comfortable pastoral havens. One of Joe's main problems with Jim Peck is the mess he makes, the refuse and garbage and junk he leaves lying around Joe's pastoral Arcadia. Jim's aggressive and goatish maleness offends Joe. The motorcycle he rides is quite literally the machine in the garden. Jim Peck invades Arcadia with his machine and all its masculine overtones, while Marian Catlin by contrast exists as an advocate of the feminized landscape, passive to the point of absurdity, refusing either to eradicate pests or to cultivate the edenic garden in any way. Already wounded by disease, she awaits the final denouement of her "natural" death, refusing to take any steps that might prevent it in order to protect her unborn child. In between these two, in something like a bizarre parody of Jefferson's yeoman farmer, comes grumpy, negative Joe Allston, a man who has lived his life in books, entering in one memorable scene with a vast king snake on the end of a pitchfork looking like a strange reversal of an allegory of the Garden of Eden.[76] Clearly Stegner has more in mind here than a simple narrative tale.

Joe has called Jim Peck Caliban. Following his own analogy, he is Prospero. The "island," as Joe has told us in "A Field Guide to the Western Birds," is "on the prow of a California hill" and life is Eden-like:

> Here I sit on this terrace in a golden afternoon, finishing off an early, indolent highball...a Pebble Beach pasha, a Los Gatos geikwar. What I have done for ten percent was never like this.
>
> This terrace is a good place to lie and listen. Lots of bird business, every minute of the day.[77]

The island is full of music, like Prospero's, and like Prospero, Joe has arrived late in life at this particular pastoral idyll. When Jim–Caliban arrives, he tells Joe that he has been there before. Like the snake Joe unearths, the garden has had its previous occupants who claim as much right of possession as Joe and his wife. When Marian arrives, with her charm and her delight and wonder at all around her, the analogy is complete. Marian–Miranda even likes Caliban. She likes everyone. "O brave new world!"[78] Indeed.

And this, of course, is the point: the brave new world is America, and Joe Allston's tragedy on a California hilltop is the tragedy of America writ small. Stegner wrote this novel in 1967 when the Vietnam War was at its height. The end of the year saw a half a million American troops in Vietnam, more than 10,000 killed in the preceding twelve months. The campuses were boiling. The suicide of Joe's son might be read as a metaphor for the thousands of young men dying in Asia. "Youth-in-Asia" was a catchphrase of the war protesters that Stegner, as a professor at Stanford, could not have failed to have heard. The suggestion that Joe's son Curtis killed himself in what was simply an absence of the will to live echoes the idea of euthanasia. In my view the very absence of any mention of the Vietnam War in this book makes its presence as a subtext all the more likely, considering the times and Stegner's close association with the young.

The other narrative subtexts, the failed pastoral, the innate evil of nature—the howling wilderness—are explicit in the text. Joe's view of uncultivated nature would have met with the approval of any early American agriculturalists:

Do you really like the woods and pastures as kind old Mother Nature designed them...did you ever dig underground in these parts? It's underground that you really meet the evils. Ever examine the roots of poison oak? They're dead black, with red underbark, and if you cut one with a shovel or an ax it squirts out juice that will put you in bed for a week. Or these wild cucumbers. I dug one up once, just to see where all that vile vitality comes from that can sprout these tentacles twenty feet long. You know what's down there? A big tumor sort of thing as big as a bucket, an underground cancer. I very much doubt that any of these things are the friends of man.[79]

Joe is persuasive, but he is *not* an early American farmer, and his perceptions are clearly those of a diseased, or at least deeply embittered, imagination. One might describe any wild thing in equally pejorative terms. His hidden disease is in sharp contrast to Marian's, which eats at her physically as Joe's does spiritually.

Joe never repudiates his attitude toward nature, but at the end of the novel he acknowledges the validity of Marian's point of view. She urged him to think of the force of life and he responded with the insistence of the darkness inherent in it. The book finishes in an uneasy truce which mirrors the uneasy truce with nature required by life in the West.

Think of the force of life, yes, but think of the component of darkness in it...

And so? Admitting what is so obvious, what then? Would I wipe Marian Caitlin out of my unperfected consciousness if I could? Would I forego the pleasure of her company to escape the bleakness of her loss? Would I go back to my own formula, which was twilight sleep, to evade the pain she brought with her?

Not for a moment. And so even in the gnashing of my teeth I acknowledge my conversion...I shall be richer all my life for this sorrow.[80]

Stegner's conclusion reinforces the idea that the pastoral is not truly an escape, and that lives led in society—Marian has brought Joe out of his hermit-like existence—albeit more painful, are more worth living. No man is an island; or to put it another way, fallen man, out of the garden, is more human and whole than his simplistic edenic counterpart. To search for the simple pastoral Arcadia is to yearn for an innocence which denies life. The garden flatters the imagination and limits, then kills, the human spirit, according to this interpretation. This point is made with great force in the sequel to *All the Little Live Things*, *The Spectator Bird* (1976). This view of the idealized landscape differs from the idea of nature as innately regenerative posited by Thoreau, and is distinct from

Stegner's own position that the preservation of wild landscape is integral to the preservation of the human spirit.

The Spectator Bird

Four years on from the action of the previous novel, Joe, morose as ever, is meditating on the imminent death of a friend when a postcard from Denmark sends him into a reverie about a trip he and his wife took more than twenty years previously. The novel is so structured that Joe's reminiscences take the form of readings of a diary to his wife, Ruth. As in *Angle of Repose*, Stegner has created a novel within a novel. Ostensibly to look for his family roots (Joe's mother, like Wallace Stegner's, was an immigrant Scandinavian servant girl), the trip is really an escape. The Allstons' son has recently killed himself, and the trip is gloomy and despairing. Joe and his wife are horribly seasick throughout the voyage.

Like Melville's Ishmael, Joe is an orphan, a Manhattanite, bereft of ancestors and offspring, depressed, perhaps suicidal, embarked on a dangerous sea voyage. Like Elsa Norgaard going west, Joe and Ruth's trip east is one punctuated by sickness and death. A returning immigrant dies on the voyage, leaving his American widow alone to live with unknown Swedish relations. Stegner's comment on the foolhardiness of trying to recapture a dead past nods again in the direction of Melville:

> Oh, his poor dream. Oh, his poor fifty years of dull work with its deferred reward. Oh, his poor dim dependable unimaginative not very attractive life that was supposed to mature like a Treasury bill. Ah, Bertelson, Ah, humanity![81]

Joe inadvertently witnesses the immigrant Bertelson's funeral the next day. A storm is raging and Joe witnesses a scene which consciously reminds the reader of *Moby Dick*. Joe sees

> an appalling turmoil of water, an uncreated waste without order or end or purpose...
>
> Then out of the corner of my eye I saw the glint of moving oil-skins out on the foredeck...They hulked like conspirators bent away from wind and rain, and in my scared condition I had the wild idea they were planning like a lot of Lord Jims to abandon ship and let all the pilgrims perish...They fell back into a ragged line, two of them bent and lifted, and there went Bertelson down the plank and into that appalling sea.
>
> There is no word for how instant his obliteration was...by the time I was back in my berth the *Stockholm* was beginning once more to drive her nose into the seas.[82]

The pleasure one takes in Stegner's intertextual references does not minimize the serious intent of such references. Stegner clearly wants his reader to think of both Bartleby *and* Ishmael in this sequence. We have the negativity and blankness of the strange denizen of the Dead Letter Office opposed to another orphaned Ishmael. However, unlike Ishmael, Joe has gone to sea in order to arrive somewhere, but like Ishmael he is seeking to recover his equanimity by any means, no matter how desperate—in his case in a renewed connection with his rural, ancestral home. In a similar "pastoral of failure," to use Leo Marx's term,[83] he loses, rather than gains, his peace of mind in Denmark, and only in returning to his home in the West achieves a kind of peace. This is an interesting reversal of expectation and inevitably reminds the reader of Nick Carraway abandoning the corrupt East in order to return to the "vast obscurity beyond the city, where the dark fields of the republic rolled on under the night."[84]

Once in Denmark Joe and his wife become the lodgers and friends of the separated wife of a quisling nobleman. A cloud hangs over the delightful Astrid which the Allstons assume is a result of her husband's wartime activities, but when they are eventually taken to the family estate, the bizarre truth comes out. The estate is picture-book perfect, the house grand, the farm cultivated on scientific principles: "Everything was as Eigil said—nature improved, cultivated as carefully as his bacon hogs and pine plantings. Even the scrub woods were carefully *cultivated* scrub woods."[85] Joe is disturbed by the perfection of nature produced by the scrupulous cultivation of the estate, and the ominous figure of Astrid's brother, Eigil, compounds this. Through a series of revelations the reader learns that Astrid and Eigil's father experimented with human eugenics. The father's suicide was the result of the revelation that he had committed incest with his own daughter—not Astrid—and that Eigil continues the practice with his own offspring.

Joe's discovery of the corruption of an old world he had previously idealized interestingly reaffirms the immigrant dream of a new world, yet Joe's mother left a corrupt European world only to find a poverty-stricken American life, poor, however not corrupt. Astrid, paradoxically, is unable to leave the corruption which surrounds her owing to her sense of duty and honor, and Joe, revealing another ubiquitous Stegnerian motif, is unable to protect her.

The Spectator Bird deals with many of the same issues as *All the Little Live Things*. Stegner again uses the technique of an unreliable first-person narrator, as he does in *Crossing to Safety* and *Angle of Repose*. While there are significant similarities between Lyman Ward, Larry Morgan, and Joe Allston, their voices are not the same and Joe's irony despite personal tragedy contrasts with Lyman's stony bitterness, and Larry's nearly detached observer stance in *Crossing to Safety*—perhaps the closest we get to Stegner himself.

Like *All the Little Live Things*, *The Spectator Bird* is a novel which works on many levels. As in *Angle of Repose*, Stegner has constructed a story within a story, allowing a dialogue between the present and the past and the different perspectives of the narrator. While on the narrative level the novel is a story of loss and recovery—the death of Joe's son followed by Joe falling in love with Astrid; and loss accompanied by resignation—leaving Denmark and returning to life with Ruth—its subtexts are the relationship between the new world and the old; the past to the present; and male configurations imposed upon a landscape perceived as feminine. All three subtexts weave together in the section of the novel dealing with the visit to the castle at Bregninge, Astrid's ancestral home.

In the treatment of Eigil, Astrid's brother, we see the convergence of two of the subtexts mentioned. Eigil represents the old ways, power, privilege, authority. Like Oliver Hutchens in *A Shooting Star*, he is superficially attractive, athletic, controlling and dominant, and many times a father. This emphasis on the fertility of arguably the two most loathsome characters in Stegner's canon is interesting. Stegner's spokesmen, Larry Morgan, Joe Allston, Lyman Ward and Bruce Mason, have either one, often problematic or difficult, child or none. (Stegner himself had only one son, with whom, as I have mentioned, he had a challenging relationship.) Eigil's virility, however, unlike Oliver Hutchens' "goatish" behavior, is expressed in cold-blooded pursuit of a genetically "pure" strain. Like his father, he practices his genetic experiments on both his farm animals and the local peasantry, some of whom are his own children. His rigid control of nature and manipulation of landscape carried out to its extreme is obscene and horrifying. Under the smooth surfaces of Eigil's model farm lies corruption. Eventually Joe discovers, and Astrid confirms, that both Eigil and his father have practiced incest.

Joe's reaction to this revelation is telling. When he believes that Astrid has been a victim of her father—rather than the unfortunate Miss Weibull, who in fact was his victim as well as his illegitimate daughter by a peasant woman—he does not sympathize, he blames:

> Also, what kind of story will she cook up for us? Who wants to sit and listen to some fable about Miss Weibull? I can just imagine it. There she will sit, a Lorelei in sensible tweeds...
>
> Shall we believe your story about being the wronged wife of a traitor, or was that a lie too? And did your husband leave you for another woman, or did he finally find himself unable to bear the long unyielding disgrace of being married to you...
>
> It makes me sick.[86]

The usually ironic and sensitive, if grumpy, Joe shows himself to be as intransigent as Lyman Ward when faced with his unfaithful ex-wife, or Oliver Ward rejecting Susan on the never-proved (and never made explicit in the novel) assumption of infidelity. This tendency to blame the blameless suggests the idea that any failures in the natural world are somehow intentional.

In *The Green Breast of the New World*, Louise Westling discusses the "subtle rhetoric of blame" which informs Fitzgerald's view of the New World in *The Great Gatsby*: "Fitzgerald suggests that this voluptuous landscape was purposive; it flowered and its rustling leaves 'pandered in whispers' to seduce the Dutch sailors."[87] I suggest that it is this same "rhetoric of blame" which Joe is exhibiting towards Astrid. Her father and brother have tried to control the natural world and women; women and the natural world are somehow to blame for the very crimes committed against them. Through this analogy Stegner is suggesting that male dominance of a feminized landscape allows blame for the perceived failure or loss of control to then be placed on the landscape itself. This is a large point and can explain a great deal about attitudes to landscape; the lack of responsible stewardship noted by Stegner and others; the sense of victimization felt by denizens of the landscape, such as McCarthy's boy protagonists who feel that the land has somehow failed them; the willingness, in some quarters, to treat landscape like a commodity to be used and used up.

The Spectator Bird, though dealing with this issue, at first reads like a parable or fairy tale; there are long voyages, castles and witches. There is even an evil ogre hiding by the gates of the castle. In one respect this seems like a simplistic vision of the corrupt old world by the new. But Stegner's new world is not seen as innocent and free of trouble. The novel opens with an impending death and is informed throughout by the suicide of Joe's son. It is for this reason that I suggest that the novel may be read as an allegory, but as an allegory of the treatment of landscape. James Hepworth comments,

> Stegner writes, "We are a wild species, as Darwin pointed out. Nobody ever tamed or domesticated or scientifically bred us." But Count Eigil Rodding sees no reason why he, fully armed Cultural Hero, should not play Doctor Faustus and do just that. To manipulate the gene pool...he has copulated with his half-sister and their daughter. Now in his mid-forties, Eigil looks forward with his "amber eyes" to his golden years when he can rape his grand-daughters.
>
> In this sense, then, *The Spectator Bird* is an environmental novel... that gives a few little twists of its own to those worn out phrases, "crimes against nature" and "population control."[88]

Setting the main action of the novel in Europe may slightly obscure the point that Stegner is making with regard to the American landscape, and the horror of Eigil's crimes against women may seem to outweigh his crimes against the environment, but I believe Eigil's treatment of women is analogous with an attitude toward the natural world which he exemplifies.

The conclusion of the novel, with its story-book ending, followed by Joe's recollections of one last midsummer evening on a haunted island, sets the work again in the realm of allegory. "And they lived happily ever after" is all but stated as Joe and Ruth go in search of the double moon-rainbow from their hilltop fortress. The story and the story-within-the-story have both been closed at the same time. The search for sanctuary and a safe place has once again come to an uneasy conclusion. The conclusion of the novel is quiet resignation:

> The truest vision of life I know is that bird in the Venerable Bede that flutters from the dark into a lighted hall, and after a while flutters out again into the dark. But Ruth is right. It is something—it can be everything—to have found a fellow bird with whom you can sit among the rafters while the drinking and boasting and reciting go on below; a fellow bird whom you can look after and find bugs and seeds for; one who will patch your bruises and straighten your ruffled feathers and mourn over your hurts when you accidentally fly into something you can't handle.[89]

The green retreat functions as a prison, in Denmark and back home in California, and Joe eventually rejects it and embraces something else, resigning himself to the ambiguities of life. And perhaps that something else is what the bird finds, leaving the lighted hall, flying out into the darkness, into the impenetrable vastness of the starry night. The conclusion of *The Spectator Bird* shows Joe beyond the fatalism of *All the Little Live Things* and suggests something closer to an "angle of repose" in his relationship with the world.

In this novel, Stegner has opened up the issue of male dominance of a landscape perceived as feminine in very broad terms. It is an issue which will have relevance throughout the McCarthy section of this book. This provides us with another link between Stegner and McCarthy, and between the pre- and post-1960s view of western American landscapes. Although Stegner's interpretation may be seen as a view painted in very broad brush-strokes, it is nonetheless important and may be mentioned again with reference to Kolodny's previously noted comment that the American landscape often fell victim to "suppressed infantile desires unleashed in the promise of a primal garden."[90] It is this primal garden which John Grady Cole searches for, and almost finds, in *All the Pretty Horses*, and its dark twin, the "cauterized waste,"[91] of *Blood Meridian*.

Crossing to Safety

Crossing to Safety, published in 1987, was Stegner's final novel, published six years before his death in 1993. Superficially, this novel seems distinct from earlier work. Wisconsin and Vermont are the primary settings, rather than the Californian or western settings the reader expects in Stegner. The structure of this novel is again a series of memories interspersed with authorial narrative. Larry Morgan, the speaker, is arguably the truest representation we have of Stegner himself. In fact the novel was originally written as a memoir for Stegner and his wife, not intended for publication. The events are almost wholly autobiographical, but as in *The Big Rock Candy Mountain*, Stegner's other largely autobiographical work, meaning is given to what might have otherwise seemed like random events through the imposition of a novelistic structure.

In brief, two academic couples, Larry and Sally Morgan and Sid and Charity Lang, share a rural retreat in Battell Pond, Vermont, as an antidote to the fact that Larry, already poor, has lost his job. In Vermont, Sally develops polio and nearly dies, remaining crippled ever after. The story returns to Vermont at several points. This pastoral sanctuary is a deception. It is in the Vermont idyll which the couples share that the really awful events of the novel happen: severe illness and death—the despoiled Eden once again. Significantly, Larry and Sally finally move to New Mexico, the sort of landscape that makes demands which Arcadia never does. Yet Larry calls Battell Pond, "the place where in the best time of our lives friendship had its home and happiness its headquarters."[92] And this is right. Eden is edenic because of what it was, not what it is. Stegner is telling us that Eden, not New Mexico, is a place that cannot be lived in, not because of what it is, but because of what it does to people. To extrapolate: the pastoral landscape carries within itself the seeds of its own destruction, at least in fictional terms, because the pastoral for Stegner's characters represents the end of striving; the pastoral therefore represents death. Therefore, in constantly seeking sanctuary, Stegner's characters are striving for the impossible. Joe Allston is probably most aware of this, and most embittered by it, but Larry and Sally Morgan are also aware that the quest for perfection results in sterility. Certainly all of Stegner's Arcadias have had their serpents in them. In the pastoral novels the green retreat is worse than a prison; it is the end of life, literally and metaphorically.

While most of Stegner's characters spend their lives looking for a sanctuary, Sid and Charity Lang already have one. And yet it sometimes seems more like a prison, such as during the war years when Charity embraced pacifism and insisted her family ignore the outside world. Sid seems thoroughly disenfranchised from what Stegner has described in his seminal essay, "History, Myth and the Western Writer," as "the legitimate inclination of the sexes," comprising "male freedom and aspiration versus female domesticity."[93]

However, the question asked by this scenario is: why did Charity Lang so need to control? I suggest that in Stegner's configuration of the "legitimate inclination of the sexes," Charity, representing domesticity, civilization and the garden, reveals that sanctuary can only exist by sacrificing freedom. And of course Charity is a recognizable type. She is the Virginian's Molly; Miss Watson, civilizing Huck; she is Teal Eye, with her silent blaming of Boone Caudill. She is the eternal western feminine in this particular male configuration, blaming, controlling, ultimately destroying, but in the process destroying herself. Is this what the pastoral of failure means: the endless repetition of a war between the sexes played out on a landscape of hopeless striving? *Crossing to Safety* might suggest so, but I do not suggest that Stegner is endorsing this model, simply that in representing these two perpetually warring types in Charity and Sid, he reveals the futility, rather like Joe Allston endlessly trying to eradicate ineradicable pests, of trying to order the unorderable, and thus suggests that in our treatment of landscape in the West we must always take the middle road between radically opposed contraries.

Throughout *Crossing to Safety*, Stegner reminds us that Vermont should be Eden. The morning after his arrival at Battell Pond, Larry says,

> Thus to awaken in Paradise. We hadn't earned it, we didn't deserve it, we didn't belong there, it wouldn't last…I felt like the grubby child in Katherine Mansfield's story when she got a glimpse of the rich girl's dollhouse before being hustled away. *I seen the little lamp.*[94]

One positive statement is preceded with four negatives. An orphan like Joe Allston, Larry knows that whatever is too good to last, won't last. He fights fate with boundless literary energy. And yet, he has seen the little lamp. He knows that he will carry with him that knowledge of Eden, even into the darkness beyond the garden.

The irony is that Larry, unlike the little child in Katherine Mansfield's story, had more than just a vision of the little lamp. In the novel, he achieves far greater success than the Langs. Sally's illness is mitigated by the fact that Larry and Sally have a much stronger and more supportive marriage than Sid and Charity. The Langs may own the dollhouse, but the little lamp that the child in Mansfield's story thought the best and most important part of the dollhouse belongs to Larry and Sally.[95]

*   *   *   *

Stegner set one other novel in New England. *Second Growth*,[96] published in 1947, is set in rural New Hampshire. The model of the "summer people" returning year after year to a rural or village idyll is here presented for the first time. The novel is a divided narrative, and might possibly be considered a short story cycle. Carl Bredahl suggests that divided narrative, "rejects the impulse to enclose,"[97] enclosure being characteristic of eastern writing. Therefore in choosing divided narrative as a vehicle to tell an eastern story, Stegner has nonetheless put a western stamp upon events, and indeed the conclusion of the novel—a bookish young boy leaving the village for parts unknown—is a characteristically western finale.

Second Growth is interesting academically for the counterpoint it provides to *Crossing to Safety*. New England is here most definitely not Eden. In this novel one meets characters who will reappear in the Stegner canon throughout his career: the bossy society woman; unworldly academics; passive wives of eccentric husbands; farmhands; smart boys in limiting provincial places. At this stage in his career, Stegner had not yet become "good on women's issues," as Comer describes him. Neither is his use of landscape particularly significant. *Second Growth* is not an uninteresting novel, but does not bear comparison with either *The Big Rock Candy Mountain*, the greatest of his early works, or the later novels.

Crossing to Safety also employs divided narrative to some extent, thus reiterating, in Bredahl's terms, a western character despite the eastern setting. It is interesting that both of Stegner's New England novels use this form, whereas none of his western works do.

In conclusion, *Crossing to Safety* again represents the lifelong search for a safe place, and the realization that sanctuary lasts only in the memory. In this, his final and most eloquently understated novel, Stegner reminds us again and again of this fact, but reminds us as well that in the unending struggle which is life, seeing the little lamp is sometimes enough.

The Non-Fiction

I have suggested that the search for sanctuary in Stegner's fiction undercuts and re-examines both the myth of the frontier, and to some extent, the frontiersman; that rehistoricization of the western American past has in Stegner one of its most important spokesmen in the second half of the twentieth century; that in his fiction the theme of the search for sanctuary in a hostile world is paramount. In this section I will examine how these themes ramify in some of Stegner's non-fiction: essays, history, and biography. This is not an exhaustive survey of Stegner's non-fiction, though that is certainly a project waiting to be undertaken, but rather an examination of those aspects of the non-fiction which speak most directly to the issues discussed in the earlier part of this chapter, and with which Stegner was most deeply involved.

Richard Etulain has written, "The career of Wallace Stegner, historian, biographer, novelist, and spokesman on environmental issues, is the most crucial link between the western regional and post-regional literatures."[98] Accepting Etulain's premise means that by the time of Etulain's writing, western literature had begun to lose the taint of "regionalism" and that the issues raised in what had once been a predominantly local literature were beginning to be perceived as national in character. This did not, however, wholly remove the stigma from the inescapable flaw of regionalism as perceived by the established literary elites

The issues of land and water use and the boom-and-bust mentality were considered to be solely western issues, at least in literary terms. Because the frontier formed a component of the broad structure of the American identity it may be argued that these specifically western issues were *always* national in character, or had been historically, particularly as the frontier had been a mutable line which gradually moved westward. Etulain's remark suggests that Stegner's work questions some of the more contentious western myths, creating a climate in which what had been thought of as predominantly regional literature, and the criticism of that literature, could be brought into the mainstream of American letters. Supporting this, Krista Comer states:

> The initial parameters through which Stegner thought about western literature were conscientiously historical in an era that valued New Critical, "text as all" practice. In a field in which "no totalizing theory" existed, Stegner's was a welcome metanarrative...Stegner brought in a new historicism, and, with it, a new dignity to western criticism...Critics could thereafter formulate a meaningful regional literary history through a realist-based aesthetic and make a convincing case for the inclusion of many serious western writers who were not finding their way into the literary canon.[99]

Comer's remarks again highlight the importance of Stegner as a threshold writer, taking us across the border from one tradition to another, making possible the wide developments in western literature and culture which his work anticipated. Therefore Stegner, through work which included fiction, essays, history, biography and nature writing, as well as through a distinguished academic career, brought into the light areas of western literature which previously had languished under the shadow of the umbrella term, "regional literature." In doing this he also invited a re-analysis of areas of western history which had passed, almost unexamined, into folklore. I also argue that Stegner, being a threshold writer, takes us from the older, myth-based perceptions of the West to the borders of postmodern perception of western history exemplified in McCarthy's works. Stegner takes western fiction out of the limiting category of "regionalism" and reveals that western literature's concerns were in fact in many cases truly national in scope.

The marginalization of western literature and western authors, a marginalization which he helped to end, was always one of Stegner's particular concerns. In "Coming of Age: The End of the Beginning," he states:

> The single fact of our preoccupation with landscape is enough to make us unintelligible to or beneath the notice of critical opinion schooled in one or another variety of abstract expressionism...
>
> Western literature differs from much other American literature in the fact that so much of it happens outdoors. It also differs in that the influence of Europe's ideas, Europe's fashions, and Europe's history is much fainter.[100]

This suggests that the problem the critical establishment has had with western writers has mainly been one of setting. I suggest that in fact setting in western literature is a more profound issue than simply a question of where the action of the novel is placed. Landscape in the West is in many cases, both in literature and in life, the repository of a deeply felt spiritual sense: an awareness of the numinosity and sacred quality of the land. This is a point which I accept is analytically subjective, and which veers dangerously close to the regions of myth itself. It is, however, a point which I believe is integral to an understanding of both Stegner and McCarthy's works, and one which will be discussed further.

An aspect of the question of western landscape which further informs this discussion is made by Mark Busby in "The Significance of the Frontier in Contemporary American Fiction," in which he examines the elements of western literature which appear in contemporary American fiction, in other guises. He concludes:

> Contrary to what many critics have stated about contemporary American literature, significant elements of frontier mythology continue to appear in American fiction. And those elements cut across the categories popularly used to classify contemporary American fiction...I do not mean to suggest that the frontier has arisen Phoenix-like in these novels. Rather, like Proteus or Coyote, it has simply taken on new shapes to adapt to new circumstances.[101]

This supports Slotkin's argument that the archetypes of the frontier mythology continue to inform American literature and culture. If one accepts this point, the significance of Stegner's work both as a writer and as an advocate for the demythologizing of western myths is made even more evident.

In his important essay, "History, Myth, and the Western Writer," Stegner laid down what Krista Comer has described as a "critical blueprint" for the reading of western fiction. In 1967, Stegner wrote, "The

Western, horse opera, has actually been studied in considerable detail, though it must be admitted that critics rarely approach it from the near or literary side."[102] Stegner goes on to make the distinction between the "Western" and "western" literature, the former being a "demonstration of a set of mythic patterns," the latter simply occurring in the western part of the United States. He argues that the "Western" has mythologized the past of the West so much that twentieth-century westerners had no sense of a usable past, or of "any continuity between the real western past which has been mythicized almost out of recognizability and a real western present that seems as cut-off and pointless as a ride on a merry-go-round that can't be stopped."[103] In other words, the myths of the past have once again reached out and crippled the life of the present, in this instance cutting the present free from the obscured history which formed it, and therefore failing to inform current action with the experience acquired by the tragedies and successes of the past. Stegner's argument suggests that by the marginalization of western literature, which has been the result of considering "westerns" and "western" literature as one, those works which have critiqued the dominant western mythology have been simply merged with the works whose historical configurations and myth structures they sought to examine. In addition to disallowing the importance of western American writing—by classifying all works with western settings in the category of dime-novel descendants—this over-simplification also minimizes the importance of the link between modern western writing, and the classic works of the canon which originally examined and critiqued the already dominant myth structure.

In the same essay, Stegner also mentions the "tone of nostalgic regret" which pervades western literature. This supports Stegner's environmental concerns:

> It is a tone that may seem odd in a new country, and yet it may express something quintessentially American: our sadness at what our civilization does to the natural, free, and beautiful, to the noble, the self-reliant, the brave. Many of the virtues of the typical western hero are virtues seen as defeated, gone by, no longer honored.[104]

In this quotation, Stegner's variety of American exceptionalism is not open to the accusation of jingoistic nationalism—quite the reverse. Stegner's awareness of the failings of the "American dream" far outweighs any belief in its innate value. What we have in Stegner, as in McCarthy, is regret for what might have been. This is a point previously made by Stegner in his novel *The Big Rock Candy Mountain*, in concluding that his father might have been the sort of man who once had a place in the pioneer world, but that his virtues belonged to an earlier age. Here in "History, Myth, and the Western Writer," written twenty-four years after *The Big Rock Candy Mountain*, Stegner is suggesting that some of the frontier virtues exemplified in even such a man as his father do in fact have value, and that their absence in modern life is a loss rather than a gain. This "nostalgic regret" applies equally to the western hero, with his myth-centered overtones, and the western landscape, which in Guthrie's Boone Caudill's words is "all sp'iled" by the incursion of civilization.[105] Yet Stegner is all too aware of the dangers both of and for the man of the myth in a society which does not have room for his species of western heroism. This is a major theme in McCarthy's western novels, as I will discuss in the McCarthy section of this book.

In Where the Bluebird Sings to the Lemonade Springs: Living and Writing in the West, Stegner addresses most of the most significant issues of human relationship to the western landscape. In his introduction, he states:

> The remaining western wilderness is the geography of hope, and I have written, believing what I wrote that the West at large is hope's native home, the youngest and freshest of America's regions, magnificently endowed and with the chance to become something unprecedented and unmatched in the world...
>
> But when I am thinking instead of throbbing, I remember what history and experience have taught me about the West's past, and what my senses tell me about the West's present, and I become more cautious about the West's future...
>
> Visionary expectation was a great energizer of the westward movement...But exaggerated, uninformed, unrealistic, greedy expectation has been a prescription for disappointment...Ghost towns and dust bowls, like motels, are western inventions. All are reflections of transience and transience in most of the West has hampered the development of stable, rooted communities.[106]

Three points which lie at the centre of Stegner's environmental concerns are explicitly stated in this quotation. First is the idea that the West is "the geography of hope." If the West is, or was, any such thing, it requires what Stegner has characterized as stewardship, unselfish protection of natural places. Undoubtedly, part of the reason for the perceived rightness of the title "geography of hope" for the western half of America was the perception of "virgin land"—vast tracts of space, seemingly free for the taking. This is a view Stegner ultimately repudiates, but the power and influence of which he acknowledges. The other aspect of the West which entitles it to be called by such an epithet is the very grandness of the landscape: the sublimity and magnificence of a "world as it had taken shape and form from the hands of the Creator,"[107] quoting the nineteenth-century explorer William F. Butler.

Secondly, Stegner says that "Visionary expectation was a great energizer of the westward movement." The geography of hope is thus coupled with the language of dream and vision: "The West never got over its heightened romantic notion of itself."[108] In the chapter entitled, "Living Dry," Stegner elaborates upon this point:

> It has been misinterpreted and mistreated because, coming to it from earlier frontiers where conditions were not unlike those of northern Europe, Anglo-Americans found it different, daunting, exhilarating, dangerous, and unpredictable, and entered it carrying habits that were often inappropriate and expectations that were surely excessive.[109]

The landscape was the repository of the ambitions of the settlers. But what was clear was that the projections of settlers accustomed to a pastoral landscape were inappropriate for the arid regions of the West. And yet the projection continued, deeply rooted in the sense of national identity. Stegner continues:

> Insofar as the West was a civilization at all between the time of Lewis and Clark's explorations and about 1870, it was largely a civilization in motion, driven by dreams. The people who composed and represented it were part of a true Folk-Wandering, credulous, hopeful, hardy, largely uninformed. The dreams are not dead even today, and the habit of mobility has only been reinforced by time.[110]

Hopefulness, reinvention, freedom from the shackles of history, limitless possibilities in a land seeming to be limitless; these then are the components of the "visionary expectation" about which Stegner writes.

The final point in Stegner's remarks which I would like to address is that of the transience of the West, which has hampered the development of "stable, rooted communities." Stegner writes:

> Transience in most of the West has hampered the development of stable, rooted communities and aborted the kind of communal effort that takes in everything...
>
> The deficiency of community is as apparent in the cities as in the small towns—perhaps more so. Western cities are likely to have an artificial look, and why not, since so many of them are planted in an artificial environment maintained by increasingly elaborate engineering...
>
> Deeply lived in places are the exception rather than the rule in the West...Successive waves have kept western towns alive but prevented them from deepening the quality of their life.[111]

Stegner is talking about the arid western states where a boom-or-bust mentality often made transience inescapable: settlers in places such as eastern Montana at the turn of the century simply had to move on when rainfall failed and crops did not grow. They had no alternative except starvation. Thus "moving on" when things didn't turn out became a regular feature of some western lives. Stegner's own family did it many times. One must not forget that it was also the quality of hopefulness which, for some, actually made transience exhilarating. If things didn't work out, there was always the hopeful possibility presented by the new. This echoes a remark made by Stegner's father, in the persona of Bo Mason, in *The Big Rock Candy Mountain*, when, in yet another effort to find his own Big Rock Candy Mountain, he uproots his family, this time to Saskatchewan. In trying to convince his wife of the wisdom of yet another move, he expostulates:

> "The difference is that this is *new*, see? It isn't even scratched." He grew almost violent, trying to show it to her as he saw it. "Why, God knows what's up there," he said. "There might be coal, or iron, or oil, or any damn thing under that ground. Nobody but cowpunchers and surveyors have ever been over it. And a railroad coming right through it."[112]

Like Cather's Jim Burden, Bo Mason sees in newness the limitless scope for opportunity. Cather's Divide was more amenable to settlement and habitation, though the life was hard, but Stegner's Saskatchewan had to be seen with the eye of faith. Like so many western landscapes, appreciation of the short grass plains of Saskatchewan required a perception not based on more traditional pastoral imagery, and attachment comes slowly. However, the dream of the Promised Land persisted. The geographer Yi-Fu Tuan says,

> The first glimpse of the desert through a mountain pass or the first plunge into a forested wilderness can call forth not only joy but, inexplicably, a sense of recognition as of a pristine and primordial world one has always known. A brief but intense experience is capable of nullifying the past so that we are ready to abandon home for the promised land.[113]

What is interesting about American spaces in regard to Tuan's remarks is that not only experience but simply the idea of the seemingly mythic western spaces was enough to "nullify the past" for many hopeful western settlers, including Stegner's father.

* * * *

Describing his early life, Stegner says that he was aware of being "a target" of an inevitably hostile world. He portrays the world of his boyhood in Saskatchewan as a time when "exposure was like paralysis or panic."[114] And indeed the brutal plains weather is a killer, then and now.

His characters are continually seeking the "safe place" in a world which again and again proves that no place is safe, or at least not for long. However, frightening as the landscape of his boyhood could be, Stegner loved it and realized that it taught him how to live in nature. The landscape of Stegner's childhood had a dual character, the dangerous, wild side seen as masculine, the side offering sanctuary seen as feminine, exactly as Stegner viewed his home life. In his later years Stegner's efforts at conservation of the fragile wildernesses of the West reflected this sentiment, prefigured in his fiction, that safe places were under threat.

Whereas humanity has been previously been perceived as the target of a hostile environment, in the latter half of the twentieth century the environment became the target of hostile, or indifferent, humanity. The safe haven must be protected from those who once sought shelter in the natural world. The American wilderness has reverted to the function of the green haven of pastoral poetry, a role which it has had, and lost, many times in the history of the continent since discovery.

The shifting perception of the vision of the West is discussed in Stegner's exhaustive biographical history, *Beyond the Hundredth Meridian: John Wesley Powell and the Second Opening of the West*. Powell wrote his *Report on the Lands of the Arid Region* in 1878. He was head of the US Geological Survey, and was one of the first men to navigate the Colorado through the Grand Canyon. Powell understood the implications of aridity beyond the 100th meridian. He was aware, in a practical, rational way, of what the Indians had known intuitively about places for centuries: there are lands that will not be lived in. Powell would have been appalled by the developments today mushrooming in the desert, draining the precious water resources and damaging the fragile desert ecosystem.

In the chapter, "The Plateau Province," in *Beyond the Hundredth Meridian*, Stegner describes a desert area which Powell surveyed:

> It is the Plateau Province, comprising all of eastern and southern Utah, part of western Colorado, and part of northern New Mexico and Arizona, that concerns us, since it is what primarily concerned Powell...It is scenically the most spectacular and humanly the least usable of all our regions.[115]

This is clearly, a land not to be lived in, as is much of the West, but to be admired and preserved for itself and the appreciation of future generations. Contemporary writers described the lands that Powell surveyed in fabulous terms. The nineteenth century, schooled by the myth of the frontier, wanted to believe the interior West was the land of Canaan, that it was possible to irrigate its desert lands, that it was the Big Rock Candy Mountain. Boomers like William Gilpin, who comes in for much criticism in Stegner's book, encouraged this sort of belief. In *Beyond the*

Hundredth Meridian, Stegner is telling the familiar story: the voice crying out in the wilderness, to which no one will listen in time.

As a result of the Powell book, Stegner developed close links with Stewart Udall, Kennedy's Secretary of the Interior—one of the few prominent American politicians of his era with a sense of environmental vision. Thus Stegner's work, though not overtly political, had consequences in the public arena. By challenging the dominant ideological stand on the environment, Stegner effectively challenged the entire structure of the western pioneer ethos with its unspoken reliance upon an exploitable landscape, seen as a market commodity. In this way Stegner questioned the quasi-mythic belief in the West as the Promised Land, open to all comers tough enough to take it. However, unlike his onetime student Edward Abbey, Stegner never advocated radical or violent action against legally sanctioned environmental vandalism, and his moderate stance gave his views more credibility in the mainstream than the fiery Abbey was ever to achieve.

Stegner's environmentalism has been described by T.H. Watkins as Stegner's "third career," along with writing and teaching.[116] I believe it can be argued that these careers may be unified, in certain of their aspects, under the umbrella term "stewardship of the landscape," to which Stegner devoted his formidable talents in all areas. Stegner worked for preservation of the western landscape; he taught many well-known nature writers when he was Professor of Creative Writing at Stanford; almost all of his own writing is infused with an environmental ethic to some degree. Watkins emphasizes the "depth and emotional character of Stegner's commitment to the land...a visceral thing...call it love."[117] This is a concept perhaps not readily accessible to conventional academic discourse, but I believe that Watkins has got to the heart of Stegner's environmental commitment with this emphasis on its personal validity and deep significance for Stegner. What I have described as epiphanic moments in Stegner's writing reinforce this emotional quality to his environmentalism. However, Stegner's environmentalism was also rooted in political action, action which bore fruit with the successful objection to the damming of the upper Colorado at Dinosaur National Monument and Echo Park in 1950, spearheaded by Stegner and others. Watkins writes,

> "In a realpolitik sense, the movement [the Conservation movement] came of age during Echo Park," the historian Stephen Fox has written. "The conservationists, perhaps to their own surprise, beat down powerful federal bureaus and private commercial interests."[118]

Stegner himself said that until the issues around Echo Park began to emerge, he had been relatively innocent about large-scale western development, even dams—thoroughly part of his era, an era in which industrial progress was almost universally viewed as a good thing. Watkins notes:

> There was still innocence enough left for Stegner to be infected, too. "Nobody can visit Boulder Dam itself without getting that World's Fair feeling," he wrote in an article for the *Saturday Review* that year [1946]: "It is certainly one of the world's wonders, that sweeping cliff of concrete, those impetuous elevators, the labyrinth of tunnels, the huge power stations. Everything about the dam is marked by the immense smooth efficient beauty that seems peculiarly American."[119]

However, working alongside this admiration for industrial grandeur and American know-how was a profound appreciation of wild places, and particularly of the grand, arid regions of the West, which had long been part of Stegner's makeup, and which had, with his biography of Powell, received the sort of historical framing which Stegner understood. The ramifications of Powell's exhortations to a heedless public about the need to preserve the public domain, and the dangers of treating arid landscapes as though they were arable, rang alarm bells for Stegner in the 1950s, watching as the Army Corps of Engineers and the US Bureau of Reclamation planned dam after dam on the wildest of the western rivers.

Water issues hold a particularly important place in Stegner's works, because of his awareness of the natural aridity of the West, but also because of a deep attachment to mountain rivers. For Stegner the western mountain rivers were not simply a natural resource, they were holy places, filled with mystery and wonder:

> All I knew was that it was pure delight to be where the land lifted in peaks and plunged in canyons, and to sniff air thin, spray-cooled, full of pine and spruce smells, and to be so close-seeming to the improbable sky. I gave my heart to the mountains the minute I stood beside this river...
>
> ...It was rare and comforting to waken late and hear the undiminished shouting of the water in the night. And at sunup it was still there, powerful and incessant, with the slant sun tangled in its rainbow spray, the grass blue with wetness, and the air heady as ether and scented with campfire smoke.
>
> By such a river it is impossible to believe that one will ever be tired or old...it is purity absolute.[120]

This deep and personal attachment to the natural world of the West has all the hallmarks of religious devotion: the landscape is regarded as the highest good: pure, sublime, personified in a way which renders it full of agency, capable of responding to its devotee in kind. This is the wellspring of his environmental activism, an activism which challenged both the myths of the West, and the power base of successive governments intent on treating what was still in some sense regarded as "frontier" as an exploitable commodity.

To extrapolate from Stegner's western environmentalism a subtext of anti-mythic activism may seem like an untenably broad leap of the imagination. However, frontier mythology carried to its extreme ends inexorably led to the Dust Bowl, decimation of the Native American populations, the creation of a culture of conspicuous waste and consumption, the effects of which we are only now beginning to understand fully. An aggressive pursuit of Manifest Destiny led to many of the same results, with the unfortunate addition of a willingness to take the frontier mythology, with all its violent and dominant overtones, coded as "The American Way," abroad, to places such as Vietnam, El Salvador, Nicaragua, and, now, the Middle East. In Stegner we see the awareness of the dangers of this way of thinking, in environmental terms particularly, through the lens of western experience and an appreciation for the grandeur of the inspiring, exploited, and fragile western environment.

The non-fiction which I have discussed here reiterates and supports many of the themes found in the fiction, and particularly emphasized Stegner's importance both as an environmentalist and as an advocate for the importance of the re-historicization of the history of the West. In addition, much of the non-fiction points out the importance of the inclusion of western literature in the traditional canon of American literature. Through his non-fiction Stegner articulated many of the premises and themes which are present either overtly or subtextually throughout his fiction canon. Additionally, in the non-fiction Stegner had a forum which may have reached a wider readership than the fiction. For one concerned with questions of environmental preservation, such a forum was essential, and indeed much of the Stegner material used by environmental advocates comes from the non-fiction rather than the fiction.

Stegner's Environmentalism

I have discussed the environmental aspects of Stegner's writing throughout his canon, but I would like to present an overview before concluding this chapter. Stegner's environmentalism was initially rooted in personal experience of childhood on the prairies of Saskatchewan. His life in a luckless homesteading family shaped his perception of the realities of frontier life, and the limits of landscape; the Stegner family was financially ruined, after years of backbreaking toil, by the natural aridity of the climate they tried to defy. Brett Olsen writes of Stegner's experience of homestead life in Eastend, Saskatchewan:

Bearing witness to Eastend's ugly side helped shape Stegner's budding environmental conscience...George Stegner certainly partook in such wanton destruction throughout his life, whether ruining fragile plains topsoil or chopping down a grove of two-hundred-year-old oaks on his property to sell as firewood. Wallace Stegner once said of his father, "he died broke and friendless...having in his lifetime done more human and environmental damage than could be repaired in a second lifetime" (*Wolf Willow*, 250).[121]

This early experience of the limits of the environment was coupled with an appreciation of its grandeur, and what I will describe as its "sublimity."

In the 1950s when Stegner's environmentalism began to become a larger part of his life and work, there were few legal protections for the environment. A post-war economy hungry for resources saw the West as it had been seen a hundred years earlier: inexhaustible, exploitable, expendable. Mark Harvey writes, "This placed a premium on the eloquently written nature essay, for wilderness activists in the 1950s and 1960s were really public relations personnel for the cause."[122] Stegner was an invaluable advocate for the environmental movement through his eloquent and persuasive writing. He believed absolutely in the concept of "stewardship" of the land, and Harvey suggests a religious, or at any rate spiritual, construct on this, which is possible, particularly given his adolescent formation among the Salt Lake City Mormons, whom he greatly admired for their sense of social responsibility, while not sharing their religious beliefs. Stegner himself never articulated any specific religious philosophy in his writings, and in keeping with a deep attachment to nineteenth-century thought, particularly Transcendentalism, rather advocates what I would describe as an understated pantheism with regard to nature. In "The Gift of Wilderness," Stegner underlines this sense of responsibility to the land and the necessity of taking the land on its own terms: "We need to learn to listen to the land, hear what it says, understand what it can and can't do over the long haul; what, especially in the West, it should not be asked to do."[123]

The sense that the land is a living thing, and must be treated as such, clearly links Stegner with Transcendentalists Thoreau and Muir, both of whose rhapsodic descriptions of natural experience, like Stegner's, describe experiences which are much more than simply appreciation. Stegner is also linked with modern environmentalists, Leopold, Carson, Abbey and others, whose concerns for the natural world include a perception of its mystery, its power, its unknowability. All believed in protection of the land: Stegner's concept of stewardship. Reverence, sometimes fear, are the terms I would choose for these writers' approach to the natural world. This sense is present implicitly in much of Stegner's later fiction, particularly *All the Little Live Things* and *The Spectator*

Bird, and is explicitly expressed in many essays and memoirs, as well as in *Angle of Repose*. Stegner's active environmentalism lasted until the end of his life. It is interesting that while he always considered himself a westerner, he asked that his ashes be scattered in Vermont, near his summer home—the heart of New England and the home of the Transcendentalists—the setting of his last novel, the prophetically titled *Crossing to Safety*.

Stegner's attitude toward the natural world was protective and respectful, and his protection of it, through his writing, vigorous. In addition, there is a spiritual dimension to his advocacy of the natural world, which I have previously mentioned and to which I would now like to return. This spiritual or metaphysical aspect of his sense of the natural world is a further link with the Transcendentalists. This aspect of Stegner's work has been examined by Susan Tyburski. Tyburski stated that, for Stegner, "true or total appreciation of wilderness can only be obtained via an unconscious route."[124] Tyburski's argument links Stegner's appreciation of wilderness with the religious concept of epiphany. In reference to the opening of "Overture: The Sound of Mountain Water," she states,

> Stegner's early experience of mountain water, and thus of wilderness as a whole, is awe-inspiring, and closely parallels the religious occurrence of epiphany. The mountain stream confrontation is similar to the proto-typical religious experience described by Rudolph Otto, and paraphrased by Mircea Eliade in the latter's introduction to *The Sacred and the Profane*. According to this study of common religious experiences, the Divine was not perceived simply as an abstract idea, but as a "terrible" and very vivid power. The religious manifestation was itself a "frightening and irrational experience," characterized by a "feeling of terror before the sacred, before the awe-inspiring mystery, the majesty that emanates an overwhelming superiority of power; and religious fear before the fascinating mystery in which the perfect fullness of being flowers" (Eliade 1957, p. 9).[125]

I doubt whether Stegner himself, with his characteristic understatement, would have employed Eliade's terminology. However, there are many moments in his works in which the sense of an awareness of sublimity, perhaps not called divinity but in my view interpretable as such, is present. And to one familiar with the western places described by Stegner, this sense of awareness is unquestionably real. While the sublime in landscape is undoubtedly more than Burke's rather limiting definition, it is useful to consider it. The sublime, according to Burke, partakes of the terrifying, the vast, the magnificent, the powerful, the loud, the painful, and so on: "It is productive of the strongest emotion which the mind is capable of feeling."[126] This description fits the monumental, inspiring, strange, and sometimes bizarre western landscapes of which Stegner wrote, and whose preservation he regarded as essential. Tyburski further discusses Eliade's concept of "sacred space," in which one receives "'the revelation of a reality other than that in which he participates through his ordinary daily life...Within the sacred precincts the profane world is transcended...' (Eliade 1957, pp. 24–26). For Stegner the wilderness is such a sacred place."[127]

This transcendence of the "profane world" is central to our understanding of Stegner's attitude towards nature and landscape. In landscape and nature Stegner sees that which is utterly real, connected to our primal sources of existence, and that which without question must be respected and preserved. Mark Harvey is equally explicit about this angle of Stegner's attachment to nature and the environment:

> Drawing on nature writers after and including the Transcendentalists, Stegner identified wilderness with the divine. While he did not put such thoughts in Christian terms or those of any organized faith, he did touch on spiritual and sacred themes. In the first place, he maintained that wilderness comprised the purest form of nature, remnants of God's original creation.[128]

I agree with Harvey's analysis, and while there is rarely direct explication of this spiritual dimension within Stegner's canon, there is an abiding sense of reverence, wonder, and joy in the presence of the natural world which suggest not only epiphanic moments such as those experienced by his character Susan Ward in *Angle of Repose*, but also an overriding sense of belief in the rightness of the natural world as it was created.

Susan Tyburski quotes from an uncollected article published in *Rocky Mountain Magazine* in November of 1981, which makes quite clear Stegner's feelings about places in the natural world:

> Perhaps the most eloquent expression of Stegner's vision of wilderness can be found in a recent article, "Dead Heart of the West: Reflections on the Great Salt Lake"...Throughout this essay, Stegner describes the various magical qualities of the Great Salt Lake, and then examines its stubborn survival in the midst of encroaching civilization, "refusing to be bent to the uses of the tourist or any industry." He concludes, "...in maintaining themselves against us, Great Salt Lake and the salt desert teach us to acknowledge limits. Another hundred years we may come to recognize this as a holy place." This statement could apply to any of our country's remaining wilderness areas, for, ever since his first experience of the sound of mountain water, these areas have been holy places to Wallace Stegner.[129]

Tyburski's quotation from this article, which I can find in no other source, is, as far as I am aware, the most unambiguous statement of Stegner's belief in the absolute sanctity of wild places. The giving of "holy" status to the Great Salt Lake and the salt desert also point to an aspect of Stegner's connection with nature which he rarely makes explicit, but which suggests a personal belief in the power of nature no less profound than that of John Muir or Henry David Thoreau.

In *Wolf Willow*, Stegner's memoir of boyhood on the Canadian prairies, Stegner describes the landscape he first perceived in these terms:

> The drama of this landscape is in the sky, pouring with light and always moving. The earth is passive. And yet the beauty I am struck by, both as present fact and as revived memory, is a fusion: this sky would not be so spectacular without this earth to change and glow and darken under it. And whatever the sky may do, however the earth is shaken or darkened, the Euclidean perfection abides. The very scale, the hugeness of simple forms, emphasizes stability. It is not hills and mountains which we should call eternal. Nature abhors an elevation as much as it abhors a vacuum; a hill is no sooner elevated than the forces of erosion begin tearing it down. These prairies are quiescent, close to static; looked at for any length of time, they begin to impose their awful perfection on the observer's mind. Eternity is a peneplain.[130]

Stegner's experience on the Canadian prairies taught him that nature was violent, powerful and pitiless. It also gave him an appreciation of aspects of nature which are often ignored or neglected. *Wolf Willow* celebrates his childhood home in Saskatchewan, a little-visited area which one might easily find uninspiring were one not alive to the living power of the landscape and its minute detail.

Stegner's enlightened appreciation is contrasted with that of the frontier boomers, typified by Bo Mason, who saw the natural world as something simply to be used for profit. Describing the influence of rural Saskatchewan upon his younger self, Stegner wrote,

> For her [his mother's] sake I have regretted that miserable homestead...But on my own account I would not have missed it—could not have missed it and be who I am, for better or worse. How better would a boy have known loneliness, which I must think a good thing to know? Who ever came more truly face to face with beauty than a boy in a waste of characterless grass and burnouts who came across the first pale primrose on a coulee bank, or on some day of great coasting clouds looked across acres of flax in bloom? Why, short of exile, would anyone ever submit to the vast geometry of sky and earth, to the glare and the heat, to the withering winds? But how else could he have met the mystery of nights when the stars were scoured

clean and the prairie was full of breathings from a long way off, and
the strange, friendly barking of night hunting owls?[131]

In this passage, Stegner touches again upon one of his primary themes:
the transformative power of nature, and the sublimity of the western
landscape. While he modified his hopeful vision of the West—"youngest
and freshest of America's regions"—he never lost the sense that the natural world possessed a kind of divinity.

This sense of the grandeur of the West is not unique to Stegner. The
Native American writer Scott Momaday discusses this attitude toward
the West:

> For the European who came from a community of congestion and
> confinement, the West was beyond dreaming; it must have inspired
> him to formulate an idea of the infinite. There he could walk
> through geologic time; he could see into eternity. He was surely
> bewildered, wary, afraid. The landscape was anomalously beautiful
> and hostile.[132]

Though Stegner was native-born, he came from an immigrant background in which such feelings towards the western landscape might well
have shared psychic space with those feelings of estrangement familiar
to immigrants such as some of Cather's sad European exiles. By the fact
that he does not have those feelings of estrangement, though he does
respect the power of the landscape, I believe one can suggest that Stegner
has further links with Native American sensibility which, once again,
refute Elizabeth Cook-Lynn's criticisms.

The transformative agency which Stegner attributes to the natural world is developed thematically in *Angle of Repose*. In the novel,
Stegner reveals his connection with the Transcendentalists, particularly
with Emerson's essay, "Nature,"[133] and with Thoreau's *Walden*.[134] His
descriptions of the Sierras also have much in common with those of John
Muir, the great Sierra naturalist and late Transcendentalist, author of
The Mountains of California.[135]

I have stated that Stegner belongs to a tradition of environmental
writing which began, in America, with Thoreau. While there are earlier
exponents of nature writing in American letters, it is fair to say that
Thoreau represents the clearest progenitor of the Transcendentalist
interpretation of this tradition, a tradition to which I believe Stegner
also, in part, belongs. It was this deeply held belief in the transformative
power of landscape, and his devotion to that landscape, like John Muir,
which spurred Stegner's environmental work and which made Stegner
such a valued advocate for protection of the fragile western wilderness.
His famous "Wilderness Letter" is very specific about the importance of
the preservation of the wilds:

Something will have gone out of us as a people if we ever let the remaining wilderness be destroyed...Never again can we have the chance to see ourselves single, separate, vertical and individual in the world, part of the environment of trees and rocks and soil, brother to the other animals, part of the natural world and competent to belong to it.[136]

This is the voice, albeit less irritable, of Joe Allston, raging against the havoc and destruction caused by the exploitative building plans of his neighbor, in *All the Little Live Things*. It echoes Charity Lang in *Crossing to Safety*, lamenting the building of a tourist attraction on their pristine, Walden-like lake. It is a voice also heard in the fulminations of Len MacDonald, seconded by Sabrina, in *A Shooting Star*, against the money-making schemes of Sabrina's brother, Oliver. It is, however, not an explicit theme in *Angle of Repose* or *The Big Rock Candy Mountain*, novels of pioneering people, except retrospectively. In his conversations with Richard Etulain, Stegner made a point which addresses this surprising omission.

There is among environmentalists a sentimental fringe, people who respond...with a blind preservationism in all circumstances...You manifestly can't go that far, though it would be nice, visually and in other ways; people do have to live, too. Some kind of compromise has to be made.[137]

This emphasis on compromise is what separates Stegner from both the deep ecologists on the one hand, and the more radical of the feminist ecocritics such as Collard and Contrucci, on another. Balance, the "angle of repose," is his ideal. Stegner is thus asserting that there is a middle ground, and that the land, certainly in agricultural terms, must support the people who live on it. He does not regard use as necessarily inconsistent with appreciation. His attitude towards the landscape is best expressed in his own description of stewardship: looking after the landscape, but recognizing that in real terms the landscape must look after us too. In this role as steward of the landscape, a significant change has occurred. In the search for sanctuary from a hostile world, the roles have been reversed. The natural world, once considered intrinsically hostile by Anglo-Americans, has become the sanctuary, that which needs to be protected from the ravages of civilization itself. Frontiering has come full circle.

Stegner's belief in "the middle ground" in development may in some ways explain the strange aberration in his writing career entitled *Discovery!* Virtually unknown by most Stegner readers and critics, this book is an odd addition to Stegner's canon, probably rightfully forgotten, written on commission for Aramco between 1968 and 1971, published in the company magazine, and republished in the fascinatingly obscure Middle East Export Press in 1971. Even Jackson Benson, the most adulatory of Stegner critics, allows this oddity barely half a page in his comprehensive volume, *Wallace Stegner: His Life and Works*.

Reading *Discovery!*, one is first and foremost aware of Stegner as an historian. Of all his works, it is most reminiscent of his biography of John Wesley Powell. Stegner was an accomplished historian, and it is a mark of his skill as a writer that this book, a history of Aramco's involvement in Saudi Arabia, is strangely compelling reading. Clearly Stegner was aware of the contradictions in the fact of a man with his environmentalist credentials writing a book praising one of the great exploiters, but it is the human side of the story which grips Stegner. The book is full of anecdote and history, character study and cultural observation. Nonetheless, the subject was one with which Stegner was clearly uncomfortable, at least to some degree. The half-apologetic comment, describing the way in which the Saudis were led into a western style of consumption, is telling: "Think of this as good or bad, as you will: it is what the Saudis themselves wanted—what ultimately they will not be denied."[138] And yet was Stegner not perceptive enough to see that "what the Saudis wanted" meant only what the elite, and now absurdly rich, upper class of the Saudi population wanted? Could he not notice, after a sojourn in the Middle East undertaken in order to write the book, that the ordinary people gained precious little from the oil bonanza?

There are other troubling aspects of this book: the constant reference to "pioneering," used in terms of oil exploration; the total lack of any mention of Saudi women (perhaps their state seemed so extraordinary as to be simply out of his ken, and it is also likely that during his sojourn in Saudi Arabia he had very little contact with Saudi women, if any); the tacit acceptance of the privileges of the Saudi royalty. It is, in short, a surprising book, and one that is rarely mentioned in Stegner criticism, though it bears a Stegner hallmark: manly men fighting impossible odds in remote locations. It was the undoubted grit and determination of the oil explorers which fascinated Stegner, and it is on individual triumphs and tragedies that the book mainly dwells. And clearly, the romantic aspect of the project in its early days was appealing to a man of Stegner's sensibilities. Also, the hard work and drive of the early oilmen was something Stegner, with his pioneer upbringing and respect for hard work and self-discipline, could relate to, and something which he admired. And yet, it is a troubling book, particularly in its tacit support of the global spread of American power. However, Stegner does make the point that in the early days the oil companies were independent of governmental control or influence, and that they frequently acted, in many cases, as ambassadors of the good things capitalism brings to remote backwaters: medicine, technical expertise, egalitarian institutions. However, I would not wish to suggest that, for all its value in terms of history and the undoubted picturesque quality of many of its institutions, Saudi Arabia, known for its vile history of repression of women and brutality towards criminals, is in any way a regime to be emulated, nor do I suppose it was any better seventy years ago. There is, therefore, something quite disquieting about this book. That Stegner should have used his massive talents on such a project is puzzling. "It was magical," Stegner states, referring to the transformation of Saudi Arabia, "from camels to Cadillacs."[139] And because it is Stegner saying it, we are inclined to believe in its truth. Stegner had his blind spots, certainly. By suggesting that oil exploration was akin to pioneering in the West, which he does many times in this book, with references to western geography, history and customs, he momentarily slips back into the unchallenged terrain of Manifest Destiny and the myth of the frontier.

This book is one of the mysteries of Stegner's canon, an aberration at best, a critical mistake at worst. It shows once again that Stegner was a man of his times in many ways, despite his undoubted environmentalist credentials.

*   *   *   *

Stegner's reverence for the natural world also suggests an equality of man and nature, seen in a positive way in Stegner's works, akin to McCarthy's complex concept of "optical democracy," which will be discussed in the following chapter. However, in brief, while McCarthy's optical democracy posits an equality of mere objects in the natural world, no thing (or being) being of greater value than another, Stegner's vision posits an equality of sentient beings, equally sharing a fragile environment. Stegner's "equality" of man and nature is my premise. I believe that throughout Stegner's canon, such concepts as being a "target" of nature point to a respect for the natural world, which in our commodified, comfortable, twenty-first-century existence, we rarely feel. Nature as a natural enemy may seem a quaint anachronism in much of the western world, yet Stegner's experience as a pioneer child taught him that not only did nature have the power to give life, and to spiritually uplift, but it also had the power to destroy. However, Stegner's sense of being a target of nature as a pioneer child never results in an adversarial relationship with the natural world—as it does for his father, who angrily chops down and plows up whatever he feels is in his way. Rather, Stegner's experience gives him a sense of communication, a possibility of "dialogue" on some level with the natural world, for he is not only a target of nature's wrath, but also of its beneficence. This possibility is reiterated throughout Stegner's environmental writings, particularly *Wolf Willow*:

> Once, standing alone under the bell-jar sky gave me the strongest feeling of personal singularity I shall ever have.[140]

I toy with the notion that man is like the river or the clouds, that he can be constantly moving and yet steadily renewed.[141]

I feel how the world reduces me to a point and then measures itself from me. Perhaps the meadowlark singing from a fencepost—a meadowlark whose dialect I recognize—feels the same way. All points on the circumference are equidistant from him; in him all radii begin; all diameters run through him; if he moves, a new geometry creates itself around him.[142]

As the prairie taught me identity by exposing me, the river valley taught me about safety.[143]

Heartless and inhuman, older than earth and totally alien, as savage and outcast as the windigo, the cannibal spirit, the wind dipped and swept upon them.[144]

Wearing any such path in the earth's rind is an intimate act, an act like love, and it is denied to the dweller in cities.[145]

In each of these excerpts, nature is given agency, and in each of these it is an act of giving—even the savage windigo wind gives, though its gifts are undesired—which its relationship with humanity is posited upon. In Stegner's world view, I suggest, nature's agency is largely beneficent, even if the young Stegner felt "targeted" by it. Stegner's environmentalism, therefore, is a personal position, born of experience and appreciation, rooted in Transcendentalism, environmental activism, and a deeply felt personal connection with the natural world.

Conclusion

Wallace Stegner's importance as an American writer lies not in the narrow epithet "Dean of Western Letters," which he was sometimes called. Rather, his significance lies in the fact that in his fiction he examined the received mythology which surrounds much of western history. He suggested new parameters with which western fiction might be read and understood as a vital component of the traditional canon. He became a spokesman for environmentalism, and brought environmentalism to the forefront in western writing, particularly with his use of the historical precedents found in the life of John Wesley Powell, and in many of his environmental essays. In addition, Stegner brought the issues which profoundly affected women's lives in the West to the forefront as early as 1943, long before the works of feminist critics such as Annette Kolodny, Melody Graulich, Jane Tompkins, and Krista Comer appeared on the critical landscape.

Stegner belongs to a long tradition of American writers which begins with Cooper and Hawthorne, Melville, Twain, Guthrie and Steinbeck, among others, who, through their critique of the frontier mythology, examine the underlying suppositions which inform, and often control, much of American life. By examining these suppositions, he reveals the shallow thinking underlying some of the most deeply held tenets of the American identity, and the historic precedents for catastrophic environmental disasters which must inevitably follow current misuse of natural resources.

Like John Wesley Powell, the subject of his comprehensive biography, Wallace Stegner might have been a voice crying in the wilderness, but through his enormous energy and vast narrative powers, he reached not only a fiction-reading audience, but also a general and political audience as well. Through his non-fiction and environmental writing, he helped preserve much that would have been lost. He also awakened vast numbers of people to the realities of the water issue in the West, and the ramifications of the continued application of the frontier ethos on the fragile western landscape.

In his fight against the marginalization of western literature and western writers, Stegner was in the vanguard. The current explosion of creative energy and recognition of western writers taking place in the western states surely owes something to Stegner's continued advocacy of the rightfulness of the place of western writers within the canon. In addition, as head of the creative writing program at Stanford University from 1945 till 1971, he personally nurtured such diverse western talents as Ken Kesey, Ivan Doig, Larry McMurtry, Wendell Berry, and many, many others. This alone would have earned him the accolade "Dean of Western Letters," but added to his other achievements, in literary and personal terms, it seems too modest a title.

In his continued iteration of the plight of women in the frontier West, a position reached by personal experience as a pioneer child of a long-suffering, abused mother, Stegner challenges some of the most deeply held misconceptions and myths of frontier life. Particularly in the short fiction set in Saskatchewan and Montana, Stegner exposes the arduous brutality of pioneering life for both men and women, and questions the basis upon which all land, even the most inhospitable, was thrown open for settlement. The pioneer, riding off into the sunset to find brave new worlds, is shown to have left behind a destitute wife and two starving children. The rhetoric of the frontier is exploded in these stories, and it is also examined in the Mormon histories.[146] The fact that Stegner's women are not seen as the conventional symbols of entrapment recognizable in other western fiction asks the question posited by Kolodny of why we have been unable to develop a model of mature masculinity on the American continent. It is answered by Stegner's suggestion that frontier virtues, as exemplified by Bo Mason particularly, not only are inadequate to deal with modern American life, but always were inadequate in dealing with the frontier itself. Therefore, the persistence of the mythology of the western heroic type is doubly destructive, reaching out to provide a misinterpretation of the past, and to obscure the reality of the present—and is likely to poison the future.

Krista Comer states that "Landscape is the single most telling signature of western identity." It is "analytically slippery...the wild card of western discourse."[147] What Comer is suggesting is that despite being a physically stable entity, landscape itself is subject to many different sorts of interpretations, and the constructed meanings imposed on it are therefore multiple, and indeed arbitrary—up to a point, that point being what the land itself will tolerate in terms of usage—and are constructed to serve particular interests. Throughout his canon, Stegner affirms these statements and in his environmental essays explicitly challenges many of the hoary myths associated with the western landscape. In his fiction, however, he looks specifically at the transformative effect of the western landscape on the individual.

Stegner's could be called an enlightened nineteenth-century sensibility, with strong links to the environmental tradition in Transcendentalism. As I have said, it was a sensibility to which he was historically, culturally, and by inclination bound. We see these links most explicitly in *Angle of Repose* in the fiction. The protagonist, Susan Ward, is narratively linked with some of the major figures of the northeast Transcendentalist tradition, as was Mary Hallock Foote, the real woman upon whom Susan Ward was modeled. Her awareness of nature is, like Stegner's, based on a reverence which has a distinct spiritual dimension. And her experiences of epiphanic moments in nature are in certain ways similar to Stegner's own, some of which I have noted in reference to *Wolf Willow* and *The Sound of Mountain Water*. Buell's description of environmental fiction in the Thoreauvian tradition suggests that the "non-human environment is present not merely as a framing device but as a presence that begins to suggest that human history is implicated in natural history."[148] This also describes Stegner's environmental work. However, Stegner's own admiration for Thoreau, though genuine, was qualified. In an essay titled, appropriately, "Qualified Homage to Thoreau," he states,

> What I miss in him, as I missed it in the more extreme rebels of the 1960s, is the acknowledgement that their society shaped them, and that without it every individual of them would be a sort of Sasquatch, a solitary animal without language, thought, tradition, obligation, or commitment.[149]

Stegner was vividly aware of a sense of indebtedness to culture and society. His parents were uneducated, and his early life was one of deprivation and poverty. For him, education was a way out of a world in which he felt, quite rightly, out of place, under-valued, and limited. What is remarkable about Stegner, however, is his lack of bitterness about his own humble roots, and particularly, his lack of malice toward a father who was by all accounts, brutal, wasteful, and cruel. That Stegner was able to regard his upbringing in Eastend—on first acquaintance a desolate, lonely, remote, and rather uninviting place, even today—into an experience which gave him the ability to form a deep and profound understanding of the natural world is evidence of his innate connection with landscape, even as a small child. His love for landscape was not learned, it was part of his very makeup, the "signature of his identity." In addition, as an environmentalist, he was aware of the effects of unregulated exploitation of the western landscape, and this awareness resonates through both his fiction and non-fiction works.

In his treatment of landscape in his fiction, Stegner effectively reconceptualizes the myth of the frontier in the elusive search for sanctuary which occupies many of his characters. In the revelation that sanctuary is a temporary state, that Eden has become debased, Stegner illustrates the disillusion which accompanied the end of the frontier.

Yet Stegner's final message is not one of disillusion or despair. He reminds us, again and again, that though sanctuary may be fleeting, we do sometimes receive it. The image of the bird in the Venerable Bede's history, flying through the lighted hall, with which Stegner ends his novel *The Spectator Bird*, is for Stegner ultimately one of redemption and hope. A watcher of spectator birds all his long life, Stegner offers us this vision of hope.

3 McCarthy's Western Fictions

An Overview

In this chapter I will look at Cormac McCarthy's critique of the myth of the frontier in his western novels, *Blood Meridian*, *All the Pretty Horses*, *The Crossing*, and *Cities of the Plain*. I will also address McCarthy's view of the continuing commodification of the western landscape. I will examine the relationship of the novels to the Vietnam War, an event which, with the attendant upheavals of the 1960s and early 1970s, marked a sea-change in cultural awareness in America. Finally I will discuss questions of the landscape in its female aspects and the relationship of attitudes toward the land to attitudes toward women as revealed in the western novels. While aspects of these points have been discussed by other critics, my aim is to focus on them in order to discuss McCarthy's perspective in relation to Stegner's. Therefore the focus will be somewhat different from other critics, revealing the connections and contradictions between the relative positions of the two writers. The link between the positions of these authors, and the development in thought either side of the ideological turning point of the Vietnam War era thereby revealed is my final aim. As I stated in my introduction, my justification in studying these two authors as a pairing is that they offer a correlation between beliefs before and after the cultural watershed of the 1960s and early 1970s in terms of their handling of the issues of landscape, nature, and the myth of the frontier, as expounded by discerning thinkers with similar concerns.

Both McCarthy and Stegner critique the myth of the frontier and its effects on landscape and people. However, I believe that the change in American thought, and loss of connection with the mythic substructure which had upheld so many of America's most deeply held beliefs, caused by the sea-change in thought of the 1960s and 1970s meant that McCarthy's critique could not have been written before that period, and Stegner's could not have been written unselfconsciously after it, although as I have pointed out, while Stegner continued writing after the advent of the postmodern era, his perspective remained firmly rooted in the previous era to which he was by education, experience, and inclination bound.

Finally I believe that Stegner's concept of numinosity in landscape has echoes in McCarthy's view of landscape as a necessary component of identity for the cowboys of *The Border Trilogy* in terms of possession, which cannot be achieved, in John Grady's case; and an almost mystical, though inchoate connection in Billy's, which is undermined by the loss of the natural world as seen particularly in the episode of the wolf, and later by Billy's placelessness at the end of *The Crossing,* and in the final part of *Cities of the Plain.* The substratum of these relationships lies in the concept of "optical democracy," an equality of all things, posited in *Blood Meridian,* though that concept seen in *Blood Meridian* is almost wholly negative, whereas a sense of the equality of the natural world and the people in it is, in *The Border Trilogy,* a much more benign concept.

I suggest that these concepts are two sides of the same coin, one seen from a perspective of cautious hope, the other from, if not quite despair, pessimism. Neither author's perspective is absolutely homogeneous, however, and Stegner has dark and desolate moments in his works just as McCarthy's perceived nihilism is often lifted by both descriptions of nature and the redemptive qualities found in his characters.

In relation to the myth of the frontier, I will argue that McCarthy's main protagonist in *The Border Trilogy,* John Grady Cole, is himself a critique of the hero of the traditional "western" novel. The significance of this critique lies in the fact that McCarthy uses the imagery of the frontier myth—the cowboy on a quest, the man alone against nature and/or racially defined enemies, the impossibility of understanding or cooperation between the sexes, and violence—to radically redefine our understanding of the significance of those ideas, and thus to re-examine western myths and, crucially, their political and environmental implications. My emphasis here will be on the environmental aspects of McCarthy's work in relation to Stegner's, and the relationship between their relative positions vis-à-vis landscape.

In McCarthy's western novels, the role of landscape and the natural world is one of opposition to the world of men; landscapes oppose the myth men seek to follow, acting as a barrier to their goals, not actively but intrinsically. As Vereen Bell has noted, "The human beings constitute one protagonist and the natural world another. Narrative and description collaborate with each other in conventional ways, but what is ultimately important is that, even ontologically, they compete."[1] That is to say, there is a tension between the "natural" and "human" worlds which is only occasionally mitigated. The worlds compete on the most basic levels. They might even be thought of as opposites. And yet the symbolic appeal of the West is ever present, and especially so to McCarthy's characters in *The Border Trilogy.* Neil Campbell writes: "McCarthy's west is a borderlands both geographically, but also metaphorically, a space for physical and philosophical migration, where issues of life and death, myth and reality, dream and actuality intersect and cross like his characters in its landscapes."[2] That is to say that the landscape, while offering "coordinates of identity," at the same time takes them away, shifting in its meanings even as the cowboys travel through it. The opposition of landscape to humanity in McCarthy's works is central to the western novels, and absolutely significant to their meaning. I believe this suggests, in McCarthy, an equivalence in which man is not the measure of all things, but simply a component, and perhaps not the most important one, of the whole. This is a very long way from the triumphalism of Manifest Destiny in the West, which trumpeted the inevitable victory of the American people over the landscape and its inhabitants, and in which John Grady Cole, at least initially, believes. In addition, McCarthy's position links him with Stegner's earlier position which posits if not an equivalence of the human and the not-human, at the least suggests an essential importance to the natural world which in turn calls forth respect and protection.

Therefore, I suggest that Stegner and McCarthy in their distinct modes are examining similar issues with regard to the western American landscape. While they appear to be writers in radically different traditions, I believe that their underlying concerns are remarkably close, as is their political stance with regard to the environment. In McCarthy's work, as in Stegner's, the author is creating a space through which the reader may examine the dominant ideological ethos of a particular historical period, as Holloway has argued.[3] My goal is to find how these spaces overlap.

McCarthy's Critique of the Myth of the Frontier

The myth of the frontier, while it has had huge cultural power, is nebulous, difficult to pin down, open to different interpretations and, like the western landscape, often the object of oppositional desires. Thus the meaning of the western landscape is troublingly opaque for those who wish to categorize it. Neil Campbell has noted its "multilayered" quality and the lack of an overriding metanarrative of the West.[4] However, this lack of metanarrative may paradoxically lead to a better understanding of the West in all its actual and ideological complexity. The fact that the West, particularly in recent years, has become the locus for any number of competing histories has made it fertile territory for fresh analyses of its past: analyses which newly challenge and examine the verities of previously accepted history.

Campbell has further noted that the "westward urge of nation-building"[5] in some respects created "a managed set of images and stories that would become the West's official history." This "official history" and "set of images" are that in which the young cowboys of McCarthy's *Border Trilogy* believe. Their tragedies hinge upon the fact that, for them, there are no alternatives to these images, and when this lack of reality reveals itself, the cowboys have no other world in which to live than that of an unstable fantasy. We know that throughout western history certain images became embedded in western consciousness: the endless frontier; the lone man regenerating himself through violence; invisible, long-suffering, passive women; the inevitably dark-skinned, adversarial "other"; and so forth. Remaining largely unquestioned owing to their essential importance in initially structuring frontier society, these images later became almost totemic in significance, and hence remained in place as cultural guideposts until the frontier era was over, and beyond. This suggests that as mythic imagery formed western identity, western identity then became fixed within that very imagery. Hollywood, taking over where the dime novels left off, gave this mythic imagery truly iconic status, creating an alternate reality which took over from actual history, and became the accepted "history" of the West for many, thus crucially reinforcing the myth of the frontier. Therefore, the images of landscape commonly associated with the West are often cinematic ones, creating a further distancing from an ever more remote reality. These images have had a profound resonance within society, creating an idealized space which seems to offer authenticity. Jane Tompkins suggests that,

> The West functions as a symbol of freedom, and of the opportunity for conquest. It seems to offer escape from the conditions of life in modern industrial society: from a mechanized existence, economic dead-ends, social entanglements, unhappy personal relations, political injustice. The desire to change places also signals a powerful need for self-transformation...a translation of the self into something purer and more authentic, more intense, more real.[6]

It is this quest for authenticity which McCarthy's characters, John Grady Cole and Lacey Rawlins, embark upon when they ride out, like "the old waddies" on their quest for a new frontier in Mexico in the first novel of *The Border Trilogy*, *All the Pretty Horses*. Paradoxically, in their quest for authenticity, the boys assume roles—the traditional cowboy—which are, for both of them, false. We hardly need to remind ourselves while reading this book that these are not desperadoes, but boys, neither of them orphans, trying to become something which never truly existed. What John Grady imagines he is becoming is something like a romanticized version of *Blood Meridian*'s Kid. When similar aspects of the previous novel's truly dark reality begin to emerge, as in the prison at Saltillo, the young cowboys look like what they are, teenagers caught up in something much bigger and more dangerous than they had anticipated. The quest for an alternate reality enacted by John Grady and Lacey in *All the Pretty Horses* is in fact a quest for what is actually a simulacrum of reality. So haunted are the boys, particularly John Grady, by a self-imposed imagery, that what begins as a teenage adventure becomes a search for reality itself.

McCarthy critiques western mythology from the inside of the genre, critiquing not only mythology but also the ideology which accompanies it and gives it its power. According to Sara Spurgeon, he writes

> from the perspective most commonly associated with the histories, stories, and myths about American frontiers in the popular imagination. Yet he savagely subverts the very myths he evokes so lovingly. Like Joseph Conrad, he both reproduces and critiques imperial ideology, at once problematizing and romanticizing traditional tropes in a complexly postmodern vision of a future tied with bonds of blood to the legacy of the mythic past.[7]

It is this subversion and problematizing which is evident in the various quests which John Grady Cole and Billy Parham embark upon in the course of *The Border Trilogy*. The obstacles which the boys encounter reveal the hollowness at the heart of their enterprises, enterprises which are based on an understanding of the West formed by mythic tropes.

Another vision of the western frontier, imagined by Billy and John Grady and critiqued in *The Border Trilogy*, is the image of a violent and degraded historical frontier presented in *Blood Meridian*, which though not entirely historically verifiable, is probably a more realistic picture of the frontier West than that in which the mythmakers might like to believe. *Blood Meridian* belongs, in part, to that tradition described by Leslie Fiedler as "gothic in theme and atmosphere alike," as do certain aspects of *The Border Trilogy*. This is a tradition in which Fiedler places many of the works of Melville, Hawthorne, Twain, and Cooper, works in which he suggests "the Faustian bargain" is at the heart of the novel.[8] In common with *Moby Dick*, *Huckleberry Finn*, and Cooper's Leatherstocking stories, McCarthy's western novels are a "womanless milieu,"[9] as Tompkins has described the West, in which young male companions struggle against intransigent evil and an arbitrary universe in which their fate is insignificant. Clearly "Faustian bargains" are made in McCarthy's novels, but in a world in which there is no "beyond" to appeal to, either for good or ill, the value of these bargains may be questionable: how does one bargain with the powers when those powers seem to be themselves utterly arbitrary, random, and often without meaning?

Robert Jarrett refers to *Blood Meridian*, the first of McCarthy's four western novels, as a "revisionary western,"[10] one which revises our concept of what the western is and does, presenting us with characters that radically alter all our previous assumptions about idealized western history. The inarticulate Kid, with his taste for "mindless violence"[11] is the heroic cowboy reversed; the depraved and amoral Judge, Jarrett suggests, is "representative of the ideology of the historical period of Manifest Destiny,"[12] the doctrine of the rightness of unchallenged white settlement of the country from coast to coast, and laterally, beyond the borders of the continental United States. In addition, according to Jarrett,

> The judge thus represents an impulse or drive toward conquest that is not inherently irrational but inherent in reason itself—a drive that the historical period itself reveals...The judge represents a will, implicit in the western mind and the historical impetus behind the American Western expansion, to wield an absolute power over nature.[13]

This desire to control nature, personified in the violent, amoral character of the Judge, suggests McCarthy's concern with westering America's effect upon the landscape, which I have suggested is one of his major concerns and which I believe links him with Stegner. Jarrett's remarks also imply a postmodern perspective of this desire to control nature exhibited by the Judge. Certainly the Judge's scrupulous recording of natural phenomena, which he then destroys, suggests a denaturing of nature which is consistent with a cynically postmodern view of the world. There is a horrible irony in all of the Judge's actions which suggests this as well. This implies that McCarthy is suggesting that the early western mind felt that nature might be dominated by humankind. However, Jarrett's comment might be taken to imply that the postmodern eye sees this for the first time. As I have suggested in my earlier comments about Stegner, this sort of critique of the West was already well underway before both McCarthy and the New Historians began theirs, and well before postmodernism appeared as a major player on the critical scene. Earlier critiques were perhaps less dramatic than *Blood Meridian*, though certainly A.B. Guthrie's *The Big Sky*, for example, offers in Boone Caudill a protagonist almost as violent and alienated as McCarthy's Kid. While the frontier myth may not have made obvious the sort of aimless destructiveness we find in the Kid, works such as Guthrie's, rooted in historical fact, remind us that the actors in the Western drama were often violent toward landscape, its creatures, and people. As Spurgeon comments, "McCarthy presents a counter-memory, a sort of anti-myth of the West, illuminating especially the roots of the modern American relationships between Anglos and non-Anglos and between humans and the natural world."[14]

Jarrett's previous comments also suggest that for McCarthy, the conflict between the natural world and man is central. By revising the tradition of the western in *Blood Meridian*, McCarthy is able to comment upon this conflict, giving the reader a perspective, which while not entirely new, is nonetheless philosophically challenging. As Jane Tompkins states: "In Westerns the obsession with landscape is finally metaphysical."[15] If this is so, McCarthy is, in his western fiction, writing about a landscape whose meaning for his characters remains troublingly ambiguous. It is not clear in *Blood Meridian*, for example, whether the West represents possible salvation gone badly wrong, or simply a track-less void—morally, spiritually, and physically. That is to say, one is not ever sure of the *intention* of the landscape, and the characters that move within it. This lack of intentionality lies at the heart of McCarthy's oeuvre. We are given the impression that landscape may be possessed of some meaning, but that meaning evades us.

Blood Meridian creates an inversion of the monomyth, as defined by Joseph Campbell, one strand of the myth of the frontier, so often invoked in American myth and literature. As Spurgeon notes,

> The scalphunters as a group can be read as playing the part of the sacred hunter, dark versions of classic Western heroes from the Deer-slayer and Daniel Boone to Buffalo Bill, leaving their communities to enter the wilderness for renewal and regeneration through the act of hunting and killing.[16]

The myth is therefore questioned from the outset of the novel, the humanity of the scalp-hunters' "prey" altering irrevocably the heart of the myth. On the contrary, the scalp-hunters of *Blood Meridian* are not heroic; they are simply agents of chaos and destruction. Equally, they enter a realm alien and strange, a wilderness in which any regeneration achieved must be suspect. They enter a place which is, "like some demon kingdom summoned up or changeling land."[17] This "demon kingdom" that the scalp-hunters travel through resembles the aspect of the hero of the monomyth's journey to the wilderness or the land of the dead. Yet on their return to civilization they do not bring redemption for either the community or themselves; rather they return, led by the sinister Judge Holden, a filthy, depraved, dangerous rabble, regenerated only in further violence. The nameless Kid sees them as

> a pack of viciouslooking humans mounted on unshod indian ponies riding half drunk through the streets, bearded, barbarous, clad in the skins of animals...the riders wearing scapulars or necklaces of dried and blackened human ears and the horses rawlooking and wild in the eye and their teeth bared like feral dogs...the whole like a visitation from some heathen land where they and others like them fed on human flesh.[18]

Humanity has here become feral, less than feral, beyond feral: reduced to some depraved state which mimics the wild, but lacks the dignity of the natural world, and it is controlled and led by the avatar of science, the Judge. The world represented by the visitation of the scalp-hunters is one in which ordinary life becomes its opposite. Spurgeon comments: "The natural order of the original myth governing the relationship between humans and nature has been upset so profoundly that even the horses are seen as feral, feeding on human flesh instead of grass."[19] So deranged that even their horses are carnivorous, the scalp-hunters represent disorder incarnate, denizens of a world in which nature has turned against itself. Spurgeon further suggests that the scalp-hunters represent a reversal of the heroic man of the monomyth, the sacred hunter figure. Their "scapulars" of human ears further imply this travesty of the religious. Additionally, the ears also act as "receipts" for those they have killed, suggesting that "the native people to whom those ears belonged are viewed by the scalphunters more as natural resources than human beings, just another part of an infinitely exploitable landscape."[20]

This attitude of brutal exploitation toward an available landscape continues with a prefiguring of the scalp-hunters' coming atrocities as McCarthy describes a scene in the local market. What might be ordinary becomes horrific as parallels are drawn with the scalp-hunters and their prey, as we see

> the flensed and naked skulls of cows and sheep with their dull blue eyes glaring wildly and the stiff bodies of deer and javelina and ducks and quail and parrots, all wild things from the country round hanging downward from hooks.[21]

This barbarous scene reveals a correspondence between the future activities of the scalp-hunters and the treatment of wild nature; as they will scalp Indians and Mexicans, so nature will be treated. The equation is made between the scalp-hunters' perception of what is non-white, or non-Anglo, with that which belongs to the natural world. All such may be taken freely and treated badly. I suggest McCarthy is equating the scalp-hunters' rapacity with the rapacity of a population who, likewise proponents of the doctrine of Manifest Destiny, would do to the land and its creatures what the scalp-hunters did to the unwary Indians or Mexicans whom they encountered.

Spurgeon's interpretation of the scalp-hunters as "profane" hunter-heroes describes a reversal of the monomyth and posits a stark reality:

> Here is the bloody tie binding America's mythic past to its troubled present, here in this mythic dance is the violent birth of the National Symbolic that has made heroes out of scalp-hunters and Indian killers and constructed the near-extinction of the buffalo and massive deforestation as symbols of triumph and mastery, the proud heritage of the modern American citizen.[22]

Spurgeon's analysis of McCarthy's intent in *Blood Meridian* reinforces my previously stated assertion that McCarthy's aim, like Stegner's, is at its core politically motivated. Written at a time when America was beginning to learn the true horror of atrocities perpetrated during the Vietnam War, it is not surprising that *Blood Meridian* is as grotesquely violent as it is. Similar things happened clandestinely in Vietnam. The correspondences between *Blood Meridian* and Vietnam will be discussed more fully in the next section of this chapter.

Additionally, in *The Border Trilogy*, the frontier myth is undercut and critiqued relentlessly. Jarrett suggests that McCarthy is offering the reader a pastiche, "a postmodern version of parodic satire, with the essential difference that the satire is 'blank' or 'amputated of the satiric impulse' by failing to provide a coherent ideological alternative to the pastiche."[23] However, David Holloway has convincingly argued that the pastiche present early in the trilogy is itself pastiched by that present in the final volume, *Cities of the Plain*, to which Jarrett did not refer, creating an "implosion of pastiche in the Trilogy as a whole."[24] This implosion thus renders the characters and their story more, rather than less, authentic, and forces the reader to confront through this authenticity the very issues with which the characters grapple: the commodification of nature, landscape, and humanity itself in an aggressively capitalist world—the myth of the frontier gone badly wrong.

If McCarthy and Stegner's projects are political, this implies a desire, if not to change—though certainly Stegner was active in seeking change—at least to critique a dominant national ethic. This ethic is often personified by the image of the "wilderness man," the ancestor of many American heroes, memorably described by D.H. Lawrence as "an isolate, almost selfless, stoic, enduring man, who lives by death, by killing."[25] This is the heroic lone man in the wilderness, the man of the myth, characterized by Stegner in his description of Guthrie's Boone Caudill as

> an avatar of the oldest of all the American myths—a civilized man recreated in savagery, rebaptized into innocence on a wilderness continent...The moral of his lapse from civilization is that such an absolute lapse is doomed and sterile, and in the end the savagery which has been his strength is revealed as his fatal weakness.[26]

This character, which Richard Slotkin described in his analysis of the Daniel Boone myth in *Regeneration Through Violence*, is a stock character in American fiction. He and his kind are present in classic westerns, and it is this model that McCarthy's young cowboys in the trilogy are initially emulating. Through them, McCarthy is critiquing this model and revealing the hollowness at its heart, revealing the *actuality* of such characters in *Blood Meridian*'s Kid. Stegner's Bo Mason has elements of the character as well, but in Stegner the man of the woods is not so much a character as an implication; his very existence posits both the possibility of personal re-invention and the economic freedom of a land in which everything is up for grabs. That the man of the woods is iconic goes without saying. He is a powerful symbol, perhaps the most powerful symbol in American history and culture. Stegner's historian's perspective is useful here.

In his story, "Genesis,"[27] Stegner pits the idea of heroic individualism against that of community spirit, which runs throughout his canon. Community spirit realistically wins out in a world in which the landscape is both hauntingly beautiful and murderously dangerous. Perhaps one of the major differences between McCarthy and Stegner is that Stegner's stories are set in landscapes that kill. In McCarthy's world it is people that kill, the landscape forming a backdrop for the brutalities of humanity rather than the reverse. Even in *Blood Meridian*, McCarthy's novel which takes place in the harshest landscapes, there is never really a sense that, although it could, the land will kill the scalp-hunters or their many victims; rather, they will kill each other. The desert reflects their own diseased interiority, not the reverse.

In this sense we see a forward movement in the progressive demystifying of the myths of the American West. Stegner takes the myth of the lone man and holds it up to the reality of the brutal landscape in which that lone man would have to exist, if he existed as he is imagined. His conclusions are evident. The western hero simply could not live alone in the western landscape in anything other than a state of primitive barbarity, all heroic characteristics lost, as George Ruxton noted in 1849,

> The trappers of the Rocky Mountains belong to a "genus" more approximating to the primitive savage than perhaps any other class of civilized man. Their lives being spent in the remote wilderness of the mountains, with no other companion than Nature herself, their habits and character assume a most singular cast of simplicity mingled with ferocity, appearing to take their coloring from the scenes and objects which surround them...They may have good qualities, but they are those of the animal..."White Indians."[28]

Ruxton's conclusions, somewhat like Stegner's, are certainly not adequate with relation to Native Americans, but they do express the contemporary view of the lone man of the woods—a far cry from Natty Bumppo or Daniel Boone—stripped of mythic overlay. Stegner's landscapes are formative of the individual, as is clearly seen in his writing, but his emphasis on the need for community shows a balance in his perspective. He acknowledges the power of the myths of the West, and their undeniable appeal, as well as the evident agency possessed by natural places, and such places' transformative power, yet he tempers and moderates all his conclusions with the reality engendered by the effect of a frontier upbringing on a sensitive, intelligent soul. McCarthy's young men, on the other hand, live the myth and the myth only. Cooperation has failed in a world more disparate from its roots, indeed a postmodern world, in which the myth has become the only reality; the simulacrum is the thing itself, since the reality is gone. The reality has disappeared with the landscape. As the landscape becomes degraded, so too does the frame of support for the western mythos disappear, leaving only the signs of that reality which in Stegner's lifetime was still evident. McCarthy's interpretation shows us what the myth devolved from the reality looks like in a postmodern world.

The once largely unquestioning acceptance of the lone man of the myth of the frontier and his kind suggests a much less complex society than now exists. Yet the image of the frontier man as an American ideal continues to be re-invoked for political purposes, despite the enormous complexity of twenty-first-century America, as I will discuss. McCarthy's young cowboys in *The Border Trilogy* believe in the image of the frontier man, the old waddies, the myth of the frontier, discussed above. They seek confirmation of identity, an identity based on these mythic images, in landscape. The desired landscape is that which will give their identities substance. They are victims of the mythmakers. They believe the mythic past is reality, and indeed a reality which still exists for them or, in John Grady Cole's case, can be acquired through acts of predation toward the Mexican landscape which replicate nineteenth-century attitudes towards non-American people and property. But like true twentieth-century children, Billy Parham, in *The Crossing*, and John Grady Cole, in *All the Pretty Horses* and *Cities of the Plain*, do not know the difference between the movies and real life. They search for a western landscape in which they can be the imagined people they see as models. They do not see themselves as the Kid of *Blood Meridian*, but rather the heroes of classic movie westerns. The survival of their identities depends upon the landscape and natural world offering them an image of self which fits the one that they imagine. Having no other models of identity, their quest is the most grave: the alternative to identification is annihilation. Robert Jarrett states: "John Grady Cole and Billy Parham both experience a loss of initially stable identity based on a mythicized past. This loss of identity mirrors the gap that separates contemporary man from authentically historical existence."[29]

This point is vitally important in my examination of these characters, suggesting that if the boys' identities are based on a myth, the loss of the myth equates with a loss of identity which then cannot be regained. What they are left with are hollow images and lives devoid of inner meaning. Both Billy and John Grady lose innocence and identity through their journeys in search of self, through landscapes in which the traditional bildungsroman is reversed, according to Jarrett. Coming of age is transformed into a vanishing into meaningless landscapes without recognizable landmarks. The landscape around them refuses to provide the answers the cinematic western landscape does: there is no sense of closure when the boy-protagonists find themselves in inscrutable western landscapes which have either become alien, or been degraded by the progressive exploitation of the western environment. The dramatic finale to *The Crossing*, in which Billy Parham witnesses that most iconic of postmodern symbols, a nuclear explosion at Los Alamos, seems undeniably symbolic of these failures of landscape. Looking for meaning, Billy finds only annihilation, not only of landscape, but of an entire way of being human. The nuclear age has surely ushered in some of the most appalling possibilities for large-scale evil which have ever confronted the human race. Jarrett has suggested that these endings are, in postmodern terms, a "principled refusal of the totalizing *grand recít* or 'master narratives,'"[30] and cites the "inadequacy of mythic cycles to coherently structure the protagonist's experiences,"[31] specifically in *The Crossing*. Sensing this inadequacy, yet believing in the myth nonetheless, McCarthy's young cowboys are exiles in their own country, indeed in their own lives. Additionally, Stephen Tatum argues that the landscape teaches the cowboys certain things about the "ephemeral nature of the world," its beauty, horror and utter indifference to humanity:

> However much his characters desire secure foundations, their fate is to traverse a fluid, liminal landscape, usually blinded or confused precisely because their philosophical abstractions, their schemes, categorizations, and names, and their inherent prejudices and passions prevent them from truly seeing the world as it is, much less their place in it.[32]

What they learn through their travels is that there is no place for them. Rather than alter the way in which they live, and lose their mythic archetypes, the boys fight a losing battle, with modernity, with landscape, with life itself.

I believe McCarthy's point in pitting his boy protagonists against a world they neither understand nor fit in is this: a certain cohort of society purports to believe (unlike the boys, who truly *do* believe) that American identity is based in the imagery of the western masculinist myth of the endless frontier, combined with appealing chivalric notions of romance which identify the "true" cowboy, or western heroic man. This cohort is largely represented by what Michael Moore archly describes as "stupid white men,"[33] that is, the powerful political and business elites for whom it remains useful to have a population—in this case represented by John Grady Cole and Billy Parham—which believes in the rightness of their actions, and for whom the images evoked by the propaganda surrounding those very actions call forth a wellspring of emotional loyalty and nostalgia for a lost golden age of righteousness and moral clarity. The usefulness of having a population which believes in the myth and acts upon its tenets lies in the fact that the frontier myth tacitly allows for levels of violence and exploitation unacceptable in ordinary life. In its belief in the endless frontier, it also tacitly supports the idea of the sort of enterprise that often masquerades under the guise of "rugged individualism," often in economic terms a covert description of exploitative behavior with regard to the landscape. It is a small step from believing in the rightness of the frontier myth and the doctrine (however covert) of Manifest Destiny, to believing, for example, in the rightness of the actions of other cowboy-manqués, such as George W. Bush. It is an even smaller step to believing, as John Grady Cole does, in however benign a fashion, in the inalienable right of white American males to take what they like. In a word, the frontier myth supports the doctrine of Manifest Destiny which in turn supports American exceptionalism and expansionism by both military and economic means. John Grady Cole and Billy Parham are emotionally attached to the model of western manhood and the frontier, and believe in its truth. To deny the rightness and actual existence of the identity based on this model, for them, results in loss of identifiable self. At the end of *Cities of the Plain*, Billy Parham is working as a movie extra, acting the role of an old cowboy, the only role which his life has taught him to play. Billy functions only within a particular narrative structure: the cowboy of history. As David Holloway has noted,

> The "ownership" of identity, the ordering of human relationships, the meaning of history itself once again turn upon the arbitrary ownership of narrative, the arbitrary meanings that the act of representation may or may not inscribe in any given set of historical circumstances.[34]

That is to say, Billy, playing the role of a character from his own life, has literally lost the plot. As McCarthy's cowboys represent the misguided personification of the myth of the frontier, then I suggest that McCarthy is saying that American society as a whole has lost the plot as well. To extrapolate the boys' failure of identification to the culture at large is to reveal a scenario of vacancy and illusion at the very heart of the life of the society. This suggests that the world in which Billy finds himself at the end of *Cities of the Plain*, post-Manifest Destiny, post-Vietnam, post-1960s, is not only a world in which his identity is merely a role to be played, but also a world in which "traditional" American identities which rely on an idealized version of America and the West have become merely roles. This further implies that the loss of coordinates of national as well as personal identity, which were a result of the cultural upheavals of the 1960s and early 1970s, have left a society in which illusion for some has become a more real perspective than reality, and in which a deep nostalgia for a perceived golden age cripples the present time.

McCarthy's West and Vietnam

Although I have already discussed the Vietnam War in relation to the myth of the frontier, I would like to add a few more points to my argument specifically in relation to McCarthy's *Border Trilogy* and *Blood Meridian*. I will also briefly consider McCarthy's recent novel, *No Country for Old Men*, with reference to the very obvious connection made to Vietnam by the fact that the protagonist is a Vietnam veteran, and one of the hired killers in the novel is also a former soldier.

McCarthy's fiction has always revealed a dark vision, but it is in *The Border Trilogy* novels, with their accessible storylines, amiable characters, romantic interest, and apparent connection to the ever-popular western tradition, that we see not only the darkness, but also the historical framing of that vision. Written after the Vietnam War, but crucially set mainly just prior to and after the Second World War, the loss of identity which plagues both John Grady and Billy mirrors the loss of direction felt by the nation collectively, during and after the Vietnam War. As Noam Chomsky has written, the Vietnam War had, in addition to the devastation of Indochina itself, consequences which extended far beyond the region.

> [It had] considerable impact on world order and the general cultural climate...[It] accelerated the breakdown of the post-World War II economic system...[and] also contributed materially to the cultural revival of the 1960s which has since extended and deepened. The notable improvement in the moral and cultural climate was a factor in the "crisis of democracy"—the technical term for the threat of democracy—that so dismayed elite opinion across the spectrum, leading to extraordinary efforts to re-impose orthodoxy, with mixed effects.[35]

Writing in this climate, in which the attempted re-imposition of cultural orthodoxy became a priority, McCarthy's western novels examine exactly what that previous orthodoxy was and what it represented. John Grady Cole's quest for a cowboy past is in itself a quest for a perceived orthodoxy, but one which he wants on his own terms. However, *Blood Meridian*, particularly, re-evaluates the mythic past so admired by those who regarded America's present, post-Vietnam, as a falling away from earlier ideals. *Blood Meridian* clearly attests that the perceived orthodoxy of mythic images of the western past was false. The *Border Trilogy* novels take this re-evaluation one step further, looking at the effects of the unexamined myth upon mid-twentieth-century characters who live in that era to which even later "orthodoxists"—I am thinking particularly of Ronald Reagan and his ilk—wished to return—the cultural twilight zone of America in the late 1940s and 1950s.

In the *Border Trilogy* novels, the boys begin their wanderings from fixed homes in which they had, however unacceptable to themselves, roles. As they travel further from these places, in search of an identity which they have imagined, they lose their original stability. In *The Crossing*, Billy's parents are murdered; at the end of *All the Pretty Horses* John Grady loses all connection with his remaining family. In this way the boys lose their moorings, social and cultural. I believe that McCarthy wrote these stories in the aftermath of a historical epoch when the country lost its way and wandered further and further from the ideals upon which it was founded—employing frontier myth and idealism in aid of ever-less justifiable foreign adventures. In short, the effects of the 1960s and early 1970s transformed the vision of those who had previously seen the American West through the tropes of myth and symbol, and indeed also of those who saw the country more realistically, but still believed in its relative benevolence. McCarthy re-examines those myths and symbols in *The Border Trilogy*, revealing the essential hollowness at their centre.

What exactly the frontier myth represented in real terms is disclosed in *Blood Meridian*, the prequel to *The Border Trilogy*, hugely violent and disturbing, full of surreal images of unimaginable violence. McCarthy has set this novel in the glory days of the doctrine of Manifest Destiny, which I have described as the political twin of the myth of the frontier. Barcley Owens argues that McCarthy's novel, set in the late 1840s, from just after the Mexican–American War through the 1870s, is the story of the Vietnam War.[36] Even if one chooses to dispute this supposition there are striking parallels, in such grisly details as the collecting of human ears and scalps as war trophies. *Blood Meridian is* a story of Manifest Destiny, and it may also be read as a story of Vietnam. However, McCarthy's allegory goes beyond Vietnam, and discusses, metaphorically, the post-Vietnam sensibility, a new sense of mistrust and cynicism towards authorities, both cultural and political, many of which seemed, in the wake of Vietnam, to have shown if not moral turpitude at least moral vacancy when confronted with the events of the war, their causes and aftermath, and the rhetoric of both the frontier and the founding fathers which had been cynically and spuriously used to justify them. In *Blood Meridian*, Glanton's gang's loss of connection with both their own histories and any connection with lawful activity mirrors the chasm between America's purported ideals and its actual activities in Vietnam and the consequent dislocation of identity of the nation as a whole, a dislocation which I believe endures.

The idea of an inherent American *right* to Mexico's land, and the scalp-hunters' "right" to both Mexican and Indian scalps in *Blood Meridian*, clearly echoes the Cold War and Vietnam era mantra that America was making the world safe for democracy, at any cost, a thinly coded way of saying safe for American economic interests. Of course, this was also the logical extension of the doctrine of Manifest Destiny. This policy was formulated as early as the post-World War II period, as Chomsky has argued, suggesting that American policy in Vietnam was simply an extension of this earlier formulation of American economic hegemony at all costs.[37] While McCarthy's scalp-hunters in *Blood Meridian* take human scalps, their modern counterparts, Chomsky's argument suggests, "scalp" the economies of weaker nations. (And, as Michael Herr chillingly points out in *Dispatches*, the original action of actual human scalping sometimes happened in Vietnam.)[38] The doctrine of Manifest Destiny, considered defunct with the settlement of the continent and the closing of the frontier, is thus revealed as the underlying philosophical rationale for America's continuing exploitation of its weaker, resource-rich neighbors, and parallel exploitation of the environment. This environmental exploitation has been discussed in American literature before, but rarely with the epic scope and narrative grandeur of *Blood Meridian*. Indeed, Sara Spurgeon suggests that the treatment of the land in *Blood Meridian* has a direct corollary with events in Southeast Asia. Here she refers to the scene of gunpowder-making and subsequent Apache-slaughter:

> This scene with its savage rape of the earth and resultant "butchery" (134) of the Indians, is a brilliant condensation of McCarthy's violent counter-memory of the winning of the West, his anti-myth of the frontier, deconstructing the forms of national Fantasy so often and so fondly used in building the space of the National Symbolic and shaping the attitudes that would come to justify American devastation of the natural world, genocide of native peoples, and imperial adventures from South America to Southeast Asia.[39]

That is to say, in *Blood Meridian*, by invoking the memory of a past many Americans held to be unassailable, and deconstructing it in such a way that all its overtones and ramifications become clear; McCarthy is reconstructing a space through which we may re-examine more recent history and find parallels.

The level of violence in *Blood Meridian* makes the Vietnam parallel more evident, as well as the creation of space in which to view Vietnam, as Dan Moos writes,

> *Blood Meridian* is a Western, but it is a Western in which we would rather not believe. McCarthy's nightmare world of death and destruction reflects little of what we have come to accept as the violence of the West...In the traditional Western, those upon whom such justice is served do not get scalped or sodomized, roasted or skewed...
>
> Unveiling the violence of Manifest Destiny, McCarthy presents us a kind of memory or a history we believed long masked.[40]

As *Blood Meridian*'s characters commit acts of carnage for no recognizable reason, so too did the dislocation of reality and protocol in Vietnam allow American soldiers to commit atrocities previously unimaginable in wartime. The revelation of the massacre at Mylai, in March 1968, as well as the exposure of some of the methods routinely used by the "special forces"—Green Berets—left the country reeling in horror and disbelief. As *Blood Meridian* reveals a previously masked history, so too did the often heroic reportage of the Vietnam War reveal not only brutal truths, but also a capacity for otherwise "normal" soldiers to engage in behavior that was a far cry from the heroic idealism of the myth of the frontier. Even members of the military opposed political involvement in Vietnam, and the comments of General David Shoup, given in a speech in 1966 and quoted by Chomsky, are revealing in their open disdain for the war, even before the massacres at Mylai:

> I believe that if we had and would keep our dirty, bloody, dollar-crooked fingers out of the business of these nations so full of depressed, exploited people, they will arrive at a solution of their own. That they design and want. That they fight and work for. [Not one] crammed down their throats by Americans.[41]

There could hardly be a more damning indictment of America's presence in Vietnam. The hawkish sentiments attributed to the army at large were largely a product of the politicians, led by Kennedy in the first instance, in his enthusiasm for another proxy battle in the Cold War, asserting American hegemonic sway over Southeast Asia.

Kennedy actively created an atmosphere of crisis during his brief presidency[42] which, coupled with his conscious self-styling as "a new frontiersman," made him and his role deliberately emblematic. But this cynical exploitation of frontier iconography had a paradoxical result, as Roper states:

> The Vietnam War fractured the political consensus of the United States in the 1960s, and after Kennedy's assassination that conflict now led a generation of Americans to challenge the worship of such traditional icons, and in turn all but destroyed the nation's belief in its established historical myths.[43]

Therefore, the employment of frontier iconography as a justification for the war in Vietnam not only had the result of creating an atmosphere of bizarre unreality during the war, but also guaranteed that when the war was over and the iconography thus used re-examined, it too would be seen to be flawed in its very inception, necessitating a re-evaluation of the very tenets of American identity. This re-evaluation took on epic proportions, and I believe that *Blood Meridian*, first published in 1985, is an attempt to assess American life, post-Vietnam.

Steven Shaviro suggests that *Blood Meridian*, like *Moby Dick*, is

> epic in scope, cosmically resonant, obsessed with open space and with language, exploring vast uncharted distances with a fanatically patient minuteness...Both savagely explode the American dream of manifest destiny, of racial domination and endless imperial expansion.[44]

This critique of imperial expansion under the guise of frontiering is also reflected in the repetitive character of all four western novels: the endless wanderings in the desert of *Blood Meridian*, the repetitive plot structure and action in all three novels of *The Border Trilogy*. This repetitiveness suggests alienation and fragmentation, yet with a sense of underlying purpose, albeit a purpose which is corrupted. Other aspects of the novels reflect this alienation: the cowboys reflect their own images in mirrors and windows. The theatre is a repeated motif, as well, which reinforces the idea of characters *acting* their own history, as America was once again acting out the myth of the frontier in Southeast Asia during the Vietnam War.

With regard to the Vietnam War a brief mention must be made of McCarthy's recent novel, *No Country for Old Men*. This late novel is perhaps rightly regarded as one of McCarthy's less significant works, yet it does add to some aspects of McCarthy's views. More a thriller than McCarthy's usual, deeply philosophical studies of personal alienation and dislocation, and almost certainly written to be filmed, this novel begins with an aging sheriff's recollection of a prisoner he sent to the gas chamber. This is followed by a scene of two violent murders by a psychopathic assassin. Finally a Vietnam veteran, Llewelyn Moss, tries and fails to shoot an antelope on a hunting trip, thus significantly failing in the hunter-hero's role at the very outset of the novel. He then finds a foiled drug-smuggling operation, several dead bodies and a suitcase full of money—all within the first eight pages. The pace rarely slows in the novel, and when it does it is usually to allow the sheriff to expound on how evil the world has become, or to utter some homespun words of wisdom on good manners, the moral superiority of his wife to himself, or the importance of belief in God—not the usual McCarthy fare. The sheriff is a character type we have met before in McCarthy: the Judge to whom John Grady speaks after returning from Mexico; the old rancher who helps Billy Parham; Mac in *Cities of the Plain*; good, decent, God-fearing, responsible, elderly, rural American men, possibly quite a lot like McCarthy himself. This is the first time such a character has been given centre-stage in one of McCarthy's novels, however. He is also very like some of Stegner's mature male characters, without the irony of Joe Allston or Lyman Ward. Not yet quite "a tattered coat upon a stick,"[45] the sheriff tries and fails to save Llewelyn and his young wife from the clutches of the too-evil-to-be-true assassin, the just-slightly-foreign Anton

Chigurh ("ant-on-sugar"). This causes him to reflect on his own failings and, in true "western" fashion, to turn in his badge. Passing through the text are various other characters, including: a doomed deputy; nameless Mexican drug-runners; the sheriff's Bible-reading wife; a crippled World War I veteran; a former Green Beret turned hired killer who is yet another Vietnam veteran; and a teenage runaway. Except for moments of McCarthy's signature exquisite prose, this is a novel which could have been written by nearly anybody with an eye for a page-turning plot and a good ear for colloquial speech. I am not suggesting that this is a bad novel; it is simply not a great novel, which is what McCarthy generally produces. As James Browning states:

> The master of Southwestern gothic has written his first indoor book, breaking his own prose the way John Grady Cole broke colts in *All the Pretty Horses* (1992), the broken prose and colts still lovely shadows of their former selves.[46]

Browning's comments nicely sum up the difference between this story of irredeemable evil and an earlier one, *Blood Meridian*, both of which require the Vietnam War to provide a platform from which they may be usefully examined. Additionally, Llewelyn Moss, the hunter figure, bears similarities to McCarthy's boy-protagonists in *The Border Trilogy* and has more than a passing resemblance to the character of the adult Billy (were Billy able to connect with women) in *Cities of the Plain*—the American Adam, with all his flaws, his hunting skills no longer required, living in a trailer in West Texas with a child-bride he has picked out at Wal-Mart.

The reduction of the hunter of the myth of the frontier to the figure of Llewelyn, a plain, decent, dumb, crack shot, is telling. As a figure from the pantheon of American heroes, Llewelyn would have done just fine next to Davy Crockett at the Alamo, or Custer at the Little Big Horn—not a leader, but one of the many doomed, heroic followers of man and myth. Significantly, he signed up for three tours of duty in Vietnam, a war in which one tour was considered excessive, presumably because it was the single arena in which his wilderness skills could be put to any use. McCarthy is pointing out the admirable qualities of such men, but also their obsolescence in a modern world in which not only are the antelope quicker and smarter than him, but the villains are too, and they have better weapons. There is a hint of nostalgia in McCarthy's depiction of this lost soul, however, whose only hope of redemption is a nineteen-year-old checkout girl. McCarthy likes Llewelyn, and the reader does too. Llewelyn is decent. He gets in the trouble he does because he goes back to give water to a dying drug-runner and is spotted by the rival gang which has ambushed the group Llewelyn first stumbled upon. But the new Indians don't fight fair, and Llewelyn's skills are of little avail on the twenty-first-century frontier. Peter Messent aptly states,

> In one sense there is little new about McCarthy's subversions and interrogations. The mythology of the American West has long been recognized in the academic community both as inappropriate to the fabric of contemporary American life, and flawed in the values it celebrates...The very success of McCarthy's 'Western' novels suggests how the ritualized and formulaic aspects of the frontier experience still attract, and hold considerable meaning for an American (and American-influenced) audience.[47]

Messent's point is an important one with regard to *No Country for Old Men*. Unlike the novels of *The Border Trilogy*, *No Country for Old Men* does not even suggest a romantic subtext to Llewelyn's story. He is enmired in the ugliness of contemporary American modernity in a way which the characters of *The Border Trilogy* were not. They existed almost entirely outside history, and their journeys into the past, or the perceived past, were something that Llewelyn would not have, and could not have, contemplated. Significantly the action of *The Border Trilogy* happens mainly outdoors in nature. Llewelyn's big mistake, however, is to go into nature, seeking regeneration and finding something quite different. After Llewelyn is spotted and escapes the drug gang, the novel takes place in cars, motel rooms, and towns. We never see Llewelyn in nature again, and his wilderness skills, particularly his marksmanship, do nothing to save him—although he does manage to inadvertently kill an old lady sitting in her front room with a stray bullet during a running gun-battle. I believe McCarthy's point is clear. The archetypal man of the myth of the frontier cannot survive in the new wilderness, for, like the world of *Blood Meridian*, the new wilderness is a wilderness of the soul, one in which the myth of the frontier has as much power as a child's fairy tale. Llewelyn is as much adrift as the cowboys of *The Border Trilogy* and Stegner's Bo Mason were, in a world which could not be bent to their wills. Additionally, he is a danger to himself and others. In finding the drug money he is, like Bo Mason, looking for his own Big Rock Candy Mountain—something for nothing, the archetypal dream of the child who has never grown up: all the pretty little horses. Here then is another link between Stegner and McCarthy. Stegner's description of his father might equally be applied to Llewelyn:

> [He] was a child and a man. Whatever he did, any time, he was a completely masculine being, and almost always he was a child, even in his rages. In an earlier time, under other circumstances, he might have become something the nation would have elected to honor, but he would have been no different. He would have always been an

undeveloped human being, an immature social animal, and the further the nation goes the less room there is for that kind of man.[48]

We see that Llewelyn, out of his role as marksman extraordinaire, has little success in the modern world. At thirty-six he lives in a trailer with his nineteen-year-old wife. Offered the possibility of acquiring what he knows to be drug money, he takes it, unthinkingly, and the rest of the novel is the story of his decline. Going on the run, he becomes progressively more estranged from what connection he did have with the world. He refuses his wife's advice and gets himself deeper and deeper in trouble until he is killed by the drug gang which has been trailing him, taking with him on the way a hapless hitch-hiker who came along for the ride, and ensuring the death of his wife after his own.

Near the end of *No Country for Old Men*, Sheriff Bell goes to see Llewelyn's father. In what may well be McCarthy's most explicit indictment of the myth of the frontier, Llewelyn's father says,

> People will tell you it was Vietnam brought this country to its knees. But I never believed that. It was already in bad shape. Vietnam was just the icin on the cake. We didnt have nothin to give to em to take over there. If we'd sent em without rifles I don't know as they'd of been that much worse off. You cant go to war like that. You cant go to war without God. I dont know what is goin to happen when the next one comes. I surely dont.[49]

We surely don't know either. And McCarthy's next novel, *The Road*, while not in the frame for this book, bears brief mention as it takes the argument even further, suggesting that the myth of the frontier and the desire for endless expansion at whatever cost will lead us all to an apocalyptic fate as the environment itself finally turns on us, as indeed it is beginning to do already. This is a point I will discuss further in my conclusion.

Western Nostalgia

I have argued that nostalgia for an idealized western past, often cynically manipulated by politicians and big business, such as the tobacco giants, results from the fact that the basis of traditional western identities, which had become highly romanticized by the time of the settings of *The Border Trilogy*, lay firmly in the past. The past, for McCarthy's characters in *The Border Trilogy*, is therefore the desired place; the past landscape, the desired one. As in *The Great Gatsby*, McCarthy's young cowboys are, ironically, beginning life already as "boats against the current, borne back ceaselessly into the past."[50] Their nostalgia for a past time leads not to wholeness but to alienation and fragmentation. This

fragmentation of self is reflected in a fragmentation of language throughout the trilogy, in which the cowboy protagonists are usually monosyl-
labic, at best taciturn, even in two languages. The inchoate expressions
of the boys mirror the mystery of the thing they seek: a land and a time
whose very existence is posited on myth. At some level, they know this.
David Holloway asks,

> What is the "otherwise" that the protagonists seek, and what is the
> "actual" that they wish to escape?...Throughout the Trilogy John
> Grady's quest is characterized by a quixotic resistance to the very
> materiality of the world in which he is set...This Don Quixote for
> the commodity age becomes little more than a hollow pastiche of
> the character he so much wants to be. A pastiche, because the kind
> of world and the kind of selfhood that he pursues—a self that has
> "depth" beyond a superficial exchange value—are no longer avail-
> able to him. In the end the best that John Grady can do is absent
> himself in the kind of death he always wanted.[51]

This argument suggests that, in the end, John Grady is at some level
aware of the futility of his quest, a quest for an idealized "other place"
and the concurrent fulfillment of selfhood which he purports to believe
exists within that idealized space. Thus his final annihilation of self is
in fact a willed choice in a landscape which is for him devoid of meaning, being *actual* rather than ideal. His ideal landscape exists in a world
of "picturebook horses" firmly located in the lost world of childhood
and fantasy. Rather than inscribe adult meaning on the landscapes he is
placed in, John Grady falls into a nostalgic longing for the impossible,
rendering the actual, meaningless.

An argument posited by Stuart Tannock has suggested that nostalgia
is a useful way of understanding the past. He also suggests that nostalgia
is employed in order to contrast an inadequate present with an idealized
past, which McCarthy's cowboys in *The Border Trilogy* consistently do.
This argument gives us a way to look at McCarthy's boy protagonists'
motives with more complexity. Billy Parham's idealized past is perhaps
more complicated than John Grady's, centered in a desire for a world of
natural purity envisioned in the non-human world, but like John Grady's, Billy's desires are still for that which is unobtainable:

> Invoking the past, the nostalgic subject may be involved in escaping
> or evading, in critiquing, or in mobilizing to overcome the present
> experience of loss of identity, lack of agency, or absence of com-
> munity. Some of the key tropes central to nostalgic rhetoric are
> the notion of a Golden Age and a subsequent Fall, the story of the
> Homecoming, and the pastoral.[52]

Loss of identity, lack of agency, and an absence of community are all central elements of the troubles which both Billy Parham and John Grady Cole suffer in McCarthy's novels.

Nostalgia regards the past as the proper place, the behavior of people in the past, the right way to live, according to Tannock.[53] It is also a response to an uncertain or confusing present. Tannock's argument continues to suggest that the nostalgic person not only idealizes the past, but in so doing refuses responsibility for the present, withdrawing into an alternate world, sometimes nature, to avoid confronting the real world in real time, and yet in so doing achieving some kind of ability to function in an inadequate or troubling present time:

> Nostalgia, by sanctioning soothing and utopian images of the past, lets people adapt both to rapid social change and to changes in individual life histories—changes, in the latter case, that may well lead into social roles and positions (of adolescence, adulthood, old age) in which individual agency, sense of identity, and participation in community are severely restricted.[54]

Therefore, according to Tannock, nostalgia functions as a viable way of approaching the past, and within that role provides an avenue, perhaps the only avenue, for characters such as Billy and John Grady to function. However, nostalgia has its dangers:

> Nostalgia should unquestionably be challenged and critiqued for the distortions, misunderstandings, and limitations it may place on effective historical interpretation and action; but, in the modern West at least, nostalgia should be equally recognized as a valid way of constructing and approaching the past—recognized, that is, as a general structure of feeling, present in, and important to individuals and communities of all social groups.[55]

We are therefore left with a conundrum. While we may recognize the dangers of nostalgia, Tannock suggests that its value lies in the fact that it provides us with a way of understanding and approaching the past, allowing us access to what might otherwise be inaccessible experience, and providing a kind of consolation for those who find the present intolerable. Certainly there is value in honoring those aspects of the past which are honorable. What McCarthy's young protagonists do not realize is that, like the present, the past had as many evils, disappointments, and losses as the present time. John Grady's nostalgia is fed by western imagery and Cold War fears. Billy's is the product of the "new protocols" that he, like his wolf, must endure in the new world of closing landscapes and a natural world in which acts of man wreak incomprehensible damage, as in the dropping of the atomic bomb on Japan in 1945, the year of the closing of his first story.

Nostalgic perception is therefore vital to both John Grady and Billy. Without a wholesale reframing of their imaginative worlds, they cannot escape their own imagery of a world which no longer exists even as a possibility. By this McCarthy seems to be telling us that there is no real world for the boys in which they may rest their imaginations, because the real is so utterly degraded, the past so elusively attractive. The complication in this argument, of course, is portrayed in *Blood Meridian*, which suggests an equal, indeed worse, degradation of the past. One wonders what choices the boys have in McCarthy's dark vision of a world tainted in its very conception.

The danger of a nostalgic world view is that it may influence present action. Nostalgic cowboys are one thing—though one questions the ability to achieve happiness in the real world when one's mindset is dominated by the past—nostalgic presidents, politicians, and military men are quite another problem, as recent rhetoric and action shows us. A nostalgic world view can lead to severe misunderstandings of real issues in a complex world, minimizing and reducing complexity in ways which can be dangerous in their political naïveté. Trenton Hickman argues,

> As both mood and mode, nostalgia not only allows us to feel something special for a past but to transform it by means of our sentimental narration and artistic deployment of it, making the past continuous with our own historical discontinuity by dislocating the past and creating cultural artifacts to validate the nostalgic narrative's anachronisms...Nostalgia longs for a past that never really was in order to validate its current moment in time and to obscure— subconsciously or otherwise—the absence of lived pasts that lack the appropriate present-day narrative sponsors.[56]

This obscuring of unappealing or unusable histories is what McCarthy's cowboys, particularly John Grady Cole, do constantly. Consider John Grady's idealization of both "the old waddies" and the Comanches, to whom they were opposed. The opening sequence of *All the Pretty Horses* with its description of "riders of that lost nation"[57] reveals a nostalgic subtext to John Grady's imaginings which had very little to do with the actual reality of the lives of the Comanches to which it refers, or the reality of their conflicts with "the old waddies."

Hickman's further remarks are also apposite with reference to McCarthy's dire prediction of a damned future, *The Road*.[58] He states:

> Inasmuch as nostalgia tends to make present an ameliorated past through its refractory and transformative project, it also compulsively worries about the future: Will there be one?...
>
> When it does not desire utopia or millennium, nostalgia worries that the future would end in apocalypse, defined here not exclusively in its cataclysmic Judeo-Christian sense but in its pre-Christian

> Greek sense of apocalypse as "disclosure"—namely the revelation of
> a hidden world where established spatial stories don't work any lon-
> ger...Apocalypse thus emerges as the anxiety of the nostalgic mind
> as the extinction of the spatial stories that allow it to exist.[59]

This is an important point with references to McCarthy's young cowboys. Because the past, seen through nostalgia, is the desired place, both
the present and the future become less important in relation to the ultimately desired, ultimately unavailable past. This explains, in part, why
John Grady and Billy make the choices they do. Regarding the past as
the desired place, the present and future may be sacrificed in order to
keep the dream image of the desired world intact. This also suggests that
McCarthy's nameless protagonist in *The Road* is the natural heir to the
tragic cowboys of *The Border Trilogy*, revealing the truth of the future
which the cowboys refused to acknowledge, as the current despoilers of
the environment also refuse to acknowledge the apocalyptic shores to
which we are ever more rapidly sailing.

The hollowness of character of John Grady and his subsequent death
inevitably remind the reader of his literary predecessor, Jay Gatsby,
equally obsessed with recapturing the past, acting a role which seems
to him the ideal. Gatsby is an empty pastiche of a boy's idea of a heroic
capitalist, and he is killed by the brutal realities of life in a capitalist
market economy, in which, like John Grady, the quest for an unattain-
able woman leads to destruction. As Gatsby is killed by a collusion of
events which lead to the symbolic sacrifice of Myrtle through the bizarre
medium of the yellow Rolls-Royce, and his own death at the hands of her
husband, a man economically disenfranchised by the capitalist economy,
so John Grady is killed by his belief that in the "free" market, all things,
including women, can be bought and sold. Both characters regard themselves as superior to the world which they nevertheless try to manipulate
to their own ends. In both cases a system much larger than either of them
determines their ends, and that system is largely economic. Jay Gatsby
cannot ever exist in the patrician world of the Buchanans, no matter
how rich he becomes, having not been born to his money. Similarly,
neither can John Grady stand against the autocratic world of the Dueña
Alfonsa and the Hacendado in *All the Pretty Horses*, nor can he fight
the world of corruption, control, and violence epitomized by the pimp,
Eduardo, in *Cities of the Plain*. John Grady sells everything he owns in
order to buy Magdalena's freedom from the brothel, little understanding that in the new world of commerce—which we see fully explicated
in *No Country for Old Men*—the very act of buying puts one at risk of
the shadowy merchant, whomever he may be. John Grady has, after all,
"bought" Magdalena before, colluding in the very degradation he then
tries to remedy. Previously John Grady has lived largely without money
as a means of exchange. It is no wonder he longs for a past which seems
to him to be free of the taint of financial corruption. However, one only

has to consider that the scalp-hunters of *Blood Meridian* were paid in gold for their atrocities to realize that there is no escape in the past either. And much of the old West, which John Grady so idealizes, was built with "corrupt" eastern capital, and a continuous series of "landgrabs." However, both Jay Gatsby and John Grady, while participating in the corruption around them, are innocent of it and blind to its effects until the very end. Yet that makes them no less responsible. Nostalgia may claim innocent motives, but John Grady and Gatsby ignore the inescapable fact that we are all responsible for the results of our actions whether or not we intend them. As Leo Marx reminds us, Gatsby's quest is a "pastoral of failure," and John Grady's child-like quest for an equally impossible conclusion is also doomed.

Billy Parham's quest for an idealized past is somewhat different from John Grady's, focusing on the natural world. Billy cannot save his wolf as the western landscape itself cannot be saved from the exploitations of the post-nuclear age, vividly shown in the final scene of *The Crossing* when the "false dawn" Billy observes is a nuclear weapon being detonated at Los Alamos. Billy wishes for the world to be as it was in the golden age when he rode into Hidalgo County with Boyd sitting in his saddlebow. That age ended July 16, 1945, when Billy witnesses the nuclear explosion in the aptly named Jornada del Muerto wilderness. The journey of the dead man is an apt metaphor for humanity after the diabolical onset of the atomic age, and equally a metaphor for Billy, who, with the loss of the wolf, his brother, the later loss of John Grady, and of the vision of a world he once thought was possible to reclaim, that of the imagined past of purity and free nature as epitomized by the wolf, has lost everything.

Near the end of *The Crossing* Billy meets an American who first claims to be the owner of the airplane which a group of gypsies have found, but later admits to being in Mexico because he'd "knocked up a girl in McAllen Texas and her daddy wanted to shoot me."[60] After telling any number of lies about himself he finally comes clean, and his final remark to Billy might be an epitaph for the whole of *The Crossing*: "This world will never be the same...Did you know that?"[61]

Billy did know it, thus revealing an awareness not available to John Grady, of the futility of searching for a dead past. Billy knows that all he will come away with is a travois (significantly the preferred method of transport of the Comanches, another doomed group of travelers in history) full of bones. And yet Billy's heroism lies in the fact that he continues to live, despite his spiritual investment in a nostalgic past, not courting death in the many ways John Grady does.

In summary, McCarthy has revealed the idealized western landscape as actually being the canvas upon which the bloody picture of Manifest Destiny was painted, which in modern times reveals the flawed grandeur of the western dream, the frontier myth, and its essentially illusory nature. In his characterizations, McCarthy uses archetypal American heroic types—cowboys, lineal descendants of the heroic avatars of the myth of the frontier—to shatter any illusion of either nobility or honor in that myth. For McCarthy, the ideals his teenage cowboys try to live by belong entirely to the past. McCarthy also shows the effects of the myth on the lives of his protagonists. These are likeable young men who desperately search for identity in a world in which that goal has the substance of a heat mirage on a desert highway. Controlled by forces beyond their control and understanding, their desires are almost entirely nostalgic. To exist in a world of desire for that which is wholly unobtainable is to place oneself in the realm of psychic and spiritual derangement. McCarthy's cowboys are therefore caught in a cyclical movement in which the passage of time represents not progress, but repetition. The repetitive elements in the plots of all three novels of *The Border Trilogy* emphasize this and suggest the impossibility of conclusion and closure.

As representatives of the mythical cowboy of history, McCarthy's cowboys are also descendants of the original hunter-hero, already briefly mentioned, of American history, described by Richard Slotkin, based on Joseph Campbell's model. The question of what happens when the hunt/war/rescue is over—as it inevitably was in the West—begs to be asked. McCarthy's cowboys, particularly John Grady, are by their very actions asking that question. The answer is that the hunt is replaced by another; the hunter-hero does not renew himself or find his coordinates of identity by a single act of salvation or regeneration through violence, but rather is compelled to repeat his actions again and again throughout time. McCarthy's cowboys, therefore, while appearing to enact the myth, are in fact repudiating it; and this is surely McCarthy's aim. This once again prompts the question: what is the "self" that the cowboys seek if their very seeking of it repudiates the object of their search? This is clearly a question that may be asked in terms of postmodernism. There are clearly postmodern elements in McCarthy, and this is certainly one of them. However, I return to David Holloway's statement that such terms of classification "tend to obscure the heterogeneous, conflicted, or contradictory character of the broad tendencies they name."[62] If the cowboys' quest is postmodern, it is at the same time something else. It is tragic, rather than ironic, yet it questions the metanarrative of western mythology and the myth of the frontier. But if McCarthy is experimenting in his western novels, he is doing it in a fairly regular way: the narratives are linear; the quests are not ironic parodies, but tragic failures. On the other hand, a distrust of metanarratives is clear, yet there is a return to an even older metanarrative than that of modernism: that of decency, ethical behavior, respectfulness, and goodwill. One rarely meets characters who use "sir" and "mam" so much in any other works of bestselling modern literary fiction. Sheriff Bell, McCarthy's spokesman in *No Country for Old Men*, articulates what I believe is an undercurrent throughout McCarthy's western oeuvre:

It starts when you begin to overlook bad manners. Any time you quit hearing Sir and Mam the end is pretty much in sight. I told her, I said: It reaches into ever strata. You've heard about that aint you? Ever strata? You finally get into the sort of breakdown in mercantile ethics that leaves people settin around out in the desert dead in their vehicles and by then it's just too late.

She give me kindly a funny look.[63]

This neat equation of the breakdown of society with a breakdown in mercantile ethics, the use of which term may indeed have given the young reporter some cause for surprise, is nothing less than a damning of the sort of unreined capitalism that now gallops over the smoking ruins of American decency and democracy, in Bell's—and I believe in McCarthy's, and certainly in this writer's—view. This is a similar criticism to that made by the brutally understated description of how Magdalena, the young prostitute in *Cities of the Plain*, was sold from one person to another, including members of the clergy, like any other market commodity. Additionally, in *No Country for Old Men* McCarthy refers to a lack of religion coupled with rampant consumerism, and the narcotics industry as a corollary of both, anesthetizing the emptiness created by a breakdown in traditional structures, as causative of the general breakdown in society. This may be postmodernism, but I believe that, like *The Road*'s environmental subtext of ecological disaster, it is something much less frivolous.

Leo Daugherty described *Blood Meridian* as a Gnostic tragedy. In the simplest terms Gnosticism posits, as does Manicheanism (which has been noted in reference to Stegner's Joe Allston), a dualism of good and evil in the world, neither being ascendant. As Daugherty states,

So, whereas most thoughtful people have looked at the world they lived in and asked, How did evil get into it? the Gnostics looked at the world and asked, How did *good* get into it?...Evil was simply everything that *is*, with the exception of the bits of spirit imprisoned here. And what they saw is what we see in the world of *Blood Meridian*.[64]

It is possible to read *Blood Meridian* through Daugherty's interpretation; one may also read *No Country for Old Men* with its evil archon figure, Chigurh, who like the Judge is the final arbiter of life and death, in this way. However, that might be a large enough topic for another book. Rather than embark upon that discussion, I would simply like to point out that in his Gnosticism or Manicheanism—if we accept this as an interpretation for McCarthy's western works—he is suggesting that the evil his characters encounter is the result of something more significant than any narrative posited by the breakdown of social structures relating to political or cultural mores, but rather that in our culture's haste to become something new, and in its embracing of postmodernism and the attendant commodification of life, and rejection of traditional values, it has allowed the evil in the world, always present (as vividly shown by *Blood Meridian*), to gain ascendancy. Crucially, in relation to the topics I am discussing in this book, this suggests that McCarthy is positing that the post-Vietnam era has revealed the hollowness of the myth of the frontier, which must be counted as a necessary and important step forward, but that in so doing we have also lost those valuable aspects of the frontier ethos—specifically, strength, stoicism, fortitude, integrity, courage, respect—which made the idealism associated with the myth of the frontier so appealing, and which are in themselves positive values. This also forges a strong link with Stegner's continued iteration of some of the values of the frontier ethos, despite his awareness of their often ambivalent function in practice in the modern world.

* * * *

McCarthy writes about deeply desired landscapes in *The Border Trilogy*, landscapes which exist in the case of Stegner's characters as possibilities, in the case of McCarthy's cowboys as inexpressible, idealized, imagined goals which will fulfill their search for meaning and identity. David Holloway has suggested that John Grady's idealized landscape, which he initially locates in Don Héctor's ranch, is, in fact, securely bound to the international economic world:

> Here we can begin to grasp the outline of another set of issues that point us back outward into the fictive world of the Border Trilogy as a whole, and toward the broader problem of what it is that motivates John Grady's utopian quest. While it figures as a properly ideological repressing of objective material realities, John Grady's point of view at Purísima is also motivated by the need to discover or to think of a world that lies beyond the material realities that drive him from Texas in the first place—the disappointment in bourgeois primogeniture, the commodifying of land, and the rupturing of the continuum between the degraded present and the "authentic" past of which he dreams. In this regard John Grady's ideological gaze at Purísima may be thought of as a coping strategy of some kind, a way of dealing with the absence of an outside space or "otherwise" to the material realities from which he seeks to free himself.[65]

Holloway continues to argue that this "stalling of history"[66] is caused by the impossibility of connecting past and present, and that John Grady's past and present have become unhinged. Therefore John Grady's move to Mexico is simply, "a step sideways in space," rather than the desired move into the idealized "other" of the past. Holloway's argument opens up further debate about what has caused this disjuncture. In John Grady's case I suggest that the catalyst has been loss: father, grandfather, mother (or at least maternal affection), girlfriend, and, most significantly, the family ranch with its role for John Grady. This loss is for him the most significant, leaving him free-floating in a world of economic and cultural realities which he neither understands nor desires to understand. It also highlights the perceived faithlessness of the landscape. The ranch is lost because it cannot support itself; it cannot do what John Grady desires that it do, and this is somehow its own fault, rather than a result of both historical circumstances and economic imperatives. This again exemplifies the "subtle rhetoric of blame" mentioned by Westling,[67] and also makes the landscape an object of John Grady's volition, rather than having its own agency, thus linking John Grady with his pioneer forebears.

There is a similar disjuncture in Stegner's *The Big Rock Candy Mountain*. Bo Mason seeks a landscape which he feels has been promised to him—to him and all other white American males at whom the rhetoric of national expansion was aimed. Bo is, like John Grady, hampered by the belief that he has rights to certain things: land, success, wealth. This belief sets him, by his own lights, above the law. Significantly, his lawless behavior (bootlegging) also draws him across international borders. Crossing borders for both John Grady and Bo Mason sets them, in their own estimation, beyond any law or moral compunctions. This "other" space alternates with an actual geographical space which both characters seek. The problems which beset both John Grady Cole and Bo Mason are historically problems faced by many Americans. Many westerners lost family farms and ranches in the Depression years, and the advent of large-scale ranching, as well as the oil industry, drove many small ranchers off their lands in the years after the Second World War. However, both John Grady Cole and Bo Mason suffer from another difficulty. Patricia Nelson Limerick puts it succinctly:

> Only a few Americans, lost in myth and symbol, could have imagined that life in the West was labor free. Certainly, all opportunity involved work, but the Western ideal set limits to that labor. Frontier opportunity was supposed to permit a kind of labor by which one simply gathered what nature produced.[68]

John Grady and Bo are simply following the lead set by the earliest promoters of the "New World," but their failure to learn that the frontier rhetoric, in which they both followed, was in fact only rhetoric, leads directly to their tragic ends. They are primarily seekers after something that can be defined in geographical terms, but the issues involved are not just geographical: the Big Rock Candy Mountain, a settled home, a ranch, the open range of history. Some of these may be geographically locatable; some reside in the imagination. In fact, the history of American settlement might be said to be about the desire for something, often finally unobtainable, which seems to lie just out of reach, beyond the next mountain range, across the next desert. Historically this makes sense. America was the destination of the largest migration of people in history, many of whom arrived from the other side of the world after reading a pamphlet, or hearing a casual traveler's tale. Expectation outstripped reality, again and again. America promised so much, but it began with the fabulous, beginning with the earliest explorers' accounts. Exaggeration and fantasy continued to be significant forms of western representation throughout the eighteenth and nineteenth centuries, and indeed into the twentieth and twenty-first centuries, despite the ideological corrective of the loss of faith engendered by the Vietnam era. The imagined reality of the hopeful pioneers has been superseded by a constructed, big-business-dominated reality (in John Grady's case it is the oil business which is the culprit in *All the Pretty Horses*) in which "traditional" westerners often cannot find a role, and in which western landscapes once regarded as primarily ranchland, or farmland, or wilderness, become something entirely different. The urbanization of the previously virtually uninhabitable desert Southwest is a case in point.

I believe McCarthy suggests that there was no alternative to the frontier myth for many; belief in an endless frontier, both economic and physical, was too deeply ingrained in the western psyche to easily allow for alternative ways of being. If it was abandoned, there was nothing for many to cling to in terms of ideology and belief, so the young cowboys cling to it, despite its evident falsity. In addition, the myths made complexities simple. As Neil Campbell states:

> Just as the notion of a geographic West is an unstable concept, so too is this idea of national beginnings rooted in the Frontier which apparently proceeded with efficient order across the landscape. The simple neatness of this concept reveals its mythic structure, for what it glosses over are the very complex relations...that actually existed in the various spaces of the West. The need for a national origin story occluded the recognition of the true nature of the historical processes being played out across the region and sought only to reduce these to a managed set of images and stories that would become the West's official history.[69]

While masking the contradictions, therefore, the myth also offers a sort of resolution in the very fact of its own alternate reality which is similar to nostalgia's function, as Stuart Tannock has suggested. As the myths fail them, McCarthy's cowboys become the victims of these contradictions, and both their youth and idealism leave them open to a set of expectations whose fulfillment is impossible.[70] Their identities, based in landscapes whose meanings have shifted, become equally nebulous.

Krista Comer's assertion, which I have previously mentioned, that western landscape, while definitive of western identity, is "analytically slippery,"[71] implies that despite being a physically stable entity, landscape itself is subject to many different sorts of interpretations, and the constructed meanings imposed on it are therefore multiple, and indeed arbitrary, up to a point: that point being what the land itself will tolerate in terms of usage, constructed to serve particular interests. If landscape is the "signature of western identity," Stegner and McCarthy are offering us radically different versions of that signature: Stegner's a nineteenth-century copperplate, perhaps a little smudged around the edges; McCarthy's an almost indecipherable late twentieth-century scrawl, written in blood.

All the Pretty Horses

I would now like to address the themes outlined thus far with specific reference to the first novel of *The Border Trilogy, All the Pretty Horses*. To briefly recapitulate my arguments: I have maintained that McCarthy's western novels critique the myth of the frontier. I have further suggested that the West of the myth is seen, however wrongly, as a place of freedom, self-transformation, and endless possibility. The longed-for landscape in *All the Pretty Horses* is the nostalgic landscape of the past. But it is not in any way the actual past: not one of many possible historical pasts, rooted in historical events; rather, it is the fabulous past of myth and memory, the "good old days," a configuration with only the most tangential connection to lived history. In postmodern terms, of course, the myth and the "real" are part of one another in the sense that one colors our perception of the other. They add to one another's reality in a host of definable and indefinable ways. However, I would like to argue that in *All the Pretty Horses*, McCarthy sets the actual and the myth in opposition to one another. (I also suggest that a good deal of what McCarthy considers the truth of history is seen in *Blood Meridian*, although there was a very great deal of frontiering which had nothing to do with the level of barbarism seen in that novel.) The question of the real and the mythical in terms of landscape and desire are central to *All the Pretty Horses*. It is the gradual realization of this distinction which is one of the major themes of the novel. We are alerted to this fact from the very first page:

> The candleflame and the image of the candleflame caught in the pierglass twisted and righted when he entered the hall and again when he shut the door...Behind him hung the portraits of forebears only dimly known to him all framed in glass and dimly lit...Lastly he looked at the face so caved and drawn among the folds of funeral cloth...That was not sleeping. That was not sleeping.[72]

This passage reveals several key points for understanding the novel. The flame and its image are twisted by reflection, "caught" in the pierglass, merging the real and the image of the real. "Dimly known" forebears are forever encased in glass, frozen in images which have little to do with the reality of their brief and violent lives, as we learn subsequently. John Grady's grandfather is "not sleeping" but John Grady does not say he is dead. He is not sleeping, but what is he? Living in John Grady's imagination, his grandfather points to another way of life, yet that way of life is lost forever in history. John Grady is a boy, not yet a man, yet he is as obsessed with the past as any nostalgic octogenarian. For him the past is reality, not to be looked beyond.

Aside from the revealing postmodern motif of the candleflame and its image being indistinguishable from one another, the beginning of *All the Pretty Horses* might suggest that John Grady was the boy-hero of a more traditional western bildungsroman, such as Lonnie in McMurtry's *Horseman, Pass By*.[73] Unlike *Blood Meridian*, and *The Crossing*, *All the Pretty Horses* begins apparently innocently enough, and the reader, like John Grady himself, only gradually becomes aware of the fact that this is a western story like no other. (*Cities of the Plain* also has this appearance of conventionality for the first few chapters, although the title alerts the reader to the potential of the novel, recalling the biblical cities of the plain and casting an oblique glance toward Proust, almost by the way.)

We first meet John Grady Cole at the end of all things. His earliest appearance is in a black suit for his grandfather's funeral. These are the best clothes we ever see him in. His grandfather is dead,[74] his parents are divorced, his father is physically ruined as a result of his war experiences, and his mother is selling the family ranch in order to become an actress in San Antonio. To add insult to injury, his girlfriend has left him for an older boy who has a car. John Grady is sixteen years old. His "hypos," as Melville would say, are getting the better of him.

At the beginning, we are already at the end: Texas is changing, the frontier is finished, the fenceposts across the range, prefigured in the strange epilogue to *Blood Meridian*, have gone in. These signify the limitations caused by impending modernity, as well as the commodification of landscape and private ownership—often by large conglomerates—of what was once open land. This suggests a nostalgia for the days of the frontier and the free range, but McCarthy is aware, as is made vividly clear in *Blood Meridian*, that the imagery of the frontier masked a multitude of problems. Whose frontier was it, in any case? The cattlemen's? The farmers'? The Indians'? God's? In examining nostalgia for the frontier past, one must ask, whose past? I suggest that these questions, implicitly asked by the novel, are questions of a new kind of western thinking, which while they had been voiced before, were much more in evidence in the post-Vietnam era, due to the general questioning of the tenets of American selfhood precipitated by the war and its aftermath, as I have discussed. They are questions, however, which were implicitly asked by Stegner, in the tradition of Muir, Thoreau and the Transcendentalists, whose view of the natural world allowed for, if not quite a multiplicity of meaning, an awareness that there were meanings hidden to us, and that the meaning of landscape might reside *in itself*, rather than in our interpretation of it.

After looking at his grandfather's body, John Grady goes out into the cold and desolate landscape, his unspoken ruminations interrupted by a train, symbol of the modern world which is his enemy, "boring out of the east like some ribald satellite of the coming sun howling and bellowing in the distance."[75] The train, equating modernity, is a satellite of "the coming sun." The "coming sun" in this way presages a false dawn, and itself finds a later echo in the false dawn which Billy Parham sees in a nuclear explosion at the end of *The Crossing*. But the "coming sun" is also the new age, which for John Grady means the end of the world he is trying to re-create. The train sucks up the desert in its passing as John Grady watches, feeling the ground shudder. Stephen Tatum has stated, "The image of the passing train with its brilliant headlamp concludes a leitmotif that can be defined as 'the disturbance of an existing equilibrium as a result of some motion or event.'"[76] This "motion or event," however, is the forward motion of history, by which John Grady and his kind are forever marooned. Throughout the novel mechanical modernity impedes his passage to a mythical, desired past. The family ranch is being sold, presumably to business or oil interests. John Grady's American girlfriend has left him for a boy with a car. Later his beloved Alejandra is removed from his grasp, first in an airplane, then in a train. The trip to the prison in Saltillo takes place in a truck. His friend Lacey Rawlins leaves Mexico in a bus. The machine world is always the enemy. Only the world of horses and landscape may be trusted.

In this opening McCarthy is presenting us with a situation which recurs throughout the trilogy. Innocence appears to be lost. In the attempt to retrieve it, much more than innocence is lost, and total, utter alienation and disaster results. But the "innocent" world the boys try to find never existed in the first place. David Holloway suggests that this absence of a real past qualifies much of the action in *All the Pretty Horses* as postmodern pastiche:

> Resurrecting the past as a series of images that stand as substitutes for the real, pastiche is a flattened or depthless aesthetic form in which the "original" object or identity invoked gives way to the simulation or the copy, the "original" being consigned to a prior age that is now lost or that is thought not to have existed in the first place.[77]

This suggests that McCarthy's own "incredulity towards metanarratives," as Lyotard defines postmodernism, extends to the metanarratives of American nationhood, progress, and masculinity. The absence of a basic reality behind the images which McCarthy's young cowboys seek also suggests the idea of Baudrillard's simulacrum. Seeking the past, the cowboys in fact confirm the absence of a coherent past and present reality altogether. McCarthy is thus impelling his reader to re-examine the metanarratives of the American past and to reassess them in the light of their consequences for the young cowboys and the landscape in which they act.

In *All the Pretty Horses*, McCarthy examines the traditional American romance of the flight to the wilderness in search of self, and suggests that rather than finding coordinates of identity in the search, those coordinates are irrevocably lost in the process. In a post-Vietnam world, innocent pastoral romance is no longer possible, if it ever was.

This re-examination, done in the post-Vietnam era with its radical rethinking of the previously accepted precepts of American identity, is quite different from the similar examination done by Stegner in his novels. McCarthy is coming from a position of national failure and disillusion, revealing a dark underside to American idealism which for the first time was generally acknowledged by a large portion of the population. Stegner on the other hand was writing in an era and for an audience which did not have the sense either that America had failed, or that its motivations were essentially corrupt. Rather, Stegner was writing for a readership which was still cautiously optimistic, as was Stegner himself, about the underlying benevolence of America's position in the world. That their positions have the similarities they do shows Stegner's prescience in recognizing possible ramifications of frontier ideology.

After his grandfather's funeral John Grady saddles up his horse and literally rides into the past, "where he would always choose to ride," following the trail of the old Comanche road toward Mexico.[78] John Grady cannot visually see the Comanche road, yet he "sees" his vision of it, significantly in "rose and canted light"—a vision of history. He is literally riding with the dead, living in the past, a past which he colors with his own expectations and desires. As the Comanches longed for Mexico,[79] so does John Grady see in that unknown, unfenced, mysterious and seemingly borderless landscape the possibility of becoming one with the images of the past which are at the core of his being.

The Comanches are mentioned in both *All the Pretty Horses* and *Blood Meridian*. It is not clear to what tribe Billy's fateful Indian belonged in *The Crossing*, but considering the demographic placement of the Comanches, he could easily have been a member of the tribe. Also, it is not surprising that John Grady identifies with the Comanches, since of all Plains Indians they were the most accomplished horsemen, and horses are the centre of John Grady's existence.

The objectivity with which Native Americans are treated in McCarthy's works is striking and in fact troubling. They are treated more as forces of nature rather than as actual human characters, and rarely given a human voice. McCarthy's sympathies are neither for nor against the Comanches, as far as one can tell, particularly considering their description in *Blood Meridian*, but it is clear that he views their passing as one of the many unfortunate elements of the relentless and reckless forward motion of American history, and in that sense to be regretted.

*   *   *   *

When John Grady Cole and Lacey Rawlins set off for Mexico, they are looking for a landscape that will give them, as Neil Campbell suggests, "coordinates of identity,"[80] status as cowboys of the old school. They set off like cowboys in a second-rate western, more children than the half-grown men they actually are. They are searching for a West of the imagination, more cinematic than real. David Holloway describes this aspect of their desires, revealed in many examples of pastiched cowboy dialogue:

> This faintly absurd and androcentric evocation of a lost cowboy past of hard riding and open plains is remarkable, not only because most of the novel is written in McCarthy's usual taut and elegant prose, but also because it is dialogue that expresses succinctly the hapless reaching for an imagined past that haunts the boys' journey...Such language merely reconfirms the kitsch deadness of the old west, its historical remoteness from the world of the protagonists' present.[81]

This pastiched form, according to Robert Jarrett, revises the anti-heroic Kid of *Blood Meridian*, the image of the "violently depraved westerner," while it also revises the more familiar "cowboy hero" of popular literature.[82]

Thus it is clear from the beginning of the novel that the boys' quest is problematic if not futile. Although begun with fairly conventional western imagery, the novel moves rapidly into a shifting world of evil and corruption with the journey into Mexico. The reader begins to sense from the moment the bizarre yet comical Jimmy Blevins—reminiscent of Elrod, the doomed bone-picker in *Blood Meridian*—joins John Grady and Lacey, that the conclusion will not be a happy one. Before the boys encounter any of the truly sinister characters in the novel, and while their journey still feels like a picaresque ramble, they meet the waxworkers, who offer to buy Blevins, paying for him in wax, itself evocative of shape-shifting and horror, for what purposes one does not like to imagine. This sudden shifting of the ground of the novel is followed by the debacle of the stolen horse in the sinister La Encantada, from which all subsequent disasters come. After these events and their days of wandering in the wilderness, it is no wonder that the boys see the Hacienda as a refuge, almost dreamlike, never questioning appearances and reality until it is too late.

The sense of futility and hopelessness created by the boys' inevitable reverses throughout the novel, periodically lightened by humane moments and comic dialogue, is one of the major distinctions between McCarthy and Stegner. In Stegner's novels, there is never a sense that the worst has to happen. In fact it often does, but Stegner's conclusions more often achieve the "angle of repose," the vision of compromise and completion characterizing a system of belief which I argue was possible in America prior to the 1960s, with its concurrent loss of faith in America, its myths and symbols. McCarthy's vision is far darker, more alarming, and in the end with few sparks of hope. In *The Border Trilogy*, McCarthy is writing about the re-enactment of a romantic frontier quest. Yet, he tells us in *Blood Meridian*, this quest never existed in the idealized form in which it is presented. Political expedience and contemporary mythologizing motivated actions which had very little romance about them at all. Therefore, McCarthy suggests that these competing versions of reality posit a lack of over-arching truth, one vision being no more or less real than another.

John Grady's self-conscious posing in the early part of the novel is revealing. As he and Lacey long to be romantic desperadoes, so too does John Grady wish to join the confederacy of landed ranchers—the sort who might be seen at the theatre in San Antonio. When he goes to see his mother in a play there, he makes his presence, his identity as a cowboy, obvious to the other patrons. He "stood in a gilded alcove and rolled a cigarette and stood smoking it with one boot jacked against the wall behind him."[83] If, as Robert Jarrett suggests, John Grady Cole and Billy Parham are retelling history, and "function within the novels as a pastiche, a postmodern form of parody, of the sentimental and romantic figure of the Last Cowboy,"[84] then in this image it is clear that John Grady is himself aware of enacting a role, whether he accepts its parodic implications or not. The significance of this happening in a theatre enhances this distancing from reality being enacted by John Grady. His is a role which he deeply needs to make real, whether or not he recognizes its falsity at some deeper level. His use of cowboy slang and mannerisms, his insistence on sternness and gravity (when do we ever see John Grady laugh?) inform the reader, as he has clearly informed himself, that John Grady is a cowboy of the old school, a modern desperado with a teenager's self-importance and lack of self-awareness. He has had losses and disappointments, obviously, but his way of dealing with them, virtually riding off into the sunset, is cinematic. We see him function in this way until the cinematic becomes a travesty of reality and his concept of himself as a desperado leads to truly desperate situations. His solutions to problems are solutions which might work on celluloid, but do not have much effect in real life. Lacey Rawlins, on the other hand, embraces the cowboy role with all the enthusiasm of a child, but more quickly than John Grady realizes its dangers. Lacey, however, has a home and family to return to. John Grady does not, or has convinced himself that he does not. Of course, this is because he *needs* to be an outcast to fit the role which he has assumed.

Jarrett also suggests that John Grady, and Billy, in the following novel, on some level realize they are "historical anachronisms living within the modern present."[85] Their desires to recover some other reality which both assume exists in the less modernized world of Mexico, and thus establish viable identities for themselves, is explicable in these terms. While Jarrett's point is entirely valid, and the novels contain elements of the postmodern, as Jarrett's previous quotation states, I believe McCarthy is not simply hollowing out a space in prior texts—as in the chapter summaries of *Blood Meridian*, which echo nineteenth-century literary convention—to comment ironically on them, as the postmodern project is partly described, but goes further than this to comment, through his characterizations, upon contemporary twentieth-century history. This suggests that while there are elements of the postmodern in McCarthy, perhaps most specifically identifiable in the reality shifts entailed in the many border crossings in the novels, his project remains one which is, in many of its aspects, not definable by specific theoretical terms. McCarthy goes far beyond the narrow confines of theoretical discourse, offering the reader not a multiplicity of meanings, but rather a meaning which encompasses multiple interpretations. By this I suggest that at various critical junctures in *The Border Trilogy* the reader is not being offered endless possible meanings, but rather is made aware that meanings may be seen differently by the characters and by the reader, and that there are ways in which all these interpretations are somehow true. An example of this kind of possible differentiation of meanings can be seen in the conversation between John Grady and the Dueña Alfonsa in which she describes reality as it is, as it was, and as it might have been. And John Grady's own assumption of the role of an "old waddy" does not suggest that on some level he is a Texan ranch boy, or an old waddy, or a denizen of a prior historical epoch, but rather that he himself is able to view reality from these different perspectives while at the centre remaining an almost hollow vessel, by choice, containing, but not being, all these possibilities. Another interesting example of this possibility of multiple interpretations of reality is seen at the end of *Cities of the Plain* when Billy sees a picture of a family, made from a broken glass plate and put together "in a study that cohered with its own slightly skewed geometry. Apportioning some third or separate meaning to each of the figures seated there. To their faces. To their forms."[86] New connections are made, new interpretations are possible, but the essential meaning of the picture still belongs only to itself.

While McCarthy does not specifically comment on the economic situation of westerners in the mid to late twentieth century, it is a subtext in the entire trilogy. I believe the example of John Grady as the Last Cowboy is, as well as a critique of the myth of the frontier, a comment upon the failure of late twentieth-century capitalism to provide a place in life for figures who once had a recognizable place in the market structure, figures who in fact acquired a romantic and iconic status as their actual economic importance waned. We romanticize cowboys while lamenting that their work is no longer necessary on the scale it once was. (In fact the historical cowboy was a wage-slave, tied to an arduous existence controlled by the often-absent owners of ever-larger ranches.) McCarthy questions the validity of this iconic status in the first instance, in *Blood Meridian*, but acknowledges its continued power through the further pastiche of it in *The Border Trilogy*. The fact that John Grady and Billy both sense themselves to be emblematic of some grand part of the myth of the frontier is evident throughout both *All the Pretty Horses* and *The Crossing*. Both boys are on quests of different kinds, but neither have a recognizable role to return to at the conclusion, or failure, of their enterprises. I believe that by the fact that both John Grady and Billy return from their respective adventures homeless, McCarthy is suggesting that while the cowboy may fulfill our collective desire for a heroic model, he himself is expendable, lacking individual identity. The expendability of the cowboy who is a mere pawn in the economic structure of the frontier world links him to the native in post-colonial discourse and suggests an equality between John Grady and the Comanches, who have passed out of existence, foreshadowing the fact that he may too.

In adopting the cowboy role, John Grady Cole has not only identified with the past, he has also identified with another social strata. The Gradys were owners, not workers. John Grady Cole clearly comes, on his mother's side, from a formerly affluent family fallen on hard times, one who hung portraits of ancestors on oak walls; who had servants— whom John Grady disingenuously refers to as "people who worked on the place,"[87] rather than admitting his family had servants. John Grady and his mother sit at the two ends of a long walnut table to take their meals (as John Grady will later sit at a walnut table with Don Héctor at the Hacienda), waited upon by a Mexican maid. They are not hugely rich, but they are well off enough, from a privileged background. His mother obviously married a man of a different social status: she herself stays in the fashionable Menger Hotel while in San Antonio; she has aspirations to become an actress and has previously left her husband to live in California: not the average, struggling ranch wife, certainly nothing like Billy Parham's mother. What John Grady really wants in Mexico is what his family once had in Texas. The girl he desires in Mexico is, very like his own mother, spoiled and extravagant, and used to privilege. The "spread" of her father, Don Héctor, is not just any ranch. In fact, John Grady is reaching far beyond anything in his own background. Like a spoiled child, he wants *all* the pretty horses.

The landscape John Grady desires is therefore the owned, controlled landscape, and as he desires to be a romantic desperado, he also desires to be a landowner. The failure of twentieth-century economics with regard to the Gradys—upper-middle-class ranchers not tied to larger interests—is another strand of McCarthy's argument, and one which is often too familiar to readers of American literature. The failure of the "American Dream," Jefferson's dream of a nation of yeoman farmers, has been an issue since its very inception. That McCarthy is able to treat this well-worn theme with a newness which gives the reader fresh perspectives on it is a tribute to his narrative powers.

Throughout *All the Pretty Horses*, John Grady adopts attitudes and postures better suited to a man many times his age. He is, after all, only sixteen years old when the novel begins. When he suggests to his mother that he run the ranch, she responds that he can't, he is too young and has to go to school, and in any case the ranch is not a viable economic proposition. His reaction is a meditation upon the "picturebook horses" which run on the wall above the ancestral dining table. As always in these novels, we are not allowed into the protagonist's mind. But McCarthy's implication is that these horses and John Grady's interest in them signify both the desire for the past and the desire for what he views as the power and romance of wild, untamed nature. Significantly, John Grady's grandfather, a pragmatic and experienced rancher, had referred to the horses as "picturebook horses," representing an impossibility. But for John Grady they represent another view of life, another possible interpretation of reality. In addition, they represent wish fulfillment in a larger sense. As Dianne Luce writes:

> Horses are literally what John Grady wishes for in his world, but through their associations with the idealized picturebook horses in the painting that hangs in the family dining room, and the shared vision of the horses John Grady and Don Héctor would like to create in their breeding program, and the young and ardent mares that John Grady promises to the stallion with whom he so grandiosely identifies, the pretty horses of the title come to represent any fantasy, dream, wish, or object of desire to which one might aspire or feel entitled.[88]

This sense of entitlement is a link with Stegner's Bo Mason, the protagonist of *The Big Rock Candy Mountain*, who similarly believes the landscape ought to be his for the taking, simply by virtue of his own existence as an American male. Additionally, John Grady's deep identification with the horses, like Billy's with the wolf in *The Crossing*, suggests a desire like that articulated by Wister's Virginian to become part of the natural world and "never unmix again."[89] This is a more atavistic connection than that which we find in Stegner's epiphanic moments.

There is an urgency about the boys' need to be part of the natural world in this way that is in keeping with the impatience of youth, and the sense that the natural world is fleeing, driven to extinction by modernity, like the wolf Billy so desperately tries to save. And this brings us to another observation: the boys act in ways that only very young men would. This suggests that the myth of the frontier which motivates them is essentially childish, doomed to failure. However, it also suggests that youth has the idealism to fight against impossible odds, armed with its characteristic and often admirable optimism and self-confidence.

The identification John Grady feels with horses implies that his world—or the world which he wishes to create and live in—is a better world than the one in which he actually exists. When "John Grady and his friend Rawlins depart Texas on horseback, their mode of travel [is] an implicit rejection of the mechanized southwest of the post-World War II era,"[90] according to Robert Jarrett. John Grady is a boy, playing his own version of cowboys and Indians, playing at being a man, but he is still a boy, in many ways a very young boy, playing make-believe, adopting language and gestures belonging both to another generation and to the cinematic world of cowboys.

Another essential element in this cinematic world of cowboys, which John Grady clearly bases himself on, is the repudiation of women, commented upon by Jane Tompkins. The "destruction of female authority," according to Tompkins, is accomplished when cinematic westerns "push women out of the picture completely or assign them roles in which they exist only to serve the needs of men."[91] John Grady has clearly seen too many John Wayne films and adopts the persona of the taciturn, self-important western icon. The serio-comic scene in which he meets his old girlfriend, Mary Catherine Barnett, in the street, shortly before his departure for Mexico with Rawlins, is typical:

> A person cant help the way they feel, she said.
>> That's good all the way around, aint it?
>> I thought we could be friends.
>> He nodded. It's all right. I aint going to be around here all that much longer.
>> Where are you going?
>> I aint at liberty to say.
>> Whyever not?
>> I just aint.[92]

Why ever not, indeed? Seen in this light John Grady's trip to Mexico not only is a search for the life of the "old waddies" in some mythical Mexico of the mind, but also an act of revenge on the women who have wronged him. In fact it is an attack on all the women in his life. For example, Luisa and Abuela, the blameless family servants, would have suffered terribly at his disappearance, yet the feelings of these two women, who virtually raised him, are as unimportant to John Grady as those of his mother, whom he consciously wishes to hurt. In fact, it may be argued that while John Grady lacks the psychopathology of his predecessor, *Blood Meridian*'s Kid, he also exhibits similar violent impulses toward appropriation and colonization which reveal an understanding of landscape as feminine, and in his eyes, faithless, mirroring the treatment he feels he has received from women. I suggest it is in a retributive, acquisitive sense that John Grady regards the landscape as female. Significantly, at the end of his conversation with Mary Catherine, John Grady watches her reflection in windows across the street from where they have been speaking, but it is he, not she, who "stepped out of the glass forever,"[93] tacitly asserting what he believes is his control of the situation. However, as we later see with Alejandra, and later Magdalena, John Grady is never in control of any situation regarding women.

Consistent with this idea, imagery of domination and penetration is seen throughout the novel. Molly McBride writes:

> John Grady's sexual conquest of Alejandra can be viewed as analogous to his penetration of Mexico. Furthermore, when one considers that "conquest" has both a political and sexual connotation, then these parallel penetrations take on even more significance.[94]

The fact that John Grady's desired "domination" of a foreign landscape is equated with the sexual conquest of Alejandra, both of which events fail dramatically to achieve the conclusion John Grady desires, is significant, pointing to the failure of the will towards a modern version of Manifest Destiny when its perpetrator is less ruthless than the original adherents of that doctrine. It also points out that while such successes may occur, they are temporary, leading one to extrapolate a similar conclusion to an environmental Manifest Destiny: the exploited, "conquered" environment will endure longer than its conquerors, indeed is already fighting back in a way which cannot be controlled or defeated by an environmentally irresponsible population. Hurricane Katrina, which devastated New Orleans in 2005, generally believed to have been as violent as it was because of the effects of human-caused environmental degradation, is a case in point, as are the ever more frequent hurricanes and floods which may be attributed to rising sea levels and global warming, effects of the reckless exploitation of an environment seen as passive, feminine, and subject only to the will of mankind.

At this point it is appropriate to point out that John Grady's reaction to the wounding feminine is to adopt a highly stylized, almost parodic version of what he regards as masculine, the idealized cowboy, in reaction to those aspects of the feminine which he cannot control (his mother selling the ranch, his girlfriend dropping him, Alejandra choosing father over lover). When events occur over which he has no control, John Grady becomes the horseman of history: a Texan Leatherstocking. The response to contrary events is flight to the wilderness, in which identity may be re-established by acts of heroic indifference to pain, death and danger. It is also significant that when he finally looks toward an actual female again, in *Cities of the Plain*, he chooses not a strong and willful aristocrat who has the means to defy his wishes, but a helpless, diseased, victimized child.

John Grady loses his innocent self-belief through his experiences in Mexico in both *All the Pretty Horses* and *Cities of the Plain*. This mirrors his father's loss of innocence through his terrible war experiences. Both father and son must leave the familiar Texan landscape to achieve a new, and not necessarily better, vision of the world. However, John Grady's father has had truly horrible war experiences. His view of the world has been forever altered by his experiences as a prisoner of the Japanese. It is not surprising that his vision of life is that of a man who suspects the world of evil motives. A similar theme is developed in Leslie Marmon Silko's novel, *Ceremony*,[95] in which a young Native American returns home after World War II and Japanese internment. He cannot return to normal life until he undergoes a ceremony of purification. John Grady's father has no such ceremony available to him. His connection to landscape and thus to life itself is severed, while Silko's protagonist is able, after the ceremony, to return to a life of connection with the land. Significantly, John Grady's father had the money to buy the ranch from his wife, but did not do it, rather gambled it away, his spiritual dispossession being such that he simply gave up trying to retain anything from his marriage,[96] according to the lawyer Franklin.

John Grady's father is like an older version of John Grady, a mirror image of what John Grady might have been like had he grown old. The father was naive enough to marry a woman simply because she liked horses—like John Grady's initial attraction to Alejandra, identified with the beautiful horse she rides—and self-destructive enough to sign away any share he might have had in the ranch when his wife divorced him. He tells John Grady that they are like the Comanches of history: "We dont know what's goin to show up here come daylight. We dont even know what color they'll be."[97] This suggests that the cowboys live in a state of siege, manning the fort and scanning the horizon for any aspects of encroaching modernity. However, this remark also suggests the subtext of racism underlying traditional assumptions of western, in the sense of white or Anglo-Saxon, superiority, as well as referring to the "intensified Cold War anxieties in 1949 caused by events in Mao's Red China,"[98] as Steven Tatum suggests. (Although I argue that McCarthy's point in this novel is to critique our own late twentieth-century milieu through his evocation of the ramifications of the myth of the frontier upon his mid-century characters, this reference to prior disturbances of national identity is an appropriate comparison to McCarthy's own post-Vietnam era.) McMurtry gives a similar thought to Gus McCrae in *Lonesome Dove*: "They were people of the horse, not of the town; in that they were more like the Comanches than Call would ever have admitted."[99] It might also be added that in suggesting they were like the Comanches, John Grady's father is referring obliquely to the loss of land which the Comanches, and he and John Grady, have suffered, as well as the ongoing commodification and exploitation of landscape, mentioned in the first chapter in several references to oil fields, and the diminishment of traditional ranching life.

John Grady's father's reference to the Comanches deserves a further brief comment. The Comanches were, according to T.R. Fehrenbach, those Indians who most completely adapted their lives to the horse, and lived, "permanently, exhilaratingly, on the move."[100] If one allows similarities between John Grady and his father, which I do, this suggests that while John Grady is looking for home, he is also, in some sense, desiring its opposite: a landscape in which he may move freely and untrammeled as the Comanches.

To recapitulate briefly: In *All the Pretty Horses*, McCarthy writes from a point beyond innocence of a world in which characters look towards a past they feel *is* innocent, only to find it irretrievably corrupt, based upon a myth whose referents are flawed, hollow, applicable to nothing but themselves. In this aspect of his writing, it may be suggested that McCarthy's work has postmodern elements. McCarthy's view of history, post-Vietnam, is one which cannot have any idealism with regard to the mythology of the western frontier, as I believe is clearly shown in *Blood Meridian*. Therefore, McCarthy is suggesting that the search for the lost innocence perceived in the romantic imagery of the past is futile. Stegner, on the other hand, while accepting the inappropriateness of the traditional "frontier type" in regard to both history and treatment of landscape, allows a more positive interpretation. Bo Mason, after all, is survived by a son who becomes an American ambassador,[101] and Susan and Oliver Ward do eventually achieve an "angle of repose" in their relationship.[102] Stegner's positive stance is never oblivious to the contradictions inherent in the western ethos, however, particularly with regard to landscape and the natural world.

In *All the Pretty Horses*, John Grady and Lacey initially return to the world of pastoral romance, that is, they are leaving civilization, such as it was, in rural Texas of the 1950s, for what they perceive as true wilderness, Mexico. The fact that their aim, or at least John Grady's, is acquisition does not diminish the pastoral intent, seen most vividly in the hacienda section of the novel. I am here using "pastoral" in the classic sense of a flight to the wilderness in which the self is renewed. The fact that within this flight is contained the world of the hacienda emphasizes its idyllic, dream-like quality, and links the novel to earlier quest literature. The brief chapter which encompasses the entire idyll at the hacienda stands out from the rest of the novel in its color if nothing else. The rest of the novel is a study in greys and blacks, earth tones and lowering skyscapes, death, violence, incarcerations, and tragedies. In the hacienda chapter we have a romance, dancing, rodeoing, games, conversation, decent food. John Grady is open about the fact that he is not sure if he cares more initially for Alejandra or her father's ranch.[103] The boys are invoking an aspect of the myth of the frontier—free, endless land—within a classic pastoral of wilderness regeneration; they go to the wilderness in order to establish a new frontier. Jarrett states that, "This journey into nature coincides with the protagonist's exploration of and eventual conflict with other cultures."[104] In fact the boys are enacting a racial struggle as well—mistaken in this case—of a superior race over a perceived inferior one. Their journeys into the mountains mirror the travels of their pioneer forbears. However, rather than finding a raw frontier to claim, they find in the idyllic hacienda another, different pastoral. Their "new" world is already settled, and the "virgin land" John Grady seeks is replaced by the virginal Alejandra. She is described in natural terms, "foxfire in a darkened wood," like a "chrysalis emerging."[105] She is described as a mermaid swimming among the cranes of a midnight lake. Alejandra also represents the untamed, and her mastery of the stallion allies her with the horse, "ardent-hearted," as John Grady himself. She is, more prosaically, the only heiress to an 11,000 hectare ranch. Whether John Grady ever separates these facts is questionable.

Like the first explorers of the New World, John Grady cannot believe his luck: his "new world" is literally too good to be true. The sanctuary of John Grady's childhood has failed him. In finding another, and in finding Alejandra who personifies it, John Grady is re-enacting the pioneer quest: the retreat from the old world and its failures to the wilderness and a new, perfect world, mirroring an imagined past, the idea of which is flawed from its very inception, built as it is on the false premises of simple "romantic readiness"—willingness to embrace a dream no matter how illogical, irrational, and hopeless, with which John Grady confronts the world. (At this point it is difficult to avoid pointing out that this quality of "romantic readiness" also is found in Jay Gatsby, equally doomed, intent on rebuilding the past, who creates a persona based on received images, who also bears the initials JG, and pursues a woman called Daisy, which is in Spanish alternately translated Margarita or Magdalena—the same name as John Grady's tragic girlfriend in *Cities of the Plain*.) The Hacienda of La Purísima represents the same sort of sanctuary, or "safe place," for which Stegner's characters also continually search, and like those sanctuaries, is as transitory.

The modern world with its emphasis on economic viability and market forces has taken away what a previous generation of Gradys acquired. Rather than adapt to these new circumstances, John Grady

Cole indulges in a repetition of the original act of settlement, seeking in Mexico what he has lost. The problem, of course, is that the Mexico John Grady invades was not the property of nomadic tribes, and therefore more easily conquered, but rather a settled, relatively stable society with its own rules and customs, of which John Grady is unaware. In seeing anywhere which is not America as available, John Grady attempts to re-enact the original American flight to the wilderness, unaware that the original flight and possession required a level of violence which he is clearly both unwilling and unable to duplicate. The spell at the hacienda is therefore only an interlude, followed by the unfinished business with Blevins, the wild card in John Grady's plan. However, Blevins' actions actually make little difference to the outcome of John Grady's pastoral quest. Alejandra's father would never have allowed her to marry John Grady (thus giving him the ranch) in any case.

The fact that the cowboys' arrival at the hacienda is preceded and followed by their troubles in the sinister La Encantada is significant. (The reference to Melville's "Encantadas" cannot be accidental. Melville's equally ill-named islands contain extinct volcanoes, a brutal adventurer, a female castaway, and a hermit who enslaved sailors.)[106] The boys, or at least John Grady, are "enchanted" once they reach the hacienda. Like a medieval knight, he is "in thrall" to his lady.[107] "Tell me what to do...I'll do anything you say,"[108] he tells Alejandra. Here, in adopting this quasi-chivalric role, the archetypal western scenario is reversed, the female taking the dominant role by virtue of her economic and social superiority, as in the medieval romance. If we extrapolate this image into a metaphor of Alejandra as the "new" world, John Grady as the American pioneer looking for "virgin land," the conclusion would be that after a brief spell of possession, the land reasserts its dominance, leaving the "conqueror" without a role or identity, or even a location in which to be, as happens to John Grady. Although it is true that Alejandra is not dominant in terms of her relationship to her father or society at large, her willfulness with regard to John Grady places her in a position of control in their relationship. I will mention briefly Annette Kolodny's point that America (for which we may read the West in this study) was "experienced as the daily reality of what has become its single dominating metaphor: regression from the cares of adult life and a return to the primal warmth of womb or breast in a feminine landscape."[109] Therefore the perceived betrayal of the land, for McCarthy's cowboys, would be doubly wounding: both land and the feminine are faithless. The frontier quest has come full circle. As Stephen Tatum writes,

> The would-be American Adam and his comrade are expelled from the Mexican "Big Rock Candy Mountain." Though appearing to be a sheltered pastoral enclave outside of time and history, La Purísima

and its inhabitants in reality attest to the inescapable impact of human history's wheeling changes and bloody ruptures.[110]

This suggests that McCarthy's cowboys are indeed like the Comanches, as they are like millions of others who rise and fall in the endless red tide of human history. The difference is, because they belong to what they have been taught to believe is a chosen race, they believe they can step outside history and recover a charmed and mythic past to which their birth entitles them, simply "cause I'm an American," as Blevins says, echoing the unspoken subtext of John Grady's enterprise.[111] Although this sense of entitlement might be said to extend democratically to all Americans, it is worth noting that John Grady is a member of an elite, perhaps not one of Austin's "old three-hundred," the first families given land grants under the Mexican government's concessions to Stephen Austin in 1824,[112] but an old family, whose ranch dated from 1866. Significantly, the Grady ranch was originally part of the Meuseback survey of the Fisher–Miller grant, an area whose history was checkered by the unscrupulous enticement of unwary German settlers (similar to the Montana settlers' disaster described in *Badland*)[113] in the early 1840s, many of whom starved or died of disease before reaching lands that were in fact unsuitable for farming.[114] Presumably, Anglo ranchers like the Gradys picked up the titles to such land after the Germans had finally given up in despair.

What John Grady Cole also finds, when his old world fails him, is that the "new" world he finds is in fact far older and more complex than the world he fled, and is dominated by class and elite interests that mirror the economic interests which controlled his abandoned western landscape and have made his family ranch unviable. He has substituted the Hispanic south for the West in his catalogue of desired space. The fact that this substitution reveals further layers of complexity suggests that the same was true of the West, despite the epithet of "virgin land," which was used to describe western spaces for so many decades. In the valley of the Hacienda de Nuestra Señora de la Purísima Concepción are "fishes not known elsewhere on earth,"[115] suggesting an isolated, ancient world, more ancient than even John Grady's nostalgia allows for: an unknown Eden beyond his reckoning.

At the hacienda, he encounters a social system, and a code, exemplified by the Dueña Alfonsa, far more archaic and systematized than any he has known in Texas. The violence which John Grady encounters in Mexico is arguably worse than anything he previously encountered in Texas, suggesting a deeply violent past. The Dueña Alfonsa's description of the fate of the Madero brothers during the blood-spattered Mexican revolution is indicative of a level of violence, of which John Grady was obviously unaware. (A correspondence is here established with Stegner, who depicts an uneasy veneer of gentility over what Susan Ward discov-

ers is a deeply unjust, feudal system, in Michoacán in *Angle of Repose*.)
Similarly, his experiences in Saltillo Prison represent a plumbing of the
depths of horror for a Texan teenager.[116]

The New World, even when it was an Old World, was a place of
barely imaginable violence. There never was a "golden age," the loss
of which so motivates McCarthy's young protagonists. McCarthy tells
us at the beginning of *Blood Meridian* that scalping existed 300,000
years ago. An article published in 1998 in *The New Yorker* tells how the
anthropologist Christy Turner has strongly suggested, in the face of huge
opposition, that the Anasazi, the earliest inhabitants of the Southwest,
known for their spirituality and almost utopian lifestyle, were in fact
probably destroyed by cannibalism among themselves.[117] Little changes,
it seems, considering McCarthy's dark predictions of the future in *The
Road*.

So, the flight is already downed. We meet John Grady on the day of a
funeral, just as we meet Melville's Ishmael when he finds himself bringing up the rear of every funeral he meets. We meet Huck Finn when his
world has assumed the quaint contours of childhood memories. We meet
Jay Gatsby when his dream "is already behind him, somewhere back in
that vast obscurity beyond the city, where the dark fields of the republic rolled on under the night."[118] Fitzgerald speaks of an "enchanted
moment" when "man must have held his breath in the presence of this
continent· compelled into an aesthetic contemplation he neither understood nor desired," emphasizing the deep hold of nostalgia, and the
power of illusion, on the American imagination, a hold which seems to
grow rather than lessen, with passing time, and a hold which firmly grips
McCarthy's cowboys. This may be considered a postmodern nostalgia,
a nostalgia without referent if we acknowledge the fact that much of
American frontier history has been mythicized. This point once again
brings us to the simulacrum. Frederic Jameson writes:

> The new spatial logic of the simulacrum can now be expected to
> have a momentous effect on what used to be historical time. The
> past is thereby itself modified: what once was...the organic gene-
> alogy of the bourgeois collective project—what is still...American
> "oral history," for the resurrection of the dead of anonymous and
> silenced generations, the retrospective dimension indispensable to
> any vital reorientation of our collective future—has meanwhile itself
> become a vast collection of images, a multitudinous photographic
> simulacrum...The past as referent finds itself gradually bracketed,
> and then effaced altogether, leaving us with nothing but texts.[119]

Jameson's argument may be questioned. To suggest that history has
become nothing but a vast collection of random images over-simplifies the
process of historicization. However, his point that our understanding of

history has become dominated by images, and indeed images of images, is clearly apposite. McCarthy's cowboys in *The Border Trilogy* belong to the era which Jameson has identified as the "mesmerizing lost reality of the Eisenhower era...the 1950s remain the privileged lost object of desire,"[120] though of course Billy's wanderings begin somewhat earlier. Rather than reflecting the reality of an actual time, the dreams of McCarthy's young cowboys are myths which masked a harsh frontier reality, and in fact show the absence of any reality which actually relates to their images. Their "texts" are myths made real by celluloid images and nostalgic desire. The desires of John Grady and Lacey for life on the "old frontier," according to this interpretation, bear no relation to anything *but* desire. This, then, is the "enchanted moment" which is the source of so much American, in this case specifically western, nostalgia. The "moment" itself is revealed as a cultural artifact which has been made iconic and has thereby lost its true relation to history. (This is most definitely not to say that there were not events and moments in western American history which partook of the grand, the heroic, the inspiring, the sublime, but equally there were as many events and moments which were the opposite, as *Blood Meridian* so graphically details.) It is the appeal of this "enchanted moment" which keeps alive so much frontier mythology; the idea that a moment may be recaptured, and the process, gone so badly wrong, may be begun again. It is partly the original appeal of America itself: a new world. McCarthy critiques this assumption with all its ramifications. This pastiche of what is arguably already pastiched throughout *The Border Trilogy* is discussed by David Holloway:

> This careful repetition of narrative, this pastiching of pastiche and the sceptical distancing of reader from pastiche protagonist that it engenders, moves *Cities of the Plain* some distance beyond the relatively uncluttered use of pastiche that underpins *All the Pretty Horses*. Rather than liberating the protagonist from some binary equation of past versus present or real versus copy, pastiche is here turned against itself by McCarthy and is forced to declare its ideological content. In *Cities of the Plain* the inability to access authentic experience, and the full hollowing out of John Grady into a mere hologram of the character he so much longs to be, reinforces his entrapment within a world he is powerless to overcome.[121]

This suggests that John Grady is seeking a landscape and a way of life that will right all his wrongs, and that will create an identity for him along the lines of the old myth structure. He would like to be one of the "old waddies." In addition he seeks a world in which traditional masculine, heroic values predominate. And he seeks a landscape upon which he may enact his historic fantasy of colonial dominance, which as a red-blooded American boy he wants as his birthright, or at least feels that he ought to want. In 1949, he is badly out of time, but not alone. He seeks as well a world in which to re-enact what Leo Marx calls the "distinctly American dream of green world felicity,"[122] seeking renewal in nature, but finds, as Robert Hass says, "an older and darker Arcadia"[123] during his sojourn in his own country of the mind. Leo Marx called *The Great Gatsby* our classic American "pastoral of failure." His comments might be equally applied to *The Border Trilogy*. McCarthy, like Fitzgerald,

> conveys both the enormous appeal that this pastoral motive holds for him and, at the same time, his recognition of its utter infeasibility— its seemingly irremedial impotence in the face of everyday, practical, material motives that ultimately determine what happens in a capitalist democracy...The pastoral hope is indicted for its deadly falsity, but the man who clings to it is exonerated.[124]

Like Jay Gatsby, John Grady *is* exonerated at some level, but that does not diminish the fact that his aims are colonial and exploitative. Not only is he out of time, but in seeking to enact his fantasies he revisits the territory of Manifest Destiny, never asking himself if he has any right to go to Mexico to find horses and claim land. However, I suggest that in this revisitation of Manifest Destiny, McCarthy is obliquely referring to the Cold War expansion of western power which was evident during the time of the setting of *The Border Trilogy*. In his actions and imaginings, Molly McBride states that John Grady

> is guilty of the very crime that our mythology of the West commits; that is, he glorifies an era in American history when heroism itself was defined by a racist ideology, an ideology that at once made possible the colonization of the American Southwest and justified its own brutality as a necessary byproduct of Manifest Destiny.[125]

McBride argues that John Grady is continuing—or attempting to continue—the cycle of conquest and colonization so vividly depicted, at the extreme end of its possibilities, in *Blood Meridian*. The racism inherent in his quest is implicit. That is, it is clear to John Grady in *All the Pretty Horses*, that what exists in Mexico is simply for the taking. One need only consider how a similar land-grabbing enterprise attempted over the Canadian border would have been regarded. The fact that Alejandra is an English-speaking, light-skinned Mexican may contribute to John Grady's failure. While she is Mexican, she clearly belongs to the world of affluent European Mexico, rather than Indian Mexico, of the workers and peasants, as does Magdalena in *Cities of the Plain*. Believing Mexicans to be somehow an inferior race, one whose social rules could be broken, as in his dishonest and clearly dangerous courtship of Alejandra, John Grady inadvertently enters a world of sophistication in which he is hopelessly out of his depth in all ways. Later in the novel, his remark to the admittedly odious captain who is interrogating him about the "stolen" horses, "You have it your own ignorant way,"[126] reveals a subtext of both national and racial superiority which is and was prevalent in Anglo-Americans' attitudes towards Mexicans. His next attempt at cultural colonization in *Cities of the Plain* is through the dark-skinned prostitute Magdalena, who is from the predominantly Indian state of Chiapas—not far from El Salvador and Guatemala, sites of more of America's ill-fated military ventures in the late 1980s and 1990s.

America's neo-colonial attitudes toward Central and South America are now, and have been in the past, deeply exploitative. Examples of military and economic intervention in Latin America are too well documented to require much repetition here. From the United Fruit Company's early twentieth-century domination of Guatemala, to the nearly half-century embargo on Cuba, to the all-too-believable horror stories beginning to emerge from South America of the kidnapping and murder of street children for the sale of their organs to wealthy, ill foreigners, Americans among them,[127] examples abound. Mexicans have long been compelled to sell the labor of their bodies to Americans. The fact that they may now be selling their actual bodies should surprise no one. This is as terrible as anything we see in *Blood Meridian*, and certainly the American military campaigns in Nicaragua and El Salvador bore some striking resemblances to the forays of the Glanton gang in the novel.

However, John Grady's own motives are complex; he is not aware himself of the implications of all his actions. Dianne Luce suggests that,

> The harshest view one may take of John Grady's ambition is that it is congruent with the frontier tradition of the land grab...Idealist that he is, John Grady would not consciously undertake such an enterprise, but Rawlins sees fairly clearly his complicated motives for cultivating Don Héctor and the Dueña Alfonsa. When John Grady confesses he has eyes for Alejandra, Rawlins bluntly asks, "You got eyes for the spread?"[128]

John Grady's quest is, for all its romantic overtones, economic, exemplifying the project of Manifest Destiny at its worst. His is the "legacy of conquest" described by Limerick, a legacy which robustly denied its real-life effects and its true motivations. One example of this is the fact that the beautiful stallion, which for John Grady represents all that he is trying to recapture in his imaginative "past," is in fact a commodity, bought and paid for with "a great deal of money in both dollars and pesos together with sight-drafts on banks in Houston and Memphis."[129] It appears that Mexico is as much a part of the degraded present as Texas, and as far from the utopian past which John Grady seeks. With reference to John Grady's "ideological gaze," that is, the ideological lens through which he sees and justifies his actions, David Holloway suggests that it is a "coping strategy" employed by him to deal with the fact of his disappointments: "The authentic past with which he reconnects is an idealistic simulation, one that aims to repress the spatializing of history, but offers nothing concrete or temporal in its place."[130] That is to say, the "past" with which John Grady attempts to connect in Mexico is in fact a dream, produced not by any quality of Mexico's own, but rather by John Grady's imaginative construction of it.

Unlike slavery, which had a similar economic motivation, conquest was somehow deemed to be "romantic," even noble, and spawned a host of myths and archetypes which both dictated and justified imperialistic action on small and large scales. As Limerick states, "These adventures seemed to have no bearing on the complex realities of twentieth-century America. In Western paintings, novels, movies, and television shows, those stereotypes were valued precisely because they offered an escape from modern troubles."[131] Not only does the legacy of conquest offer economic gain, then, but it also offers, by virtue of its romantic appeal, an escape from harsh reality into a world of "pretty horses"—except for the fact that the "pretty horses" turn out to be commodities like everything else. Driven from a landscape and a world he considered rightfully his, John Grady is more like the homeless, nomadic Indians who silently watch him pass at the end of the novel than he knows, displaced from history as much as they are. His actions in Mexico also reveal him as a classic American type: the man on the make looking for the Big Rock Candy Mountain. Although John Grady does love Alejandra, in a self-consciously doomed fashion, he certainly loves the horses, and the ranch, almost as much. In this he resembles the less appealing character of Stegner's Bo Mason in *The Big Rock Candy Mountain*, as I have previously argued. John Grady is clearly more sympathetic to the reader, but his goals are more naive than Bo's. Bo's goals at least had some basis in reality, however tenuous. Bo was in fact living in a frontier era in which some of his dreams might just have been possibilities. However, John Grady lives in a world in which the referents for his dreams were already lost. His actions, based on mythic archetypes, are doomed to inevitable failure.

The lullaby from which *All the Pretty Horses* takes its name adds another strand to this argument. In the song, the baby is told to go to sleep and when it awakens it will have "all the pretty little horses." This suggests the boys are enacting a dream, the result of which will be that they, like the baby in the song, get the horses and the land. This is certainly part of John Grady's unstated goal. This also suggests an infantile world view. In an infantile world view, the child gets what it wants, and feels it has a right to the objects of its desire. John Grady believes that he is entitled to the things he wants—like a baby, he is the centre of the world. As Stegner said of Bo Mason, he is "a child and a man."[132] Stegner's description could equally be applied in part, to the nameless Kid who is introduced exactly 100 years before John Grady, in *Blood Meridian*. The parodic story-book beginning of that novel, "See the child," also suggests this comparison. It might also be applied somewhat to Jimmy Blevins, the living lightning-rod, a weird, half-grown incubus of a character who comes out of nowhere to dramatically sabotage John Grady's Mexican adventure. It is also a description which fits Llewelyn, the protagonist in *No Country for Old Men*, as I have previously mentioned.

Stegner tells us that at one time Bo Mason, flawed though he was, would have been an acceptable member of society: he worked hard; he was willing to take on dangerous but necessary jobs of the kind in which a new society abounded. Equally, McCarthy's young cowboys' errand into Mexico in *All the Pretty Horses* might have met with happier results, economically, in another era. In McMurtry's novel of the Texas range, *Lonesome Dove*, the cowboys regularly sweep down into Mexico to rustle cattle. This was common practice on both sides of the Rio Grande in the 1870s and early 1880s.[133] McCarthy's cowboys are still living with the recollection of that long-defunct tradition. However, while Stegner, through his partial defense of the Bo Masons of the West, is suggesting that the frontier tradition, of which the previously mentioned cattle raiding is an example, once had some validity within its historical milieu, McCarthy implies that it was always the result of a childish, solipsistic view of the world which was as wrong in the past as in the present time. Like a child playing make-believe, John Grady, by adopting the mythic persona of the romantic cowboy hero, is able to believe in himself, until, as Dueña Alfonsa warns him, he finds that "the world is quite ruthless in selecting between the dream and the reality, even where we will not."[134] This comment most clearly shows us the distinction between the historic milieu in which McCarthy was writing as opposed to that of Stegner. By the time McCarthy wrote his critiques of the myth of the frontier, beginning with *Blood Meridian* in 1985, revelation both of Vietnam atrocities and also of other aspects of American economic aggression had made innocence in regard to the country's motives impossible. During the main part of Stegner's writing career, the questioning was of the country's motivations with regard to its own landscape and development. Stegner largely ignored the bigger picture of America's effect on the rest of the world as it was, in fact, not yet much questioned in the nation's forum.

*   *   *   *

John Grady Cole shows a way of life in transition. By the time the novel was set, the era of the cowboy as a romantic hero was long gone, if indeed we can say it existed at all. Additionally, the economic rationale for small-scale ranching was being steadily eroded by an aggressively profit-based ethos. John Grady's refusal to accept that life would never be as he imagined it is at the heart of his tragedy. Neil Campbell suggests that

The landscapes of McCarthy's trilogy reflect the characters' own position in-between worlds...This surreal, incongruous mixing of Old and New mirrors John Grady's own journey outward in search of an idea of the past, of a West of "pretty horses," truth and rugged acts of self-definition.[135]

Seeking self-definition in landscape, the desired landscape for John Grady must necessarily be one in which the actions of the individual are inevitably heroic if they are to fit into the model of identity he has defined for himself. Therefore the shame he endures for actions which he considers to be unheroic—the betrayal of Don Hector by his affair with Alejandra, the killing of the boy in the knife fight in prison, the perceived abandonment of Blevins— contributes to the dissolution of identity initially formed in response to his perceived role in the landscape and natural world, and mirrors the original displacement felt by him when he felt Texas slipping away from him. Again there is the postmodern sense of an absence of any basic reality underlying John Grady's sense of self. At the end of the novel, his whole world has gone, along with John Grady's sense of his place in it. He longs for a sense of wholeness which he believes existed in the frontier past, but reality, even in Mexico, does not reflect his dreams. As Tatum writes,

> Having been cured of his "sentiments," the orphaned Cole, as he was in the novel's opening scenes, occupies once again a liminal space between a lost mythic past and an uncertain "world to come"...Just as the novel's first image of Cole is that of his reflection in a flower vase, so its final image of him is of his *shadow* passing and vanishing "into the darkening land."[136]

Orphaned, like Ishmael, John Grady is adrift on a sea of empty signs, searching for meaning in that which has none. At this juncture, John Grady's attempts to find identity have resulted in the opposite: not only does he lack a place in the world; even his shadow vanishes in the land. In some respects modern alienation has been replaced by postmodern annihilation.

I would like to briefly recapitulate. I have argued that John Grady Cole is seeking an identity in landscape which is based on the precepts of the myth of the frontier and the doctrine of Manifest Destiny. I have further suggested that McCarthy shows us the impossibility of reconciling this desired identity with the realities of the market-driven economy of the modern-day American West. By suggesting his project is political, I argue that McCarthy sees in the continued application of obsolete patterns of behavior, which John Grady's actions exemplify, a threat to the integrity of the nation as a whole, grounding a large cohort of the population in imagery which is not only self-destructive but dangerous, not only to

America but also to those nations which fall under the hegemonic sway of the United States. I further argue that this imagery is based upon mythic and spuriously historical premises which always were grounded in an illusory idea of the American West, indeed of the country as a whole, and that these mythic and "historical" premises finally came in for large-scale questioning in the wake of the Vietnam War, when their tenets were re-invoked in aid of what is often viewed as an imperialistic conflict.

Frontier imagery was often a cover for a multitude of irreconcilable and unpalatable historical facts which were masked for a variety of reasons, principally those in aid of the continued exploitation of the western landscape and its indigenous peoples, an exploitation which, it could be argued, has continued in the fact of American dominance in much of the third world. In their desire for idealized western landscapes, McCarthy's characters reveal the continuing power of the concept of an idealized, obtainable landscape, a concept which has now gone beyond western spaces and resulted in the cultural and economic colonization of large parts of the rest of the world.

While McCarthy's western works obviously contain elements of the postmodern, I believe his project is larger than that which might be contained in the context of any particular theoretical discourse. Additionally, I suggest that McCarthy's project more concretely aims to reveal serious and dangerous tendencies in our culture and its effects on the world at large.

The Feminine in McCarthy's Western Landscapes

I would now like to turn to the issue of the feminine in McCarthy's western landscapes. I have previously suggested that John Grady Cole initially travels to Mexico as an act of revenge upon the women who have wronged him: his mother, who has denied him the ranch and insisted he go back to school; and Mary Catherine Barnett, the girlfriend who has left him for an older boy. We know the wounding caused by his mother goes deeper than the selling of the ranch. Early in *All the Pretty Horses* his father reveals to John Grady that his mother left them for a time when he was a baby. John Grady's reaction to these events is to retreat into a world of masculine fantasy and myth. As I have argued, his reaction against the wounding feminine extends to all women. Yet the significance of the fact that all women are not responsible—if any are—for his sufferings seems to escape the single-minded John Grady Cole. In addition, the landscape itself—a landscape which John Grady has felt was his by right of birth—is changing; ranching is no longer a viable proposition in a world of fenceposts, trains and cars. This issue of the changing landscape is central to John Grady's problems. Landscape is no longer the available, receptive feminine of John Grady's imaginings. Nor is the dominantly masculine life of the historical, quasi-mythic cowboy available. John Grady's response to these circumstances is to attack the feminine, first in his abandonment of those women who do care for him, then in his callous endangering of Alejandra while trying—at some level, conscious or not—to acquire "the spread" of her father. The old world of his grandfather and the "wild Grady boys" is lost to John Grady, and he never stops lamenting that loss and trying to re-create that time, by whatever means, fair or foul, are available to him. Clearly John Grady does not see himself in these terms, and his actions in relation to Magdalena in *Cities of the Plain* reflect a compassionate as well as acquisitive sensibility. Yet I suggest that Magdalena is a substitute for Alejandra, who in turn stands in for the land of which John Grady may no longer be master. McCarthy's aim is clear when introducing Magdalena during a description by the cowboys of a group of prostitutes. The cowboys use terms similar to those used to describe cattle when discussing the women. Women, in this post-chivalric world, are possessed, bought and sold like possessions. In *All the Pretty Horses*, John Grady Cole looks at Alejandra—a character much like his own mother in her strength and independence—as a way forward in economic terms, among other things. However, by the beginning of *Cities of the Plain* he has reverted to a perspective which sees females as something to be acquired, like land or horses, though he would be loath to admit that this was the case, still obsessed as he is with romantic imagery and self-image.

In *All the Pretty Horses*, John Grady's mindset is so firmly in the past that his father's disillusion seems to him to directly equate with his mother's unfaithfulness. That is, John Grady does not see his father as a victim of a masculine war, but rather of feminine infidelity. Therefore, John Grady may objectify, indeed commodify, both the natural world and the human female in it in reaction to what he regards as an attack on both his father and himself and their traditional way of life. Because he sees landscape as female, John Grady takes it as a personal affront to his masculinity and sense of self when that landscape is not available, while he is at the same time able to justify a distancing from the human female in any but the most romanticized of terms. His anger at his mother and at the world in general is the uncomprehending outrage of the child who argues that "it's not fair" that the world is constructed as it is. Therefore, when neither the land, nor the females behave as John Grady believes they ought to in *All the Pretty Horses*, he retreats to a world of fantasy and "pretty horses." As Dianne Luce has remarked, John Grady

> confuses the ardor of his desire with his right to attain its object. He has been raised to feel that his right and proper place in the world is on his family's ranch...When John Grady loses the ranch through his grandfather's death and his parents' divorce, he sets out to regain this lost paradise in another country.[137]

This is why John Grady makes the trip to Mexico, in search of all the pretty horses he feels are his right.

However, John Grady becomes powerless when faced with the human, non-animal world. His efforts are all futile; he cannot obtain Alejandra without her agreement. He cannot get out of prison without the help of Dueña Alfonsa. He cannot keep Blevins from getting killed; he cannot find the owner of Blevins' magnificent horse. His acts of heroism, admirable as they are, are nothing to his defeats.

Part of John Grady's narrative in Mexico is in fact akin to the captivity narrative, traditionally associated with the female in colonial American literature. In the traditional captivity narrative white people, most often women, are kidnapped by Indians, and their capture is followed by a long journey in the wilderness. The narrative is often considered to be a sort of divine test or judgment, linking it with the test in the wilderness of the hero in Joseph Campbell's description of the monomyth. In John Grady's case it seems to be both. McCarthy thus links his novel to the traditional canon. During John Grady's captivity he passes through a series of enclosures, each more formidable than the last. First the boys are manacled on horses. Next they are put in a fetid jail in La Encantada. Finally they reach the truly terrible prison at Saltillo. The series of enclosures suffered are repeated in the next novel of the trilogy. However, in *The Crossing* it is the female wolf that is enclosed, again each enclosure worse than the previous one—trap, cart and the final arena where she is forced to fight the dogs. Again in *Cities of the Plain*, Magdalena is imprisoned in the brothel and is seen through repeated images of enclosure, beginning with the mirror in the bar where John Grady first sees her. In *All the Pretty Horses*, John Grady is witness to both the abuse of Rawlins and the murder of Blevins, and Rawlins' stabbing. He himself remains relatively unscathed until the final denouement with the cuchillero. While violation of women was a central issue of the traditional captivity narrative, it is Rawlins, not John Grady, who is raped by the captain while in captivity.[138] John Grady does suffer a similar penetration, however, in the fight with the cuchillero.[139] Rather than negating the suggestion that this part of the novel might be considered a captivity narrative, this confirms it, given the implied feminization of Lacey (suggested by his name and his adulatory relationship to John Grady) as well as that of Blevins, who we may also assume was raped while in the jail at La Encantada.

Throughout *All the Pretty Horses*, John Grady is enacting a child's fantasy, with all the selfishness of a child, and with a child's lack of foresight. To prove his manhood, or perhaps just to express his pique, he disappears without a word to his dying father, his mother, Abuela, or Luisa. He never sends word he is alive or dead, and his brief appearance at Abuela's funeral at the end of *All the Pretty Horses* is the last anyone in his family knows anything of him till his death in the final pages of *Cities of the Plain*. John Grady hurts those who have never deliberately hurt him, and the vengeance he takes upon his mother for the fact that she has, for clearly economic reasons, sold the ranch, is terrible. John Grady's mother has her own reasons for not wanting to live on the ranch; John Grady cannot accept the fact that her desires, and feminine desires in general, are different from his own. He cannot accept that his mother has a right to sell her own property, as he cannot accept that Mary Catherine Barnett has a right to choose another boy over him. Neither can he accept that Alejandra is in fact making a mature choice in following her father's wishes rather than running off with him to an uncertain future. John Grady never matures as a character. His remorselessness with regard to his family, and his failure of conscience in relation to Alejandra, whom he puts at risk of social disgrace and possible pregnancy, mark him as kindred to his predecessor, *Blood Meridian's* Kid, in more ways than simply youth. As John Grady cannot accept that feminine desires may be different from his own, neither can he accept that his role in the landscape may be one of predator. In his desire for what he thinks he deserves because he is a white American male, he ignores the fact that his desires are in fact the legacy of Manifest Destiny. As Gillian Rose points out, "Woman becomes Nature, and Nature Woman, and both can thus be burdened with men's meanings and invite interpretation by masculinist discourse...feminine figures can stand as symbols of places."[140] Rose later adds, "The female figure represents landscape."[141] As Kolodny has pointed out, and Rose further discusses, this leads to a conflicted relationship with the land as well as with women, for men such as John Grady who do not have the another frame of reference to counterbalance the simple binary of land-as-woman and woman-as-land:

> The metaphor of land-as-woman affected men's attitudes toward the environment in complex ways, and Kolodny locates this complexity in the conflict induced by the metaphor itself. The land was imagined as mother, whose generosity and abundance were marvelous, Edenic, but which could overwhelm settlers and corrupt their efforts at self-sufficiency.[142]

For John Grady, whose mother was neither generous nor affectionate, this creates an even greater problem. The land must be faithful, since the mother was not. The lost land is represented first by Alejandra, who, like his mother, ultimately rejects him, then by Magdalena, who is killed. Her loss is intolerable, resulting in no other avenue for John Grady but death. One cannot see any avenue of escape for John Grady, trapped as he is by frontier mythology, a world in transition, and inadequate parents.

Returning to John Grady's equation of Alejandra with available landscape, David Slater writes of a type of racism historically related to the doctrine of Manifest Destiny:

In the case of the territorial expansion of the United States, and specifically with regard to the Latin other, the war with Mexico (1846–48) brought to the surface a variety of images and definitions that set off posited virtue against unmistakable vice. Mexicans were caricatured as lazy, ignorant, dishonest and vicious…The characterization of the Mexican as belonging to an inferior race also carried a gender distinction…The war…seemed to express a masculine destiny; American men, for instance, claimed that their sexual attractiveness to Mexican women was God-given…the males of a superior and expanding nation.[143]

This attitude toward Mexico and Mexicans is retained, if at a subliminal level, by John Grady. He views Mexican women, and the Mexican landscape, as obtainable, and believes himself to be above the law. For John Grady, what was regarded as obtainable was in some sense regarded as female. John Grady, Lacey, and Blevins are described as "marauders"[144] when they cross into Mexico for the first time, entering a landscape which they believe will have neither the will nor the power to deny them their wishes. Describing John Grady and Lacey's belief that "there aint shit down there,"[145] Molly McBride states:

This blank map early on in the novel becomes a metaphor for the boys' illusion that Mexico is unclaimed territory, that it is theirs for the choosing. In *Mapping Men and Empire*, Richard Phillips argues that it is "unknown terrain in which colonial desires are accommodated" and that when the heroes "find themselves off the map," they encounter a blank space onto which they can inscribe their masculine desire as well as their cultural ideologies.[146]

This inscription of masculine desire is the subtext to the relationship between Alejandra and John Grady, as well as to the uneasy rivalry between John Grady and Alejandra's father, played out symbolically in games of billiards and chess.

Apart from Alejandra's family, who are clearly in another category which even John Grady is aware of, John Grady views most Mexicans in the way he views animals. It must be added that John Grady is kind to animals—and he is not cruel to Mexicans. Yet the prostitutes in the brothel in the beginning of *Cities of the Plain* are referred to in unabashedly animalistic terms, though admittedly not by John Grady. In *All the Pretty Horses* John Grady's comment to the terrified captain, "My family's been practicing medicine on Mexicans a hundred years,"[147] implies the distinctness of Mexicans as a species in John Grady's mind. His attitude toward Mexico is characterized by acquisitiveness, and, as John Wegner notes, any notion of chivalrous behavior—which itself posits the helplessness of women—is undercut in *Cities of the Plain* by the fact that,

John Grady, the "all American cowboy," and his friends are in Mexico to buy a cheap piece of Mexican flesh. These cowboys have come to Mexico to "pick out" a woman much the same way they cut out cattle on the ranch.[148]

This behavior toward women in *Cities of the Plain* is prefigured in *All the Pretty Horses* during the scene in which John Grady, riding the stallion, feels the virility and potency of the stallion to be in his control, under his command. Significantly, the stallion is not his property, but he assumes control of it as long as he can. Dianne Luce has commented:

John Grady rides the horse because it gives him the illusion of potency, both in the sense of control and in the sexual sense. He speaks to it with blasphemous hubris arrogating to himself the attributes of the God of Job.[149]

For all his youthful attractiveness, John Grady is one for whom the desire to dominate is an essential part of masculine identity. This flaw is revealed by the less blatant, but equally appropriative attitude toward land exhibited by him throughout *All the Pretty Horses*. When he fails to obtain the land, John Grady settles for women, but land is what he really wants. This reiterates my previous suggestion that John Grady Cole is equating the female with the landscape. When he first sees the hacienda after riding high into the mountains, his vision is clouded by romance: "They saw below them the country of which they'd been told...They saw vaqueros driving cattle before them through a haze of golden dust."[150] Three paragraphs later, John Grady sees Alejandra, and the enchantment is complete. All is in an ambience of solipsistic wish-fulfillment and magic. The country, "of which they'd been told," already assumes a legendary, magical character. We are told that the waterfowl are like fish, the vaqueros travel in a haze of gold. The land of gold: how often in American history has it drawn the unwary, siren-like, to death and destruction. The hacienda fits into a pre-existing myth structure of which John Grady may have been unaware. Whether he knew of El Dorado or not is immaterial, he has created a new myth as he sees the landscape. The land will be his, and he will become its master, whatever way he can. I have earlier quoted Dianne Luce's remark that John Grady's actions are simply related to that of the rather innocuously named "land grab."[151] However, I suggest that the frontier tradition of the land grab was at its worst, murderous and brutal—as in the Leadville section of Stegner's *Angle of Repose*—and that in acquiescing in that tradition, McCarthy's cowboys align themselves with a sinister aspect of frontier history which in the past was too often whitewashed. This does not suggest that the land grab was still an option open to people in the late 1940s when the novel is set, but rather that the cowboys are heir to that tradition and tacitly approve of the result, if not the tactics. It also suggests that at the time of the writing of the novel, 1992, the possibilities of the international "resource grab" were becoming more evident with such events as the first Gulf War, which some observers regarded as a thinly veiled enterprise to keep American oil interests safely within the hegemonic sway of American-dominated regimes.

The fact that Alejandra comes into John Grady's field of vision at the same time that he sees the beautiful hacienda seals his fate. Like Tristan on shipboard with Isolde, the love potion—in his case the vision of all that land—has taken effect. In the following chapter which describes the brief, enchanted idyll on the hacienda, John Grady's egotism grows to monstrous proportions. He is a cowboy's cowboy: he breaks a herd of horses in four days; he obtains the favors of the daughter of the house; he rides the wild stallion bareback; he works all day on no sleep; he plays chess with the elegant and formidable Dueña Alfonsa, and billiards with Alejandra's father; he moves out of the bunkhouse away from his friend Rawlins—the only effective rein upon his extravagant fantasies. He almost makes it. His failings are the failings of the dream of the pioneers in the era of Manifest Destiny, represented by the horse-stealing Blevins, who perversely asserts that he can take what he wants, in this case the freedom of the boys to have their own Mexican adventure, because he is an American. In John Grady's case this perversity is shown by the utterly ill-advised affair with Alejandra and his belief, however unstated, that he might acquire "the spread." This is the take-what-you-can-get attitude of all the Bo Masons of American history, Manifest Destiny at its most unscrupulous. Had he not lied to Don Héctor about Blevins, John Grady might have at least retained his position at the ranch. But Blevins, both the "human lightning rod," as Dianne Luce refers to him, and the representation of blind imperialism—stealing back what he has already stolen from another—has crossed his path and drawn trouble down on all three boys. Blevins is problematic because, as Luce states, "His assertion that the older boys should allow him to ride with them because he is an American is an ominous echo of the ethnocentrism and racism at the heart of *Blood Meridian*'s violence."[152]

Luce's argument suggests that, like Blevins, John Grady fails by believing that the feminine landscape and the female herself were his for the taking, simply because he is an American. Therefore John Grady reenacts the tragedy of the worst events of the discovery and early exploration of the new continent, as well as the later tragedies of Manifest Destiny. I return to Richard Phillips' point: John Grady regards Mexico as "blank space," that is, space which is not owned by white Americans. Molly McBride has convincingly argued that for John Grady the penetration of Mexico and the hoped for acquisition of land which may follow are both related to his equation of female and land: "John Grady continually attempts to penetrate entities, both physically and psychologically...Thus John Grady's literal crossing of the border is closely aligned with his penetration of the figurative "land" of Alejandra's body."[153] It is in this sense that John Grady regards the landscape as "feminine," and in this sense that he believes he has a right to it. He may look upon it with the "masculine gaze." John Grady's feelings about land and women are clearly entwined. Gillian Rose has written,

> The sensual topography of land and skin is mapped by a gaze which is eroticized as masculine and heterosexual. This masculine gaze sees a feminine body which requires interpreting by the cultured knowledgeable look; something to own...The masculine gaze is of knowledge and desire.[154]

While no one would suggest that the young, unsophisticated, John Grady Cole was possessed of the "cultured knowledgeable look," there is in his unassailable confidence a certain "knowledge and desire" which informs his actions and creates both his hubris and sense of entitlement. And both of these derive from the fact that, like Blevins, he is an American, and male. As the explorers felt that America was "virgin land" because *they* had not seen it before, so John Grady feels, ominously, that what exists beyond known boundaries is not subject to known rules, hence his expedition into Mexico, which is, paradoxically, obeying the American "rules" of myth-driven hegemonic dominance. While the "land grab" would be impossible in the US, as presumably would be the relationship between a rich girl and a (now) poor boy, in Mexico, outside the bounds, it was felt to be allowable. In this what Luce has described as John Grady's hubris is effectively unbounded, but so too is the hubris of the society from which he comes. However, in John Grady's case, he is immediately punished for his arrogant acquisitiveness.

By the time John Grady embarks on his particular errand in the wilderness, the landscape no longer carries the overtly feminine overtones which early explorers attributed to it, but as a feminized space—that is a space which was perceived as open for male acquisition and upon which masculine desire may be inscribed as McBride has suggested—is the last refuge of an embattled and archaic masculinity. Unlike Billy Parham in *The Crossing*, however, John Grady does not spend extended periods in the wilderness, but rather passes through unknown landscapes, searching for sanctuary in recognizable havens: the hacienda; Mac's ranch; the little blue house he rebuilds for Magdalena. Each of these havens is a falling away for John Grady, as the first trip to Mexico is itself in reaction to the loss of the beloved Texan ranch, childhood and family. While the hacienda is beautiful, it is not Texas, and it is not John Grady's; Mac's ranch is equally unobtainable, and under threat by government acquisition. The final, tragic refuge, the little blue house John Grady pathetically rebuilds for Magdalena, is, in its touching absurdity, again an attempt to return to childhood. Yet it represents containment and control of the feminine as well. John Grady has built a doll's house for a woman who is to him little more than a doll. The idea of Magdalena living all alone on the high plains, while John Grady spends his days with Billy, roping cattle and being a cowboy, is a return to the bad old days of the frontier, in which women led lives of maddening isolation and deprivation, mainly indoors, while men enjoyed the freedom, despite the undoubted hardships, of the open landscape.[155]

John Grady's overarching desire is to control the feminine, landscape or woman. The fact that he is generally a fairly benign, non-violent young man does not diminish the implications of this desire, nor the tragic results in the case of Magdalena. Like his precursor, the Kid of *Blood Meridian*, John Grady may be a minor character in the larger tragedy, but he plays a part nonetheless. Louise Westling has discussed this problem:

> Characters in twentieth century American literature [are] haunted by the lost dream of Eden in the New World...They all participate in cultural habits of gendering the landscapes as female and then excusing their mistreatment of it by retreating into a nostalgia that erases their real motives, displaces responsibility, and takes refuge in attitudes of self-pitying adoration.[156]

While John Grady has not been guilty of any serious depredations against the natural world, his view of it as the available feminine implies Westling's point. For John Grady the landscape, and the creatures in it, are for his use, whatever that may be. His attitude toward breaking horses is a case in point, making them "lovely shadows of their former selves," as James Browning wrote.[157] His gendering of the landscape and nostalgia for an imagined past are equally futile, and are linked to his desire to control the feminine, with terrible consequences for himself and those around him.

*   *   *   *

One of the major problems we see in *The Crossing* is Billy's problematic connection to the female principle in life. In his relationship to the wolf he attempts to make contact with the feminine, but destroys it. According to Nell Sullivan the wolf "embodies the mythic feminine with her inscrutability, fecundity, and fidelity."[158] Sullivan further argues that, unable to subdue the feminine wolf, he finally assumes its femininity in certain respects, adopting a feminized point of view. Certainly inscrutability and fidelity, identified here as feminine characteristics in the wolf and by association with all females, are characteristics Billy exhibits, particularly in *Cities of the Plain*, when his devotion to the doomed John Grady effectively breaks Billy's heart.

Unlike John Grady Cole, Billy does not respond to the human feminine, except in the maternal feminine, and even that is at one remove: Mac's dead daughter; Betty, who cares for him on his deathbed; his dead sister Margarita. Billy seems unable to establish significant contact with living women in any way. In the few pages in which his mother appears, she is almost faceless, a figure of authority but not great affection. The Mexican girl with whom Boyd disappears is again hardly visualized apart from the traditional masculine imagery associated with Hispanic women, and is not even granted a name. Billy's reaction to her, as to all women, is incomprehension. Early in the novel when Billy, referring to women, tells the old bachelor rancher, "I guess I've got to say that I dont understand the first thing about them,"[159] it is no surprise.

Nell Sullivan suggests that through Billy and John Grady's narratives, McCarthy reveals

> destabilization of gender roles in the context of a western narrative, in which gender roles are usually very clearly defined. While women are systematically eliminated from the narrative in the trilogy, the feminine itself remains and is ultimately "performed" by biologically male characters...By divorcing femininity from women and allowing the male performance of both gender roles, McCarthy in effect creates a closed circuit for male desire.[160]

Sullivan argues that the feminine role in relation to John Grady's caricature masculinity is assumed first by Lacey, then by Billy. Billy has himself changed roles, first acting the masculine with regard to the wolf, and with disturbing overtones of zoophilia,[161] so that one almost feels Billy is looking for a *species* to which to belong. This suggests that Billy's aloofness extends only to human females and implies a homoerotic subtext to the novel, and indeed to the whole trilogy. Sullivan further states:

> With its destabilization of gender identity, The Border Trilogy could be regarded as McCarthy's most subversive work. Yet while male performance of the feminine seemingly undermines the notion of "natural" male domination, it also becomes one more strategy to contain feminine power and obviate women.[162]

This obviation of women is central to McCarthy's theme in *The Border Trilogy*. McCarthy's reason for this obviation, I suggest, is to further illustrate the failure of the traditional male archetypes which, in the latter half of the twentieth century, by their tacit acceptance as models, caused so much destruction worldwide in America's continued expansion of "frontiers," actual and cultural. Significantly, in McCarthy, the heroic cowboy cannot cope with women, and they are systematically erased from the texts; so too the myth-driven masculine model of aggressive behavior adopted by the controlling powers of the US also obviates the female response to issues such as capitalist expansion and wars fought on questionable grounds. The Vietnam War, a war waged against a traditional non-capitalist society, is a case in point. This is not in any way to suggest that men have not been opposed to these wars and acts of aggression, military and economic, only to posit that the model upon which this behavior is based is a masculine one, adopted from the archetypes of the frontier myths.

Women are that against which male identity is defined in the traditional western; in McCarthy's western narratives this goes even further as women gradually vanish from the texts altogether—or, in the case of *Blood Meridian*, are absent from the outset except as occasional random victims—or are systematically enclosed and destroyed. Sullivan has pointed out the significance of Mary Catherine Barnett's last appearance—framed in a window glass which John Grady walks out of "forever."[163] There is also the attempt to "frame" Magdalena in the little blue house. The containment of the wolf has been mentioned. Alejandra is confined within the parameters of a traditional patriarchal society, and in the end follows the rules. The Dueña Alfonsa is also confined by a social structure in which her role is immovable. John Grady's mother becomes a puppet, a figure on a stage, of whom no more is heard. Billy Parham's female relatives all die. The Primadonna in *The Crossing* ends up in a sideshow—confined, like the wolf. Unless one suspects McCarthy to be a writer of the most grotesque misogyny, one has to wonder what is going on in all these anti-female narratives. I suggest that in positing this obviation of the female in the structure of what looks like a traditional western, McCarthy is undercutting both the genre and the assumptions upon which it is based, along with the political ramifications of a culture which believes in models of heroic manhood of the frontier archetype. I believe that this is something McCarthy was able to do, post-Vietnam, when those models came into question; post-feminism, when the evidence of such misogyny in fiction would be deeply offensive were it not being used as a critique. The cultural upheavals and rethinking of traditional models make it impossible that a writer as perceptive and accomplished as McCarthy could be unaware of the implications of the obviation of women in his work. I return to my premise that McCarthy's aim is a political one. I believe he means to undercut prior assumptions which have led to the use of the myth of the frontier with its basically masculinist assumptions as a tool of the dominant political elites in their project of worldwide hegemonic domination by the capitalist system, spearheaded by America and all its attractive hyperreal imagery and aggressively marketed consumable products.

* * * *

In relation to women, McCarthy's characters clearly fit the pattern suggested by Gillian Rose:

From his position of power he tends to see them [women] only in relation to himself. He understands femininity, for example, only in terms of its difference from masculinity. He sees other identities only in terms of his own self-perception.[164]

And to this it might be added that John Grady Cole also sees both landscape and horses only as they relate to himself. In Billy we have a more feminine relationship to landscape, in which Billy himself seeks to become part of the natural world. Although McCarthy's young cowboys do not possess power in a conventional sense, John Grady, at least, seeks it, in one way or another. His attitudes toward land and nature are appropriative. However, the limitations of his self-perception mean that his perception of other identities is limited by the image of self which he has concocted out of western mythology and masculine teenage angst. While John Grady is clearly attracted to women, his choices are always bad. It is almost as if John Grady wants his choices to fail. One possibility for this will to failure is suggested by Nina Baym, writing of women in traditional American fiction:

For heterosexual man, these socializing women are also the locus of powerful attraction. First, because everybody has social and conventional instincts; second, because his deepest emotional attachments are to women. This attraction gives urgency and depth to the protagonist's rejection of society. To do it, he must project onto the woman those attractions that he feels, and cast her in the melodramatic role of temptress, antagonist, obstacle; a character whose mission in life it seems to be to ensnare him and deflect him from life's important purposes of self-discovery and self-assertion.[165]

This deflection from his purposes is certainly is the effect his chosen women have upon John Grady. Yet he deliberately chooses two women whose unavailability presents the most insurmountable obstacle to his aspiration. His youthful innocence will not allow him to consciously admit that his bad choices may be motivated by the unconscious desire to fail, but the result is failure nonetheless. This suggests that, like Billy, John Grady's attraction to the feminine is in many ways a mask for the deeper desire for both possession of landscape and for a return to the childish world of "pretty horses" which he feels has been taken from him. Therefore while John Grady Cole obviously desires the young women who are his objects in the novels, at some level he wants *not* to have them. While both Alejandra and Magdalena represent a certain kind of success, final possession of either girl would doom John Grady to a life very far removed from the image of the heroic cowboy which is central to his identity.

To reiterate, I do not agree with Nell Sullivan that McCarthy's western novels express a misogynistic attitude toward women. I suggest that McCarthy is not a misogynist writer, that through these narratives which systematically commodify or destroy women he is in fact critiquing a society, typified in the ethos of western mythology, which cannot communicate with the female in its human or environmental manifestations. As women disappear, so does the landscape fall victim to the oilmen, the nuclear testers, the fencers. McCarthy's twentieth-century cowboys cannot cope. Neither could their nineteenth-century counterparts—if they ever existed. Even a writer such as Larry McMurtry, whose western novels follow certain traditional patterns, does not show us nineteenth-century superheroes, like the Virginian, but rather ordinary, flawed men in difficult situations. McCarthy's young cowboys have seen too many western movies; they have modeled themselves on a one-dimensional, cinematic version of western manhood, one which is bound to fail them. McCarthy's final figure in *All the Pretty Horses* and *The Crossing* is a man alone, isolated in a landscape of disaster. It is only at the conclusion of *Cities of the Plain*, when an aged Billy has returned to the innocence of his long-lost childhood, that we see a return to the realm of the female, in Billy's humble acceptance of Betty's care for him. This suggests that the much-mythologized solitary odyssey of the man alone in western spaces is finally revealed as futile, and the acceptance, by that character, of the domesticated feminine world is both inevitable and redemptive. This is a point which Stegner also makes in *Angle of Repose* and *The Spectator Bird*. A similar conclusion to McMurtry's *Lonesome Dove* series occurs when the crippled Ranger Call incongruously finds some sort of peace in caring for a blind Mexican child. This suggests that in his critique of traditional masculinity, McCarthy is at one level accepting the beginnings of new power given to women through the critique of gender roles in the 1960s. Rather than a misogynist point of view, I suggest that McCarthy's western works paradoxically reveal an acceptance of the strength of women and the feminine. This is a point which certainly may be argued in the light of *No Country for Old Men* and its depiction of female characters.

McCarthy's cowboys have modeled themselves on an image of manhood which is ultimately revealed as hollow; therefore the coordinates of identity which they seek become even more crucial. Seeking identity in the myth of the frontier and the landscape, the young cowboys are not only looking for a role, they are also in some respects looking for a gender. This also bears relation to the blurring of gender boundaries in the post-1960s world. The gay liberation movement followed close upon the hippy movement as both embraced an abandonment of rigid social convention.

In *The Crossing*, Billy's roles are further confused. He first assumes a paternal role toward his brother, Boyd, but is soon relegated to the status of observer, even a supplicant, in Boyd's life. The last conversation we hear between them is telling:

> Talk to me.
> Go to bed.
> I need for you to talk to me.
> It's okay. Everything's okay.
> No it aint.
> You just worry about stuff. I'm alright.
> I know you are, said Billy. But I aint.[166]

Billy clearly isn't alright, by his own terms, and he is aware of it. Sullivan suggests that Billy's sight of the naked Primadonna which McCarthy implies changed his life by awakening nascent sexual desire is "overwrought,"[167] a mask which slips when, later in the novel he refuses to even claim knowledge of the Primadonna:

> But Billy had already seen bleeding through the garish paintwork old lettering from a prior life and he recognized the caravan of the traveling opera company that he'd seen standing with its gilded wheelspokes in the smoky courtyard at the hacienda at San Diego when he and Boyd had first ridden through the gates there in that long ago.[168]

That the Primadonna is now undergoing some grotesque degradation as "*un espectáculo*" at a village sideshow is clear. John Grady or Boyd probably would have felt compelled to rescue her from the situation, but Billy runs away. I suggest that rather than awakening knowledge of heterosexual desire, Billy's original view of the Primadonna, in which was revealed "the world which had always been before him everywhere had been veiled from his sight," revealed to him the knowledge of his lack of desire. "Nothing was the same nor did he think it ever would be."[169] Unlike the sexual awakening of the two cowboys in Annie Proulx's story, "Brokeback Mountain,"[170] in which a sublime landscape reflects the passion the cowboys feel for one another, Billy never openly exhibits active homosexuality, but the subtext of his relationship with John Grady throughout *Cities of the Plain* is, at a subliminal level, homoerotic. When the novel begins with the cowboys at the Mexican brothel, John Grady is referred to as "the boy." Billy's interest in John Grady's success with the prostitutes may be read as avuncular. He is ten years older than John Grady, after all. However, his ostensibly joking comment, "Dont listen to him John Grady"[171] when Troy suggests a particular prostitute for John Grady to engage becomes more revealing when, at the point which John Grady has seen Magdalena, significantly framed in a mirror glass, Billy quickly suggests they leave and get something to eat. This framing device, which we have seen several times in *The Border Trilogy*, is important. Women disappear into glass; John Grady's girlfriend Mary Catherine Barnett vanishes along with her reflection. John Grady sees his ancestors framed in glass. Magdalena is viewed through a mirror.

The morning after seeing Magdalena, an exchange between JC, another cowboy, and Billy, after John Grady has left the room, is revealing:

> What's wrong with him? said JC.
> Aint nothin wrong with him, said Billy.
> I meant John Grady.
> I know who you meant.
> Oren folded the paper and laid it on the table. Dont you all even start, he said.[172]

Oren's remark suggests that John Grady has been a topic of contention between the cowboys before, and that Billy has taken his part on other occasions. When Billy and John Grady set off in the truck, Billy says, "I love this life. You love this life son? I love this life. You do love this life dont you? Cause by god I love it. Just love it."[173] This suggests both that John Grady's feelings matter to Billy and that Billy needs John Grady to feel as he does. It is also arguable that the references to love are a coded way for Billy to express his feelings about John Grady. And further, Billy may feel that John Grady loves being a ranch hand, so he, Billy, will adopt the same attitude. Equally telling is the conversation between John Grady and Billy after Billy and Troy have decided not to move to Troy's brother's ranch:

> What did you think about that country down there?
> I thought it was some pretty nice country.
> Yeah?
> I aint goin nowheres. Troy aint either.
> John Grady ran the brush down the horse's loins. The horse shuddered.[174]

Billy defensively asserts that he is not leaving John Grady. John Grady's subsequent treatment of the horse suggests a sexual subtext, a tension between the two cowboys which remains unspoken, in which John Grady adopts a position of power. As in his relationship with Lacey, John Grady is aware of admiration, and is capitalizing on his position as its object. As when he enlists Billy's aid to help him obtain Magdalena, Billy is stricken, but nonetheless assists John Grady, as though he, like John Grady, "cant help it."

Billy slumped back in his chair. His arms hung uselessly by his side. Aw goddamn, he said. Goddamn.

I cant help what it sounds like.

My own damn fault. I never should of took you down there. Never in this world. It's my fault. Hell, I dont even know what I'm complainin about.[175]

As with Boyd, Billy's taking a younger man to Mexico has resulted in that man falling in love and in an essential sense leaving him. It will also once again lead to the other's death. This homoerotic subtext is present in other examples of western literature: the Virginian's relationship with Steve; the boy's relationship with Shane, in the eponymous novels; McMurtry's Gus and Call in *Lonesome Dove*; Huck Finn and Jim. It is a subtext closely linked with death, and the stories of Billy and John Grady are no exception to this. This link with death, I suggest, is due to the fact that the homoerotic subtext could never have been actualized in classic American literature, and McCarthy is clearly linking the novels of *The Border Trilogy* to that genre. Just as the possibility of miscegenation between Cora and Uncas in *The Last of the Mohicans* had to be resolved by death rather than fulfillment, so too does the story of John Grady and Billy have to end with the death of John Grady. Thematically, no other conclusion is possible.

The absence of fully developed female characters, and the implied destructive potential of most females who do appear (Alejandra, Magdalena, La Criada, John Grady's mother, the nameless girl who takes Boyd away from Billy, La Dueña Alfonsa) and the subtext of homoerotic relationships between men, suggest either full-fledged misogyny or allegory. As I have suggested, there are reasons why John Grady might be misogynistic. Although he assumes the role of the tough cowboy of western myth, John Grady's background is very different. He is a privileged child of what amounted to landed gentry in Texas. His father contracted a marriage in which his wife, the heir to her father's ranch, had complete control. The contradiction of real economic power in the hands of the woman as opposed to the traditional western image of the dominant, controlling, western male is striking. Economically, John Grady is in the same position as his father. In courting Alejandra, he is repeating the process at which his father so clearly failed, that is, in finding a female who represents the economic bonanza of ranch ownership, courting her, and successfully marrying her and gaining the ranch. The father, while he deserves our sympathy, is also passive to the point of self-destruction. One of the few characters in the novels who has actively lived in the real time of the twentieth century (i.e. his war experiences), it has undone him: "It's his own damned fault. He signed ever paper they put in front of him. Never lifted a hand to save himself."[176] What is particularly telling in the lawyer's comments here is the assumption that if he had tried to "save himself," John Grady's father could have had the ranch which belonged to his wife's family. The fact that he did not take that which in fact was not his in the first place is regarded by the other men in the story as foolish, and is presumably so regarded by John Grady himself. This male solidarity is again revealed when John Grady, seeing that his now divorced mother has checked into a hotel with a man, severs all contact with her. And yet, he is identified by his relationship to his mother's family. He is most often referred to as "John Grady," not simply John, and is never called "John Cole," which is, in fact, his name, except, significantly, when Billy breaks down Eduardo's office door in *Cities of the Plain* while looking for him. Thus we are given a contradiction. While John Grady identifies at one level with his father, on another he is his mother's son. The contradiction for John Grady is in belonging to an old ranching aristocracy while wanting to be "an old waddy." In addition, the fact that he feels that his mother is denying his birthright further fragments John Grady's already fragmented identity.

Read as allegory, the absence of developed female characters suggests a skewed understanding of the landscape on the part of the characters; as females are commodified, so is the land. It is only near the end of *All the Pretty Horses* when John Grady is nearly back to Texas that he exhibits an awareness of the contradictions inherent in his perspective of the landscape. McCarthy reveals John Grady's alienation in the scene in which he has just killed a doe and watched it die. This possibly overly emblematic moment causes him to think of Alejandra and his own position as an outsider in the world he loves but does not understand. His confusion is both of his historical time and also typically adolescent.[177]

The world, this incident seems to suggest, is finally revealed to John Grady as a place where justice does not naturally come to those who deserve it. He feels separate from the world because in some sense he feels that it has betrayed him. In a world of "pretty horses" there ought to be justice for the heroic cowboy. This view of reality reflects the fact that John Grady exists in a time when not only is his role in the world questionable, but the previously understood reality of that world has been cast into doubt by the events of the previous decade: World War II, Hiroshima, the Holocaust. Life has assumed new dramatic proportions. Everything looks different. And McCarthy, looking back at that period through the lens of late twentieth-century disillusionment and a reframing of what had been traditional givens in society—the changing role of women, the loss of a role for men, the questionable nature of America's attitude toward the rest of the world, the continuing depredations enacted upon an already damaged landscape, the breakdown of belief in traditional organized religions—imposes a further filter upon our interpretation of John Grady's feelings.

John Grady's awareness of the world around him is posited on one thing: that he is at the centre of events and it is his vision which colors the landscape around him. At the end of *All the Pretty Horses*, he sees a "solitary bull rolling in the dust against the bloodred sunset like an animal in sacrificial torment."[178] This imagery reflects both the state of John Grady's psyche, and the torment of the landscape in which the quest for human dominance of nature has created alienation between humankind and the landscape. As Judge Holden says in *Blood Meridian*, "Whatever in creation exists without my knowledge exists without my consent."[179] More attractive, less vicious, less destructive, yet John Grady's attitude toward nature and the world around him uneasily echoes the ego-centered world of the Judge who, with the scalp-hunters, in turn is the vanguard of the doctrine of Manifest Destiny with its imposition of national will upon all within its sway. "Only nature can enslave man and only when the existence of each last entity is routed out and made to stand naked before him will he be properly suzerain of the earth,"[180] the Judge has said. John Grady's absurd paean to his own power when he speaks to the stallion echoes this with its insistence upon control. The sense of omnipotent power over nature is less sinister in John Grady than Judge Holden, yet it is disturbing, and particularly so if we look at John Grady Cole, the "all-American cowboy," as representative of an attitude toward the natural world, particularly as seen in his attitude toward horses and uses of land. By revealing the superficially attractive John Grady as heir to the same cultural presuppositions as *Blood Meridian*'s scalp-hunters, McCarthy effectively explodes the mythology surrounding the idea of the romantic West. John Grady's speech to the stallion reveals a subtext of both hubris and indeed cruelty, suggesting a certain level of condescension toward the power of the natural world actualized in the horse:

> I rule the mares...I and I alone. Without the kindness of these hands you have nothing, not food, not water, not children. It is I who brings you the mares from the mountains, the young mares, the wild and ardent mares.[181]

John Grady also paradoxically exhibits a passivity which is at odds with the persona to which he aspires, the brutality of which is revealed by the previous excerpt. He allows Blevins, who is clearly trouble, to join him and Rawlins on their trip to Mexico. He gives Alejandra the stallion to ride though he knows it is dangerous. He also allows Alejandra to put herself at risk by her seduction of him. He does nothing when Blevins is shot. He is nearly killed in the prison, not taking any action to avoid trouble until Perez approaches him. He accepts Alejandra's refusal to marry him almost wordlessly—as Nell Sullivan has commented, he takes more trouble over recovering Redbo than he does trying to convince the woman he thinks he loves to change her mind. This contradictory passivity runs parallel with Billy's "craziness" in the next novel.

Billy's "craziness," or at least eccentricity, is evident to those around him in *The Crossing*. "Have you always been crazy?" the driver who meets Billy, trailing his wounded wolf, asks. "I dont know. I never was much put to the test before today."[182] Shortly afterwards, Billy turns toward Mexico, almost instinctively. He meets another rancher:

> You a very peculiar kid, he said. Did you know that?
> No sir. I was always just like everybody else far as I know.
> Well you aint.
> Yessir.[183]

He aint. And he is just beginning to realize it himself. While we have in *The Crossing*, as in *All the Pretty Horses*, something which looks like the traditional bildungsroman, the self-awareness which Billy achieves is awareness he cannot accept, hence his rejection of settled life and subsequent years of wandering in an attempt to avoid knowledge with which he does not want to deal. He does, however, attempt to rejoin the conventional male milieu with his repeated attempts to join the army on his first return from Mexico, but a heart murmur keeps him in the civilian world, a world which appears feminized by contrast with the war going on outside its borders. The world of Texas appears feminized to Billy at this juncture in the novel because it is outside the masculine activity of the war. Significantly, he has something wrong with his heart, rather than flat feet or bad eyes, suggesting, with its metaphorical implications, a profound difference in Billy. Billy's motivations are less clear than John Grady's. At several junctures during *The Crossing*, his actions seem almost random, or driven by some inner compunction whose source is obscure even to him. Why does he lead the fatal Indian back to his family ranch? Why does he defy his father to save the female wolf and then attempt to return her to Mexico? Why does he kill the hawk? And why does he chase away the maimed dog at the end of the novel? At all of these moments, Billy's actions seem to be self-destructive, or would be self-destructive if there were a coherent self to be destroyed. Rather, Billy's actions reveal a random testing of fate. We see in the incidents of the wolf, the horses, and Boyd's corpse, actions done automatically, as if the very doing of them might infuse them with meaning. However, Charles Bailey describes Billy as a tragic hero, Hamlet-like, with Oedipal leanings.[184] Seen in these terms, the ill-fated rescue of the wolf becomes an act of rebellion against the father, the wolf a representative of the feminine. Nell Sullivan has argued that the wolf is in fact the only developed female character in *The Crossing*. Considering that, her progressively more degraded confinements (traps, muzzle, wagon, sideshow, dogfight) assume alarming implications[185] of attitudes toward the feminine. Yet Billy identifies with the wild world from which the wolf comes. Even as a small boy, he had crept out in the middle of the night and seen wolves "running on the plain harrying the antelope...and the wolves twisted and turned and leapt in a silence such that they seemed of another world entire."[186]

However, while Billy does identify with the world of the wolf, he destroys that very freedom to which he aspires, reinforcing the final impotence of his actions which I have previously posited, and suggesting a corollary with the inevitability of western man's failure with regard to the western landscape. Looking at Billy's motivations in various incidences in *The Crossing*, he does want to be at one with the earth in some atavistic way, "never unmixing again," like the Virginian, reinforcing McCarthy's critique of the frontier myth which is so in evidence in Wister's novel. Billy also wants to be alone, a typical western characteristic of the archetype: the strong, silent, solitary man. Perhaps he wants to die. Like Jane Tompkins' eponymous premise, Billy may want to go "west of everything."[187] Certainly a return to a state of peaceful oblivion would solve most of Billy's problems.

When we meet Billy again in *Cities of the Plain*, he has become a garrulous, vulgar, smoking, drinking, whoring, travesty of himself. As he is an actor at the end of the novel, he is an actor at the beginning. This Billy is not the Billy we knew throughout *The Crossing*, it is Billy trying to be what he thinks a man should be. The contrast between the coarse, swaggering character we see in the brothel at the beginning of *Cities of the Plain* and the boy who takes a wolf back to Mexico cannot be attributed to age alone. The disturbing aspect of this Billy is that he has apparently so wholeheartedly embraced the worst aspects of the cinematic version of the American cowboy hero. When, in the scene at the White Lake when Billy confronts the one-eyed criada, while looking for Eduardo, and says, "aint a damn soul está, is there?"[188] the remark sounds ridiculous coming from one whom we know to be a fluent Spanish speaker, grandson of a Mexican woman. Equally in the scene with Eduardo, when Billy has kicked in the door to his office, Eduardo merely says that the door was not locked, and Billy's response, "I aint studyin your damn door"[189] is the response of an actor who has forgotten his lines. Eduardo's response seems civilized by comparison, reasonable with a horrible, unarguable rationale that Billy's inchoate passion cannot fight.

If McCarthy's aim is indeed allegorical, then *The Border Trilogy* may be, as Nell Sullivan has suggested, the most subversive of McCarthy's works to date. Not only does he subvert the myth of the frontier and reveal the hollowness at its source, but he also subverts the idea of a western masculinity itself. Images of traditional maleness are revealed to be, in fact, subliminally homoerotic at the least. McCarthy's cowboys cannot now relate effectively to the human feminine, any more than they can relate to the landscape and nature with which they have replaced it, if they (or their companions) ever could. The old ethos masked many aspects of gender relations in a wash of mythic images, as discussed previously. And the economic structure of the post-war world has made cowboys anachronisms. By the time *Cities of the Plains* opens, Jose Cavazza says "Los vaqueros de McCarthy se bajan de sus caballos y suben a sus polvorientas camionetas. [McCarthy's cowboys have got off their horses and climbed into their dusty pickup trucks.]"[190] Therefore the landscape, which was once the receptive, feminized field of action, has become adversarial as well, and *all* coordinates of identity are lost for those who dwell resolutely in the past.

In a post-1960s world where the traditional certainties of the roles of men and women, the supposed dominance of white males, and the rightness of the "American way" have been exposed as false, or at least misguided, McCarthy suggests that the entire structure of the westering American ethos was undercut, based as it was upon false principles which demanded not only racism, but also sexism. The American dream was only for white men. I think this reading clears McCarthy of charges of misogyny, at least with reference to the western novels. McCarthy undercuts masculinity in a way which Stegner does not. However, McCarthy was writing in a time in which gender roles had been radically re-evaluated by feminism. This suggests that McCarthy, in his own way, is paradoxically "good on women's issues" too, in the sense that his critique of traditional masculinity accepts that traditional "western" male roles, with their implied or evident obviation of women, have no relevance in the late twentieth and early twenty-first centuries.

I return again to my opening suggestion that John Grady's first trip to Mexico was in fact an act of revenge upon the women whom he perceived had wronged him. If this point is extended to the feminine landscape, John Grady's act of revenge upon the old world of Texas is to find a new world in Mexico. However, the new world is as contradictory and troublesome as the old one he fled.

For Billy the inscrutable feminine presents an unresolved conundrum, unable to be understood or embraced. The feminine for Billy is as mysterious as the natural world which he seeks in order to give meaning to an existence, which, like that of the wolves, has become a thing of the past. Orphaned like the wolf, unable to connect with the feminine, Billy reverts to an all-male world, the ideology of which lay firmly in the nostalgic realms of the past.

It is John Grady and Billy for whom time and the world are out of joint, not the disappointing world they leave behind, not the imagined world they seek.

Conclusion

In *West of Everything*, Jane Tompkins argues that elements of the western novel represent "a revolt against the rule of women."[191] If *All the*

Pretty Horses is viewed in this way, it falls neatly into the genre, along with the elements of male silence, desert landscape, violence, and the repression of emotions which Tompkins identifies as representative of the genre. Clearly part of its mass appeal is that it has been considered by many readers to be a traditional western novel. The novel may be read as simply a bildungsroman, a classic western tale, but I suggest that in that very fact lays the heart of its subversion. McCarthy, once referred to by a reviewer as "the master of the macabre,"[192] has appropriated the classic American myth structure, associated as it so often is with the coming-of-age story of a young man—the myth of the lone man in the West—in order to subvert it and all its attendant false histories. In this way, McCarthy offers a critique of the genre from the inside. And the fact that *All the Pretty Horses* is preceded by its darker twin, *Blood Meridian*, cannot be overemphasized. One of the elements in the novel, and in *The Border Trilogy* as a whole which undercuts the supposition that we are dealing with "western" novels—well written, rather more complex than the usual shoot-em-ups, but westerns nonetheless, it has been argued—is the relationship of the cowboys to the landscape.

The Crossing is not so much a revolt against the rule of women as a usurpation of the feminine with regard to the landscape. For McCarthy, the problem of human dominion over nature is the problem of masculine domination of the feminine world of landscape. In this sense the novel is opposed to its predecessor, *All the Pretty Horses*. In *All the Pretty Horses*, John Grady attempts to impose an often almost caricature perspective upon the acquisition of land, events, and people. All is seen through the lens of an archaic world view which posits male white Americans as the natural inheritors of the earth. In *The Crossing*, on the other hand, Billy denies the masculine world of his father by his identification with the she-wolf, and enters into her feminine realm. Everything that happens after the first crucial turning when Billy says, "Damn all of it,"[193] and turns his horse's head toward Mexico, is a result of this identification. In this sense the two novels are opposed, while the protagonists bear many similarities yet are in fact, opposites. Billy's turning toward Mexico echoes Huck Finn's final turning away from the world of the Widow Douglas and Aunt Polly, when he asserts that he would rather go to hell than turn Jim in to the slave-hunters, even though he knows to do so would be "right." (In fact a neat parallel might be drawn between Tom Sawyer and John Grady, and Huckleberry Finn and Billy.) Both John Grady and Billy turn away from civilization toward nature, coded as female in both novels, John Grady trying to conquer it, Billy trying to merge with it.

Billy's identification with nature, viewed by him as female, is part of the issue of what I suggest is his conflicted gender. He never tells anyone about the wolves he saw as a child; their meaning is clearly more profound than Billy may allow himself to say. This inarticulateness extends to his whole life. Billy is both unable to communicate and unable to understand human communication and motivations. His spell in the wilderness with the wolf seems to be the closest Billy ever comes to expressing himself: talking to the wolf by the fireside; singing to it. Although this study is limited to McCarthy's western novels, the parallel between Billy and his wolf and Lester Ballard, another outcast seeking sanctuary, in McCarthy's *Child of God*, talking to his female corpses, as though they could understand him, is uneasily brought to mind. However, Lester's status as an exile is imposed upon him, while both Billy and John Grady take on the status of exile through their own actions.

The landscapes through which the boys travel are, with few exceptions, harsh and unforgiving. This is the approach of the traditional western, and its appeal to classic, and indeed admirable, male values of stoicism, self-sacrifice, courage and strength are clear. There is a quasi-religious subtext to these values which gives their practitioners an air of asceticism, while also exemplifying arrested emotional development, coupled with an almost priestly austerity, which we see in McCarthy's young cowboys. A hard, austere, sublime landscape, as Jane Tompkins has noted,[194] creates characters who reflect it. However, this understanding of the landscape is subverted in *Blood Meridian*, where the landscape reflects not sublime austerity, but rather depraved nihilism, mindless violence in a landscape as alien as the moon. *Blood Meridian* takes the traditional male-oriented myths that John Grady Cole and Billy Parham live by, and stretches them, on a rack of historical accuracy and philosophical examination, leaving nothing to which the romantic imagination may cling. One wonders whether *All the Pretty Horses* already existed in embryo, when *Blood Meridian* was conceived. If so, it was a subtle irony on McCarthy's part to follow this terrifying, nihilistic tour de force of historical revisionism with the superficially romantic story of a teenage boy, lost loves and lost horses, knowing that, in the end, one equals the other.

In *Blood Meridian*, McCarthy gives us an otherwise unobtainable vision. While it is a modern work, it is couched in the stylistic forms of the nineteenth century, drawing the reader's attention to nineteenth-century forms of interpretation. Jonathan Pitts comments,

> McCarthy's narrator, because it is both literary and historical, does the work that Emerson's eastern poetic eye and Turner's western historical eye could not do: see the bloody facts of America for what they are...The kid leaves behind Emerson's morning redness of the American pastoral...for the violent and anonymous ship of fools and confidence-men drifting into McCarthy's evening redness in the West.[195]

Like *Moby Dick*'s *Pequod*, this particular ship has crewmen from all races and orders of humanity. And like the *Pequod*, this ship of fools is an entirely male world, oblivious to any female influence, except, of course, the overwhelmingly female entity of the sea itself. However, the landscape in *Blood Meridian* is only female in the sense of the female as victim of masculine enterprise, as Spurgeon has noted. Like the *Pequod*, *Blood Meridian* has its Ahab, its Ishmael. But its malign purpose is not merely one monomaniac's goal, Ahab's quest for Moby Dick. Its larger goal is the erasure of history itself through mindless acts of violence and annihilation in a landscape which has become reflective of the state of the scalp-hunters' own diseased interiority. Pitts states:

> The scalp hunters seem to circle endlessly in the same dry riverpan in a continuous encounter with the past, never getting anywhere except to die or to kill...In this "optical democracy," the sun-dried level plain, everything is equal and so nothing substantially meaningful. Humanity becomes geology, an endless shifting and grating.[196]

McCarthy's is a landscape in which humanity means nothing, like the "baking, parched desert landscape of barren llanos and mesas" into which "the scalp-hunting crew almost disappears."[197] This landscape is clearly not a feminized space. It is in this landscape that McCarthy posits the idea of "optical democracy" in which everything is as meaningful, or meaningless, as everything else, and in which "unguessed kinships" reveal themselves in a "hallucinatory void." This "hallucinatory void"[198] in which the scalp-hunters act, and into which they vanish, is the precursor of the feminized landscape in which McCarthy's twentieth-century cowboys search so futilely for coordinates of identity. David Holloway has defined McCarthy's vision of "optical democracy" as

> looking at landscape, and then writing about landscape, in such a way that any anthropocentric assumption of human primacy over the natural world is rejected, each human life being represented on the same quotidian level as each spider, each stone, each blade of grass.[199]

This is entirely true in *Blood Meridian*. However, in *The Border Trilogy*, the landscape reflects John Grady's and Billy's relation to the feminine, and in some way is their relationship with the feminine principle in life, particularly Billy's, as previously suggested. And initially, the relationship both boys have with the landscape is not simply anthropocentric, but also androcentric. Both boys escape into the landscape when the human feminine—or feminine principle exemplified by Billy's wolf—fails them, or they fail it. Therefore the boys' relationship with the landscape is in some ways already posited upon the models of identity previously mentioned, and the concurrent myths about the American landscape. In the landscape, and their respective struggles with it, the young cowboys encounter an equality of good and evil: landscapes are beautiful and harsh alternately; people are terrifyingly evil and profoundly good; antitheses abound. In their attempts to relate, on some level, to the feminine vis-à-vis Billy's wolf and John Grady's quest for a feminized landscape to possess, both fail. They come to recognize the random nature of both events and possibilities. They both come to resemble the land during their sojourns: both return ragged and dirty to American soil, but return they do. Their spells in the wilderness—what they consider to be the wilderness—are sojourns, not emigrations. They have endured a sort of purification through pain and loneliness, but no liberating absolution comes. Rather than "coming of age," as in the traditional bildungsroman, McCarthy offers us a paradigm in which coming of age means simply continuing to exist in a world from which meaning has been drained and from which connections are absent. When they return to America, their troubles are as present as before. Both have no place to go and embark on lives of wandering in landscapes they feel have failed them, divorced from the feminine in an almost exclusively male world.

Significantly, McCarthy's "optical democracy" is opposed to the prevalent attitudes toward landscapes which were common during the years of settlement. Anne F. Hyde has described a "history of stubborn misperception"[200] which attended these years, the strength of which may still be seen in attitudes toward development of the western landscape. By subverting this tradition of misperception with an optical democracy in which everything equals everything else, McCarthy effectively subverts the gender hierarchies of perception of landscape as well. That is, if everything equals everything else, male and female landscapes equate. The cowboys cannot play traditional masculine roles in a landscape in which meaning shifts and alters in the same way as their own mutable identities.

*   *   *   *

McCarthy's vision is bleak. By revising the myth of the frontier through his western novels, he examines causes for the particularly American malaise which found one of its most recent manifestations in the Vietnam War, and which looks set to involve the western world further in a similarly murky conflict in the Middle East. In John Grady's attack on the feminine, and Billy's hopeless identification with it, he posits the two sides of a relationship with landscape which, in his configuration, have dominated America's relationship with the wild from the earliest days of settlement.

In relation to landscape, personal perspective and experience is everything. Therefore the view of landscape and relationship to the natural world of McCarthy's cowboys relates directly to their own experiences and self-perceptions. The scarred, beaten, deprived Kid of *Blood Meridian* exists in a world equally ravaged. John Grady Cole, a child of privilege, sees a world which ought to be his for the taking. When his desires are thwarted, the world becomes an alien land. Billy Parham is an exile in his own skin, looking for a sense of wholeness in the natural world which is denied in his own soul. These are clearly over-simplifications, yet they reveal patterns of perception. For John Grady, the femininity of the landscape rests in the fact that he *desires* it; for Billy it lies in the fact that he wants to *become* it. The landscape functions as a map of identity, but like the map Billy and Boyd are drawn during their wanderings, "it was not so much a question of a correct map, but of any map at all."[201]

In this chapter my aim has been to look at several aspects of Cormac McCarthy's western novels. I have examined the novels as a critique of the myth of the frontier. I have also suggested that the novels provide us with an understanding of the Vietnam War as a manifestation of the continued influence upon American life and political policy of the mythic archetypes of the frontier. Finally, I have suggested that the novels critique an attitude toward western landscape which is manifested as a masculine view of a feminine landscape which is posited by the masculinist view of the feminine inherent in the frontier ethos.

My goal in this chapter has been to reveal McCarthy's complex attitudes to the post-1960s West. McCarthy's critique has been accomplished through the use of what initially might be considered traditional western novels. However, I hope that I have shown that McCarthy's use of this form has been employed in order to undermine the very tenets upon which the traditional "western" novel is based. McCarthy's critique reveals that these tenets, based upon the myth of the frontier and a modern version of Manifest Destiny and belief in American entitlement, are themselves responsible for a deeply corrosive approach to the West, and for the perpetuation of both racist and sexist attitudes toward both land and people, in America, and abroad in regions which may fall into the dangerous categories created by the still-living myths of the frontier with all their attendant assumptions and privileging of the rights of white American males over all others. Further, I suggest that McCarthy's critique of the myth of the frontier reveals the dangers of what has become a national creation myth when it is applied to contemporary political life.

Conclusion

Across a Great Divide

In my introduction I suggested that Wallace Stegner and Cormac McCarthy provide a hinge between thinking before and after the cultural watershed of the 1960s and early 1970s in terms of their treatment of landscape, nature, and the myth of the frontier, and have similar concerns with the social, political, and individual ramifications of that mythic structure upon the West, as well as having particular awareness of both the effects of the frontiering ethos on the lives of western women, in Stegner's case, and the ideological significance of a gendering of landscape as female, in McCarthy's.

In addition, I have suggested that Stegner and McCarthy critique the myth of the frontier in ways which, while not representing a continuity of thought, do represent a continuity of concern with similar issues. Before the ideological conflagration which was the era of the Vietnam War, concerns addressed by Stegner regarding the West were focused on environmental degradation and the effects of a transient lifestyle, posited by the concept of an endless frontier. As an historian and a novelist, Stegner was also concerned with the effect of this frontier-chasing transience upon domestic and community life, and particularly about its effects upon women, whom he regarded as fundamental in building society in a relatively new—at least to westering settlers—environment. He rightly feared that patterns acquired by more than a century of westward expansion would be tenacious and that habits and behaviors appropriate to one era would be transposed onto a later time in which they were both obsolete and dangerous. His concern was mainly with the treatment of landscape, and was also related to issues of aridity in the West. He regarded the preservation of the natural world as essential to the moral, spiritual, emotional, and physical health of the nation. His vision of a numinous natural world was central to his belief in the integrity of nature and the importance of respecting and preserving natural places, a belief which he saw flouted again and again by the persistence of frontier "use-and-use-up" thinking which refused to die, long after the historical frontier itself was a distant memory. He also took the view that Americans had a duty to be "stewards" of landscape. This is related

to Stegner's impulse of protectiveness toward the landscape and its creatures, coded as female. Stegner's other major concern was with the role
of women in the West, both historically, and in relation to how historical patterns continued to impact upon the lives of twentieth-century
women in the West. These patterns created unrealistic expectations,
and also allowed for a largely unquestioned acceptance of frontier-style
transience. Stegner regarded typically western transience as hostile to
rooted community life, which he believed was essential for social stability and personal fulfillment. Although he lived through the upheavals of
the 1960s and 1970s, Stegner's views and approaches remained largely
fixed in the perspective of the pre-Vietnam era and come from a position
of deep connection with the natural world.

Stegner's approach was a threshold which links earlier critiques of the
West with the post-Vietnam, post-1960s approach taken by McCarthy. I
have argued that an understanding of the feminine aspects of landscape
is central to both writers, and that Stegner reveals a deeply sympathetic
understanding of both the role of the female in the western landscape,
and the landscape itself in its feminine manifestations. This is an understanding which McCarthy takes further to present a critique of the depredations enacted upon the western landscape and western man in the
name of the myth of the frontier.

McCarthy's position in his western novels, beginning with *Blood
Meridian*, is initially dissimilar to Stegner's because he approaches the
historical inaccuracies and beliefs associated with westering and the frontier ethos in shocking fashion in order to discredit the idea that there was
anything positive in the original western enterprise. He focuses almost
exclusively on the violence and racism which accompanied events in
western history which have since been whitewashed, or have remained
generally unacknowledged. *Blood Meridian* has close intertextual links
with Melville's *Moby Dick*, which critiques the destruction of the natural world as early as the mid nineteenth century. *Blood Meridian*'s own
perspective on the treatment of the natural world, including its inhabitants, reveals an attitude of vicious wastefulness, and a desire for control.
We see the Judge systematically eradicating natural history in order that
he might have control over it. The control over nature as well as the
eradication of the original inhabitants of the natural world represents
the doctrine of Manifest Destiny, the twin of the myth of the frontier,
in action.

I believe that McCarthy's position, which is a far more radical criticism of the myth of the frontier than we see in Stegner, is a result of
his historical placement, post-Vietnam. Indeed, there are many elements
in *Blood Meridian* which bear direct parallels with Vietnam, as I have
argued. Vietnam, *Blood Meridian* says, is the inevitable result of *this*,
pointing a skeletal finger directly at the revealed vision of the often-
romanticized frontier era. Like events in *Blood Meridian*, many of the

horrors of the Vietnam War remained unacknowledged until forced into the light of day by survivors or participants. The endless frontier, McCarthy declares, was little less than an endless nightmare, peopled not by romantic heroes but rather by depraved criminals, largely created by a world whose binaries of white versus "other," and man versus landscape, allowed for a fatal hiatus of ordinary standards of human decency.

A similar hiatus, although one with no foreseeable end, is anticipated in McCarthy's latest novel, *The Road*, in which environmental degradation is accompanied by a total denial of civilization and humanity. The ruins of civilization show "The frailty of everything revealed at last."[1] But McCarthy's pessimistic argument is that this is humanity's truth and has always existed, though veiled from our eyes. A similarly bleak point is made in *No Country for Old Men* in which the equality of good and evil is posited in a Manichean vision of a world in which it is uncertain which side will triumph.

Significantly, in *The Road* there are images which recall the history of American settlement. From the ship registered in Tenerife, Columbus' point of departure for the New World, to the burning man who recalls the self-immolation of Vietnam War protesters, we see images from the palimpsest of American history throughout this dystopian picaresque. The nameless father in the novel observes the human ruins, reminiscent also of America's remorseless bombing of conscripted Iraqi soldiers fleeing Kuwait during the first Gulf War: "People sitting on the sidewalk half immolate and smoking in their clothes. Like failed sectarian suicides... What had they done?"[2] Indeed even the form of the novel calls into question the basic tenets of the American canon with its reversal of both the bildungsroman and the road-trip. From Kerouac's *On The Road*[3] to McCarthy's *The Road*—as the Grateful Dead so vividly reminded us at the end of the 1960s, "What a long, strange trip it's been."[4]

In the novels of *The Border Trilogy*, McCarthy focuses on the effects of the myth of the frontier on young men who are compelled to follow its tenets through lack of any other coherent approach to life. John Grady Cole and Billy Parham follow the myth of the frontier because they believe in its truth and believe that it offers them roles in life. In fact by the time all three novels were set—late 1940s, pre-World War II, and the early Cold War of the 1950s—the role of the western cowboy had lost its ever-tenuous economic rationale, and the romanticized western landscape itself was falling prey to schemes of development and exploitation, schemes which have little abated in the past half-century.

Both writers, I have argued, and I believe, have a political agenda in their works. In critiquing the myth of the frontier and its effects, both Stegner and McCarthy have aimed to derail the mythic machine which still runs wildly down the tracks of American identity, dominating national discourse. The myth of the frontier, twenty-first-century style, still incites, with its deeply emotive power, action which was often reckless and inappropriate in the early days of settlement, and which, transposed to the twenty-first century, is perhaps the most dangerous element in an increasingly fragile world both in terms of the environment and political activity. The need to let go of the national origin myths which have dominated, particularly, the treatment of the western landscape, and which continue to allow the image of the endless frontier to color American political thinking at home and abroad, has never been more urgent. Many critics both in American studies and western studies have addressed the issue of these myths, obviously, but their tenacity is great, largely because they key into pre-existing ideas, as I have argued in my first chapter. While it is undoubtedly true that American literature has been self-correcting with regard to national mythology, as Forrest Robinson has argued;[5] and while the New Historians and their subsequent critics have changed much of our perception of the western American past, finally including the histories of women and non-white racial groups; and ecocritics have turned our attention to the results of frontiering and continued exploitation of a fragile western landscape; it is still clear that in popular culture, at least, much triumphalist, Manifest Destiny-style national mythology survives. We now live in a world in which the imminent implosion of an environment we have systematically degraded is an ever-present reality rather than a distant possibility. Coupled with that awful eventuality is the largely accepted American goal of worldwide economic dominance, consisting in control of world markets—now being undercut by the rising powers of Asia—as well as incursions into foreign territory, often on the unspoken grounds of resource grabbing. In addition, America has shown little regard for the effects of its expenditure of natural resources and fossil fuels upon the rest of the world. Attacks, both real and imagined, have led to the identification of the perceived enemies of America as the "other" characterized in examples of early canonical American literature, literature which fed into the development of the myth of the frontier. Alarmingly, recent events have posited a further opposition, that of Christian versus Muslim, an opposition which neatly fits into the model suggested by the captivity narratives of colonial America, of white versus Indian. With the election of Barack Obama as president, there seems to be more hope that these many ills might be eradicated, but their roots are tenacious, and deeply embedded in a world view based upon mythic precepts.

It is for these reasons that I believe an analysis of Stegner and McCarthy's treatment of the myth of the frontier, particularly in relation to landscape and nature, is so important. Both authors provide accessible ways into what is a troublingly complex set of issues. In their respective critiques, both Stegner and McCarthy offer explanations for the durability of the mythic archetypes which have dominated western American literature, and which have provided a national "creation myth," a myth with startling power to induce action, even today. By critiquing these mythic archetypes, both authors give their readers the possibility of understanding the West and, indeed, America, free of the dead hand of the myth-bound past.

The perspectives of McCarthy and Stegner are related to their historical placement. McCarthy was born in 1933, when Stegner, already a published writer, was completing his PhD at the University of Iowa. Stegner had grown up poor, sometimes destitute, and lived through the Depression, an experience which was to mark him for life. He found in literature and culture the stability of which his childhood had deprived him. McCarthy, on the other hand, was born into a moderately affluent, educated, cultured, Catholic family. While Stegner had genuine working-class credentials, McCarthy had to slum it, like his semi-autobiographical character Suttree, in the eponymous novel, to experience the sort of life that Stegner knew first-hand. However, McCarthy did grow up in the post-war South in a place which had strong links to a dying rural past—the hillbilly country of the Tennessee mountains near Knoxville. McCarthy's country characters have the ring of authenticity which reveals close observation. Alongside this rural life which McCarthy was able to observe so minutely was the wider world, enmeshed in the Cold War, the arms race, economic domination of foreign markets—the new colonialism—and later, the Vietnam War. By the time McCarthy finally left Tennessee for Texas in 1977, there was no corner of life, no matter how remote, which could be unaffected by changes to life brought in by late twentieth-century, nuclear-armed, consumerist modernity. Both lives and landscapes felt the effect of the changes. In addition, the reaction against these changes—the campus radicalism, the new feminism, perceived cultural changes as old taboos were replaced by new freedoms, and political disillusionment—while initially limited to the campuses and cities, eventually trickled down, in some form, to all levels of society. The conflict between old ways, both the real and the mythic, and new realities, is examined in human terms in McCarthy's western novels through the medium of the ostensibly "western" novel. McCarthy critiques both the storied past which his characters desire, and "the world to come,"[6] into which they vanish.

Stegner reveals a cautious optimism regarding life in the American West. His critique of the myth of the frontier which has dominated much of that life, historically, is a valuable lens through which western American history and culture may be viewed. Stegner has a clear vision of what the West is, and is not, and gives us this vision, freed of sentimentality and myth, yet still acknowledging the power inherent in the founding myths of the West. Crucially, he acknowledges the dangers of the enactment of the tenets of the myth of the frontier upon a fragile western landscape.

McCarthy, on the other hand, through the lives of myth-obsessed young men in *The Border Trilogy*, reveals the destructive possibilities of the myth of the frontier, and its capacity to poison lives, as it has damaged the landscape. McCarthy's young protagonists live in a world in which their beliefs in an outmoded dream cause their own lives to devolve into continuous nightmare. From Stegner to McCarthy, the West goes from being the home of hope and cautious optimism, albeit with an awareness of the damaging potential of the frontier ethos, to being space upon which a nihilistic tragedy is enacted, over and over again. The landscape which, in the one case, has been among other things an agent of personal transformation, has in the other become the locus of personal and cultural derangement. The myth has become the Nightmare, its adherents lost in a space which for them will never again become place.

I have stated that Stegner belongs to a tradition of writers who, through their critique of the frontier mythology, reveal the unspoken yet accepted tenets which underscore much of American thinking with regard to the western landscape. Critiquing these accepted archetypes, Stegner reveals the deeply suspect thinking underlying some of the most firmly held beliefs about the West. Through metaphors of a "despoiled Eden,"[7] Stegner points out the flawed thinking, based upon the idea of a limitless frontier—suspect even when the country was still unsettled—which has led to some of the worst excesses in western development, and which has made so much of the western landscape an arid wasteland, and endangered much more of it.

Environmental pollution and water issues loom large in Stegner's works, particularly, *Angle of Repose, Beyond the 100th Meridian,* and *Where the Bluebird Sings to the Lemonade Springs.* The use-and-use-up mentality of early western settlers, who could simply move on, further west, has been shown in its continued implementation to be a recipe for the kind of environmental doomsday scenario which, during Stegner's own lifetime, still seemed like fiction. Now we know the Ogallala aquifer is emptying; sinkholes appear regularly in western landscapes which used to be buoyed up by ancient, underground reservoirs; Glen Canyon, the jewel of the Colorado, is no more; millions of acres along the courses of dammed western rivers annually become salinated by the effects of the dams, as the dams' reservoirs themselves inexorably silt up, an ecological time bomb which we have bequeathed to our grandchildren. As Marc Reisner chillingly points out in his study of aridity in the West,

> The reckoning has not even begun. Thus far, nature has paid the highest price. Glen Canyon is gone. The Colorado Delta is dead. The Missouri bottomlands have disappeared. Nine out of ten acres of wetlands in California have vanished, and with them millions of migratory birds. The great salmon runs in the Columbia, the

Sacramento, the San Joaquin, and dozens of tributaries are dimin-
ished or extinct...And it didn't happen only in the West.[8]

Many of these environmental tragedies were just beginning in
Stegner's lifetime, but in the history of America, the obliteration of the
buffalo, the passenger pigeon, and the beaver, among other species, all
told the story to come. As vulnerable species were hunted and trapped
to extinction, so too did the landscape itself became the victim of a
thoughtless, exploitative mentality which sees no tomorrow. In addition
to water issues, there have always been issues of pollution in the West:
Los Angeles sits under a permanent smog haze; thousands of acres of
desert landscapes in the Southwest are cordoned off, poisoned by nuclear
testing, or home to mothballed weaponry. The previous administration
told the same story of denial and prevarication, as George W. Bush and a
supine Congress fought against any legislative checks against the biggest
polluters, though alarm bells were ringing loud and clear.

In his era Stegner's was not a lone voice raised against these things,
but his was an extremely eloquent one, and one which through his fiction was able to speak to many who might not have heard straightfor-
ward environmental critiques. Additionally, Stegner was speaking up
long before the environmental movement gained momentum, initially
during the 1950s, when most of America was still unaware of the issues
he championed.

Stegner constantly reminds us of our responsibilities toward nature.
This concept of "stewardship" toward the natural world has been widely
commented upon and was related to his experience growing up as a
western child, as well as being an aspect of his attitude toward communal responsibility. Brett Olsen comments,

> Stegner stood among several other voices that have periodically risen
> above the din of rapid human progress to call for a broad-based
> environmental ethic—a human responsibility to maintain the health
> of the land...He derived his primary understanding of the land from
> the empirical, practical fact of growing up in the West.[9]

While Olsen's comments suggest a clearly enlightened sensibility, I
have also argued that Stegner's appreciation of the natural world has
what I would characterize as a distinctly spiritual dimension, and that
he recognizes, and reveals through his own memoirs and his characters,
particularly Susan Burling Ward in *Angle of Repose*, the transformative
power of the natural world, and an appreciation of the sublime in nature.
This aspect of Stegner's thinking is in keeping with the influence of the
Transcendentalists upon his decidedly nineteenth-century sensibility, a
sensibility modified by experience. While in no way adhering to any
conventional form of spirituality, I have suggested that Stegner's height-

ened awareness of the natural world is one which, like John Muir's, partook of more than simple appreciation. Susan Tyburski has argued for an explicitly mystical appreciation of landscape on Stegner's part, as I have noted earlier. It might be argued that what Tyburski characterizes as "epiphany" is also akin to what William Cronon has referred to as an appreciation of "the mountain as cathedral,"[10] which he links to our concept of the sublime and which heightens the appeal of wilderness by providing an alternative to conventional religion. Cronon states,

> This escape from history is one reason why the language we use to talk about wilderness is often permeated with spiritual and religious values that reflect human ideals far more than the material world of physical nature. Wilderness fulfills the old romantic project of secularizing Judeo-Christian values so as to make a new cathedral not in some petty human building but in God's own creation, Nature itself.[11]

Cronon goes on to suggest that this approach to nature in fact denigrates the human sense of community—which Stegner himself valued so highly—by creating an idealized natural world which is, to its adherents, more "real" than the lives they are compelled to lead away from the wilderness:

> To the extent that we celebrate wilderness as the measure with which we judge civilization, we reproduce the dualism that sets humanity and nature at opposite poles. We thereby leave ourselves little hope of discovering what an ethical, sustainable, *honorable* human place in nature might actually look like.[12]

Cronon's argument is obviously not against wilderness itself, but against our way of perceiving and appreciating it. His objections are to the imposition upon the natural world, of values more commonly associated with traditional religious observance, an imposition of sacrality which he suggests lead to the extreme positions taken up by such groups as Earth First! and the more radical animal rights activists.

I disagree with Cronon's position, at least as it may be applied to Stegner. Of course, one sees the obvious danger in sacralizing nature above humanity, and Stegner, having experienced the strangeness and solitude of raw, unmodified, dangerous nature as a child in Saskatchewan, knew just how important community was, and how various were the demands and needs of the entire community which depended upon the natural world. Stegner knew that farmers needed to farm and hunters needed to hunt, but he did not feel that it meant that visionaries could not still see visions climbing Mount Ktaadin, nor that a reverence for nature conflicted with its responsible use. Stegner always argued for the middle ground, and, as Brett Olsen points out:

His conditional acceptance of the pastoral median reflected, is some ways, a far more holistic environmental philosophy than that of some concurrent "deep" ecologists. They advocated an inclusive human–nonhuman nature relationship, while simultaneously praising nonhuman nature as the ultimate moral authority, and thereby reinforcing a duality between the two.[13]

While not regarding nature as "the ultimate moral authority," Stegner was still deeply aware of the transformative power, and the agency possessed by nature. I suggest that Cronon's argument is against those who consider themselves to have exclusive spiritual knowledge of the natural world, but whose actions express a political rather than spiritual dimension, and whose adversarial positions express a desire for the moral high ground over a population perceived as basely exploiting the natural world. And in this respect, Cronon's criticism is valid. Christopher Hitt has commented:

> Although Cronon supposes his environmentally-conscious readership will find his view "heretical" (TW 69), his impulse to critique the sublime is hardly new. Indeed, it has been the overwhelming tendency of literary criticism over the past few decades to evaluate the aesthetic of the sublime primarily as an expression of asymmetrical power relationships: between human and nature, self and other, reader and text, male and female, conqueror and oppressed.[14]

However, I would suggest that Stegner's expression of the sublime in nature has nothing to do with obtaining the moral high ground, or power relationships of any kind, although his experience of sublimity in nature informs his political goal of preservation of the natural world.

Stegner's concern with sublimity is rather an experience which defies description, belonging to what Susan Tyburski has called "the unconscious route," and Sharon Butala has characterized as "the place words stop."[15] Neil Evernden has described it thus:

> It might be fair to say that the experience of radical otherness is at the base of all astonishment or awe, all "numinous" experience. It is that shock of recognition that generates the acknowledgement of mystery that we can characterize as religious.[16]

It is this inexpressible "radical otherness" which Stegner reveals to us throughout his canon. It cannot be dismissed as either politically motivated or non-productive of environmental advocacy, for while it is related to Stegner's ever-present concern with stewardship of the landscape, on the other hand it has nothing at all to do with it in concrete terms, being an entirely different class of experience. It is this point that I believe

Cronon has missed. This class of experience, which Tyburski has characterized as "epiphanic," is what Stegner describes when he writes of an experience which occurred during his childhood in Saskatchewan:

> Strangeness flowed around me; there was a current of cool air, a whispering, a loom of darkness overhead. In panic I reared up on my elbow and found that I was sleeping beside my brother under the wagon, and that a night wind was breathing across me through the spokes of the wheel. It came from unimaginably far places, across a vast emptiness, below millions of polished stars. And yet its touch was soft, intimate, and reassuring, and my panic went away at once. That wind knew me. I knew it.[17]

Without sentimentality or self-consciousness, Stegner has here given us a moment which can only be described as epiphanic. To dismiss such moments—and there are many in Stegner's works—or to miss the point of what Stegner is saying, is to fail to understand the heart of Stegner's attitude toward the natural world. Stegner's respect for the natural world is a respect bound up in both the mystery of nature, and a respect for its independent existence, and its power. His connection with nature is most like that of John Muir, the great Sierra naturalist. This spiritual dimension of the natural world is, I suggest, the lodestar of Stegner's appreciation of the natural world.

Stegner was aware of the many influences upon our perception of the western landscape. In discussing landscape, one is speaking of the land as seen through what Anne F. Hyde calls "cultural filters" as well as visual and historical filters. In her essay "Cultural Filters: The Significance of Perception," she states:

> The West has shaping power because of its unique geography and not necessarily because it is or was a frontier. Its significance comes from the fact that in a certain part of the American continent, particularly the lands west of the one hundredth meridian, Anglo Americans came up against a series of landscapes that defied their notions about utility and beauty.[18]

This suggests that the question of the extraordinary variety and strangeness of much of America beyond the 100th meridian must be recognized as one of the determinants in the perception of western landscape. Stegner was very much aware of and alive to those qualities in the western landscape. This is not to say that there do not exist mountains as high, deserts as vast, rivers as raging, products of erosion as striking and often bizarre, as exist in the American West, in other parts of the world. It is simply to say that the combination of these effects together, coupled with the weight of expectation which attached itself to the idea of the West, created a psychological and metaphorical climate which gave enormous psychic weight to the idea of the West. In addition, the way in which settlers reacted to this new landscape was the result of a long history of cultural presuppositions which had been posited in the frontiering mind from the days of the Puritans. These, too, were factors of which Stegner was well aware. It is certain that, as Hyde suggests, the actual landscape of the West itself and its unique geography contributed and continues to contribute to the resonance of the original mythological archetypes, embodying, as it does, some of the most unusual, bizarre, beautiful, haunting and psychologically evocative landscapes on the planet. In the same way, the first pioneers and explorers to reach western America had a freedom from earlier perceptual models which had dominated the eastern colonies with their unavoidable likenesses to European landscapes. Therefore, the suggestion of "Western Exceptionalism" as opposed to "American Exceptionalism" may have validity in the sense that Hyde further suggests that the perception of the West crucially led to a redefinition of American culture and identity. It is this redefinition, as well as his own perception of the landscape's sublimity, which Stegner is alluding to when he refers to the West as "the geography of hope." However, as Stegner was all too aware from his own upbringing, the new perceptual models of the West—unlimited land and resources, freedom from history, the Big Rock Candy Mountain—led inexorably to misuse, mismanagement, and mistakes of every kind with regard to the West. Human casualties were the likes of Stegner's parents, dragged westward and driven on by hopeful, hollow rhetoric.

Stegner's understanding and appreciation of the West links him to an older tradition, as well as providing us with a path from that tradition to the critique of the West which I have discussed in McCarthy's works. Both authors have significant intertextual links with canonical American literature, and both authors are approaching similar issues, albeit from different angles. Additionally, Stegner helped bring western literature out of the literary backwater of "regionalism," putting western literature in the larger framework of contemporary American literature. Stegner's enlightened critique of the myth of the frontier takes us across the border from one tradition to another, inviting a re-analysis of areas of western history which have become obscured by a romanticizing of history. He thus provides a link between an older western fiction, and the newer perspectives of our rather complex times.

McCarthy's project, different as it initially may appear from Stegner's, leads us down many of the same western trails, but these trails have been altered by the new world in which McCarthy is writing. Through his critique of a western masculinity rooted in the myth of the frontier, McCarthy takes us from the familiar image of the cowboy on the range to something that may be described as a postmodern understanding of the loss of identity inherent in the acceptance of an outmoded mythic model based on false historical premises. However, as I have mentioned previously, I do not propose to categorize McCarthy as strictly postmodern, returning to David Holloway's observation that labeling as complex a writer as McCarthy with any particular theoretical tag tends to minimize the complexity of his work.

I have suggested that McCarthy's western fictions, by using both a recognizable narrative structure and a specific historical framework, reveal a critique of the myth of the frontier and its historical ramifications enacted under the guise of the doctrine of Manifest Destiny in *Blood Meridian*. He also critiques the continued influence of the myth of the frontier, with its subtext of modernized Manifest Destiny in *The Border Trilogy*. In addition, McCarthy's western works have an environmental subtext, revealing an attribution of female qualities to landscape in the context of male desire; and conversely applying to the human female those aspects of male desire which apply to the western landscape: acquisitiveness, control, commodification. To put this another way, as William Cronon states:

> The storied reality of human experience suggests why environmental histories so consistently find plots in nature and also why those plots almost always center on people. Environmental history sets itself the task of including within its boundaries far more of the non-human world than most other histories, and yet human agents continue to be the main anchors of its narratives.[19]

That is to say, in order to tell the story of the myth of the frontier, the writer must tell it in terms of human lives. The lives of the young cowboys in *The Border Trilogy* underline the fatal consequences of continuing to live by outdated myths. Their placelessness underscores the futility of trying to somehow re-enact a history which in turn, as shown in *Blood Meridian*, was always suspect, founded upon gender-based, racial, and national assumptions of superiority and entitlement. The barrenness of such assumptions is made doubly evident by the landscape of *Blood Meridian*. It is a "mineral waste" in which McCarthy's concept of "optical democracy" posits a very different sort of relationship with the natural world than Stegner's. As David Holloway comments,

> As defined and practiced in *Blood Meridian*, the style of "optical democracy" connotes a writing that renders all preference among objects "whimsical"...until anything beyond the uniform facticity of the moment is crowded from view. Optical democracy is a kind of writing that verges on deep ecology in its reduction of all that is animate and inanimate to a dead level of equivalence: ostensibly, that is, it is a writing in which a man and a rock become equally "thing-like." And initially at least, it is writing that thus appears to reify the

human and nonhuman world, reporting it back to us as an agglomeration of matter, a superabundance of material objects assembled together in a world where there are only objects to be found.[20]

This understanding of nature is neither Stegner's one of "being a target," nor one of "stewardship," nor does it suggest the numinosity found in his appreciation of the natural world. Rather, it suggests an indifference—even more than indifference, an absence: a "dead level of equivalence"—in which there is no communication because there is no life. While Stegner and McCarthy both posit a certain equivalence of human and non-human elements in their works, the influence of Transcendentalist thought in Stegner, with its basically positive view of life, makes a marked contrast with McCarthy's dark gaze in which all things appear equally without substantive meaning. My contention is that this is the result of the loss of faith caused by the Vietnam War and its aftermath.

McCarthy's characters, in both *Blood Meridian* and *The Border Trilogy*, are adrift, castaways buffeted by the storms of history, temporarily buoyed up by mythic waves which constantly threaten annihilation. In *The Border Trilogy*, old certainties are revealed as hollow; symbols have outlived their meanings; mythologies are without power. In its enactment of original mythopoeic events, *Blood Meridian* reveals the vast canker in the rose of the myth of the frontier. The original frontier in McCarthy's vision is a horror show of genocide, rape, and violence. The impossibility of harboring romantic notions about the Glanton gang and their like is set aside by the young cowboys of *The Border Trilogy* in their desires to be like "the old waddies." *Blood Meridian* gives us the horrible facts; the trilogy presents the durable myth. From denial to vague awareness, the cowboys in the trilogy progress to understanding, from understanding to despair and death. A landscape of disaster is the backdrop to this progression, revealing in characters' relationship to the natural world, the spiritual alienation which besets them.

In both *Blood Meridian* and *The Border Trilogy*, McCarthy radically revises the myth of the frontier through the characters' perception of disastrous landscapes. The Kid, expecting nothing, moves through landscapes which reveal nothing but the anarchic nature of life and the debased state of men's souls. John Grady Cole travels through those same landscapes a century later, with expectations of receiving something innately deserved. In the end he learns that his expectations are hollow, and yet he still tries to realize them in some way, eventually leading to his own death. Billy Parham has neither the Kid's nihilism nor John Grady's expectations. He looks to the landscape to find identity, but identity slips further and further away in a landscape which offers him no co-ordinates.

*   *   *   *

I have argued that Stegner has clear links to Transcendentalism. Robert Jarrett suggests that McCarthy offers us a "postmodern revision of Transcendentalism."[21] Jarrett argues that unlike the Transcendentalists, McCarthy's characters do not identify with the landscape, rather that the landscape itself represents personal annihilation. He states, "This greater void beyond reflects, finally, not an Emersonian or luminist contemplative merger of the soul, but death, man's fundamental alienation from his natural environment."[22] We have seen in Stegner's works this "contemplative merger of the soul" in the epiphanic episodes which I have mentioned. Wister's Virginian, who offers a closer thematic link with McCarthy's cowboys than do Stegner's characters, also seeks this merger with the world, in almost Zen-like terms. Unlike the Virginian, with his desire to "never unmix again," John Grady Cole, and to some extent the Kid, seek to contain the uncontainable landscape, rather than to become one with it. Billy Parham seeks hopelessly for identity within the natural world, and is constantly rebuffed. The landscape has become deadly, rather than life-giving, as it is for Stegner's characters, and the spiritual alienation of the cowboys is expressed in it.

The Kid is the first example of the spiritual alienation which McCarthy develops throughout the characterizations in the western novels. Yet the description of the Kid in *Blood Meridian* could fit any of the cowboys at some stage in their pilgrims' progress:

> The sun that rises is the color of steel. His mounted shadow falls for miles before him. He wears on his head a hat he's made from leaves and they have dried and cracked in the sun and he looks like a raggedyman wandered from some garden where he'd used to frighten the birds.[23]

Here the Kid is an alien in nature, his very presence an abomination, yet strangely familiar. Like the "fairybook beast"[24] he has been previously described as, his alienation offers him a role. In the previous section he has been covered in mud during a fight: in the earth but not of it. His perceptions of nature are of an adversary, never a guide. When he meets a former slaver who has taken to religion, the old man tells him:

> When God made man the devil was at his elbow. A creature that can do anything. Make a machine. And a machine to make a machine. And evil that can run itself a thousand years, no need to tend it. You believe that?
> I don't know.
> Believe that.[25]

The hermit's equation of the machine with the devil is an equation that will be made again by more sympathetic speakers. Making the slaver the spokesman for the pastoral ideal is an irony lost on the Kid, not the reader. The Kid continues on a journey under "bloodred" skies, peopled by corpses, cut-throats, murderers, and thieves. When he meets Captain White's recruiter, he is naked, under the trees by the river outside San Antonio de Bexar, his mule gorging on lush river grass. Drawn by the promise of plunder, the Kid comes away from the only attractive manifestation of landscape he has encountered, and enters the world of the scalp-hunters. He leaves the comparative civilization of the settlements, entering the "howling wilderness."[26] The use of this term, so frequently employed in the annals of exploration and early settlement, is significant. After his baptism in the river, prefiguring John Grady and Lacey's "baptism" crossing the Rio Grande, the Kid is re-enacting the original American quest: freeing the land from barbarians, realizing the American dream of a land "from sea to shining sea." During his next wanderings the howling waste becomes the "hallucinatory void,"[27] a space, rather than a place, in which all certainties are negated, all behaviors accepted. When the gang returns to the settlements, they bring the behavior of the void with them, making them ever-alien to the world of civilized man. Wandering in a landscape of disaster is the only choice left to the Kid.

Twelve years later, the Kid, now significantly aged twenty-eight—the same age as Billy in *Cities of the Plain*—shows glimmerings of humanity. After initially abandoning a group of returning settlers he was guiding east, he encounters a flagellant sect of penitents in the mountains. Days later, he finds the penitents slaughtered. Nearby the Kid sees what he thinks is an old woman sitting in the rocks. He speaks to her, telling her of his life and offering to take her to a place of safety: "He knelt on one knee, resting the rifle before him like a staff. Abuelita, he said. No puedes eschucharme?"[28]

The old woman to whom he has told his confession, to whom he appeals as a pilgrim, staff in hand, to whom he has offered help—a woman whom twelve years previously he would have instantly scalped, dead or alive—whom he has addressed in the familiar, as "little grandmother," is "just a dried shell and she had been dead in that place for years." Too late, too late. The Kid has removed himself from the possibility of redemption, and when we meet him, years later, again among the bone-pickers, soon to shoot a half-grown boy, he is back among the outcasts who people the only world to which he has access: "the planet Anareta, clutched to a namelessness, wheeling in the night."[29] The Kid from his birth is pursuing his own destruction, indeed his own annihilation. He never pursues life, unlike Billy Parham and John Grady Cole, who initially seek identity in a reality of which the truth is always uncertain. The truth, McCarthy is telling us, lies in the world of the Kid.

McCarthy tells us that the Kid represents the world which John Grady and Billy think they desire, but reveals the raw image of what their desires actually mean. John Grady's fabled landscapes are the Kid's mineral wastes. His "pretty horses" are opposed by the nightmare vision of the snakebitten mare, waiting to die and be eaten, the ponies full of arrows, the newborn foal cooked as soon as it is born. Billy's wolf is echoed in the "pale lobos" that surround the scalp-hunters' fires. Much of the language is similar in the four novels; some is identical: "You wouldn't think that a man would run plumb out of country out here, would ye?"[30] Spoken by Toadvine in *Blood Meridian*, this echoes John Grady's assertion that "it aint my country...I dont know where it is. I dont know what happens to country,"[31] in *All the Pretty Horses*: two characters, a century apart, equally lost.

Characters in *Blood Meridian* are repeatedly described as "pilgrims." They address each other as "pilgrim" in the same way that Billy addresses John Grady as "cowboy." Besides the sense of anarchic pilgrimage into the realms of the god of war, as the Judge describes it, that power which is "at last a forcing of the unity of existence,"[32] "pilgrim" connotes the Pilgrim Fathers, founders of the nation. Like the Pilgrims, the Kid, and later Billy and John Grady, are alienated from their original homes: cultural orphans. In his comments on *Blood Meridian*, Stephen Shaviro takes this argument even further: "Exile is not deprivation or loss, but our primordial and positive condition. For there can be no alienation when there is no originary state for us to be alienated from."[33] Shaviro further argues, quoting McCarthy, that the pilgrims of *Blood Meridian*, and by analogy all westering pilgrims, are beckoned onward by the horizon, "all the itinerant degenerates bleeding westward like some heliotropic plague."[34] This "heliotropic plague" then represents the glorious westward march of the American people. The landscape in which this plague of degenerates enacts their westward march is neither a howling wilderness nor the land of Canaan, but a hallucinatory void, a mineral waste, a world emptied of meaning. Like the lifeless landscape of Crane's "North Labrador,"[35] the landscape of *Blood Meridian* is timeless, lifeless, deprived of agency. This is unlike the vivid, living landscapes of the Transcendentalists, the expression of which was inherited by Stegner, but rather their opposite. In Stegner's view, and that of the luminist painters and Transcendentalists writers, landscape has an existence, even numinousness, beyond human intervention. In *Blood Meridian*'s world, the landscape is the outer representation of the darkness within: it has no agency, no meaning beyond that which is predicated by its observers and is often one of personal destruction and death, reflected in images of landscapes which offer the reader, and the characters within the novels, a descent into a "hallucinatory void," a landscape beyond disaster.

*   *   *   *

In *All the Pretty Horses*, John Grady Cole's relationship with landscape is complex. At the beginning of the novel, he has been betrayed both by the human maternal, his mother, who wishes to sell the ranch, and by the unproductivity of the ranch itself—the maternal landscape—which has precipitated the sale. While he has a sense of betrayed filial devotion to the landscape possessed by his family, he also longs for the days of no fenceposts, the open range, the world without machines. Machines are the enemy throughout the novel, as is progress of any kind. His romanticizing of the past is clear in his evening rides along the old Comanche trail

> where the painted ponies and the riders of that lost nation came down out of the north with their faces chalked and their long hair plaited and each armed for war which was their life...When the wind was in the north you could hear them...and the rattle of lances.[36]

This looks like a scene from one of the darker Hollywood westerns: if not quite romantic, at least a vision with possibilities of honorable behavior. John Grady's vision of the past does not take into account another reality, one which has been lifted from the very pit of hell:

> A legion of horribles, hundreds in number, half naked or clad in costumes attic or biblical or wardrobed out of a fevered dream... like a horde from a hell more horrible yet than the brimstone land of christian reckoning, screeching and yammering and clothed in smoke.[37]

This is the vision seen by the Kid, and from all accounts it is a vision that was, for some, probably true. The gulf between John Grady's understanding of the past, the actual reality of that past, and the future which he desires to make out of his false vision, are at the heart of *All the Pretty Horses*. His premises are based on the frontier mythology which attended much of western pioneering. This nostalgia for a half-real past can be traced to historical events, but is deeply founded in frontier mythology, with all its nostalgia for a past which existed only in literary and mythic constructs:

> What is become of the horseman, the cow-puncher, the last romantic figure upon our soil...Well, he will be here among us always, invisible, waiting his chance to live and play as he would like. His wild kind has been among us always, since the beginning: a young man with his temptations, a hero without wings.[38]

This could be John Grady Cole's platonic conception of himself. Owen Wister, like John Grady, laments not only the passing of the cowboy, but the passing of the land of the cowboy as well. But in this there lies a contradiction. Wister says, "It is a vanished world...The mountains are there, far and shining, and the sunlight, and the infinite earth, and the air that seems forever the true fountain of youth...But where is the horseman?"[39]

Wister suggests that while that the land still exists, without the horseman it has lost its meaning. Therefore the perception of the landscape through the eyes of the horseman, and the narrator who in turn perceives the horseman as part of the landscape, is what gives the landscape its heroic character. When the heroic character of the horseman goes, the landscape loses its almost magical intensity and significance in the mind of the narrator. Thus we get the mapless wastes, peopled not with heroic horsemen but the vicious, alienated outlaws of *Blood Meridian* and the lost young cowboys of *The Border Trilogy*. This suggests that for the followers of the myth of the frontier, it was not the landscape itself which had agency, as I have suggested is the case in Stegner's arguments, but rather it is the man in the landscape which gives it identity. This point crucially implies that Stegner's critique of the myth of the frontier offers us an alternative to the nihilism which accompanies McCarthy's critique. Beyond McCarthy's post-1960s perspective, there may be another way.

If we accept Stegner's belief in the spiritual dimension of landscape itself, we may, with one bound of our painted ponies, overleap the modern despair which accompanies the knowledge of the myth of the frontier's tainted origins and find ourselves in a world, not perfect, but perhaps not as entirely hopeless as a close reading of McCarthy might lead us to believe.

And McCarthy himself allows for redemptive possibility in the final closure of *The Border Trilogy*. In the end, redemption comes from the feminine, curiously, after four novels in which obviation of the female has been an issue. We find a similar closure in both *No Country for Old Men* and *The Road*, in which women provide both haven and comfort. At the conclusion of *The Border Trilogy*, we find Billy, an old man, being comforted by Betty, the mother of the family which has given him shelter, when he awakens from bad dreams:

> She patted his hand. Gnarled, ropescarred, speckled from the sun and the years of it. The ropy veins that bound them to his heart. There was map enough for men to read. There's God's plenty of signs and wonders to make a landscape. To make a world.[40]

The map of the landscape we read in Billy's hand, where once there was no map at all, reveals that Billy has connected with the life of the world from which he was once so alienated. The comfort given to him by a maternal female has taken the action of the western novels full circle. The Kid was motherless and abandoned. The only woman the reader ever sees him speak to is an ancient corpse which falls to pieces at his touch. John Grady's mother was distant, and he himself chooses only unobtainable females, locked into the imagery of western manhood, and equating the feminine with the landscape which he initially believes he can possess. Billy's mother is revealed only as a shadow of his disciplinarian father. Billy longs to connect with the female principle in nature, but cannot. And being an unlanded, working cowboy, he is economically doomed to bachelorhood. The homoerotic subtext of *Cities of the Plain* further suggests an inability to connect with the feminine on a deep level. That the final moment of *The Border Trilogy* offers the reader a vision of the redemptive power of unselfish kindness, given to Billy by a clearly maternal woman, suggests that at the end of these stories there may be a glimmer of hope. Simple human kindness, of which there are many examples in *The Border Trilogy*, offers Billy a way out of the darkness of a world without referents. Edwin Arnold has described Betty's actions as a "final absolution"[41] for Billy. The mistakes Billy has made have not been errors of pride or avarice, as one might characterize John Grady's mistakes. Rather, he has erred in trying to connect with a world he could not reach owing to the model of western manhood which he felt compelled to adopt. Additionally this conclusion suggests that the vision of landscape as the unfaithful feminine, which is posited early in the trilogy, may now have reached the same point that we find in Stegner, that is, that landscape and nature are not the object of fantasies which are "infantile, concerned with power, mastery, and total gratification: the all-nurturing mother, the all-passive bride,"[42] posited by Baym, but rather that we have reached a point at which we may regard nature as needing us—Stegner's concept of stewardship—as much as we need it. Betty's kindness at the end of his life brings Billy back to his own beginnings, and in this conclusion there is hopefulness not evident in the three previous western novels. This conclusion is also, significantly, the only one of the four western novels which occurs in a domestic setting, suggesting that the lone man of the myth of the frontier may have found a home at last.

Stegner and McCarthy open doors to a past and an ideology which retain power and remain significant in American life and letters. It is only by a clear understanding of that past and ideology that we may accept that which is valuable, reject that which is not, and move forward toward a future in which the power of myth assumes its true place as metaphorical and philosophical inspiration, rather than as catalyst for ever more catastrophic events, events which transpose the frontier dream of the past into present and future nightmare.

Notes

Introduction: A Changing Landscape

1 Lora, Ronald. *America in the Sixties: Cultural Authorities in Transition.* New York: John Wiley and Sons, 1974, p. 2.

2 Hellman, John. *American Myth and the Legacy of Vietnam.* New York: Columbia University Press, 1986, p. 128.

3 McCarthy, Cormac. *Blood Meridian or The Evening Redness in the West.* New York: Alfred A. Knopf, 1985 (London: Picador, 1989).

4 McCarthy, Cormac. *The Crossing.* New York: Alfred A. Knopf, 1994 (hereafter *Crossing*).

5 McCarthy, Cormac. *All the Pretty Horses.* New York: Alfred A. Knopf 1992 (Picador, 1993) (hereafter *Horses*).

6 McCarthy, Cormac. *Cities of the Plain.* New York: Alfred A. Knopf, 1998 (hereafter *Cities*).

7 McCarthy, Cormac. *No Country for Old Men.* New York: Alfred A. Knopf, 2005 (hereafter *No Country*).

8 See Etulain, Richard W. *Stegner. Conversations on History and Literature.* Reno: University of Nevada Press, 1996, pp. 132–33, for a summary of some of Stegner's views on modern literature.

9 Kolodny, Annette. *The Lay of the Land: Metaphor as Experience and History in American Life and Letters.* Chapel Hill: University of North Carolina Press, 1975, p. 4.

10 See Sullivan, Nell. "Boys Will Be Boys and Girls Will Be Gone: The Circuit of Male Desire in Cormac McCarthy's *Border Trilogy*." *Southern Quarterly*, Vol. 38, No. 3, Spring 2000.

11 De Beauvoir, Simone. *The Second Sex*, trans. H.M. Parshley. London: Picador, 1988, p. 188.

12 Collard, A. and Contrucci, J. *Rape of the Wild: Man's Violence against Animals and the Earth.* London: Women's Press, 1988, p. 1.

13 *Horses*, p. 128.

14 *Blood Meridian*, p. 140.

15 Rose, Gillian. *Feminism and Geography: The Limits of Geographical Knowledge.* Cambridge: Polity Press, 1993, p. 94.

16 See Baudrillard, Jean. *America.* London: Verso, 1988.

1 Myth, Environment, Gender

1 See Reisner, Marc. *Cadillac Desert: The American West and its Disappearing Water.* London: Pimlico, 2001, Ch. 12, pp. 435–36.

2   Broncano, Manuel. "Landscapes of the Magical," in Swift, John N., and Urgo, Joseph R., eds. *Willa Cather and the American Southwest*. Lincoln: University of Nebraska Press, 2004, p. 124.

3   Campbell, Joseph. *The Hero with a Thousand Faces*. Princeton: Princeton University Press, 1949 (3rd edition 1973), pp. 30–31, 245–46.

4   Wister, Owen. *The Virginian*. New York: Macmillan, 1902.

5   Hellman 1986, p. 27.

6   Spurgeon, Sara. *Exploding the Western: Myths of Empire on the Postmodern Frontier*. College Station: Texas A&M University Press, 2005, p. 4.

7   Ibid., p. 8.

8   www.sparknotes.com/biography/**troosevelt**/section8.rhtml

9   Anderson, Benedict. *Imagined Communities*. London: Verso, 1983, 1998, p. 144.

10 Ibid., p. 141.

11 Ibid., pp. 37–46.

12 Smith, Henry Nash. *Virgin Land: The American West as Symbol and Myth*. Cambridge, MA: Harvard University Press, 1950, 1978; 1950, p. 91.

13 Renan, E. "What is a Nation?" in Bhaba, Homi, ed. *Nation and Narration*. London: Routledge, 1990, p. 19.

14 Campbell, Neil. *The Cultures of the New American West*. Edinburgh: Edinburgh University Press, 2000, p. 3.

15 Ibid., p. 6.

16 Comer, Krista. *Landscapes of the New West*. Chapel Hill, NC: University of North Carolina Press, 1999, p. 11.

17 Marx, Leo. *The Machine in the Garden*. New York: Oxford University Press, 1964, p. 45.

18 Heyne, Eric, ed. *Desert, Garden, Margin, Range: Literature on the American Frontier*. New York, 1992, p. 55.

19 In Berkovich, S., and Jehlen, M., eds. *Ideology and Classic American Literature*. New York: Cambridge University Press, 1986, p. 28.

20 Turner, Frederick Jackson. *The Frontier in American History*. New York: Dover, 1996 (facsimile reprint of Henry Holt 1920 edition), p. 219.

21 Limerick, P.N., Milner, C.E., and Rankin, C.A. *Trails: Toward a New Western History*. Lawrence, Kansas: University Press of Kansas, 1991.

22 Milner, Clyde A. "America Only More So," in Milner, P.N., Butler, A.M. and Lewis, D.R., eds. *Major Problems in the History of the American West*. Boston: Houghton Mifflin, 1997, p. 35.

23 Limerick, Patricia Nelson. *The Legacy of Conquest: The Unbroken Past of the American West*. New York: Norton, 1988, pp. 322–23.

24 Stegner, Wallace. *The Big Rock Candy Mountain*. New York: Doubleday, 1943 (London: Penguin, 1991) (hereafter *Mountain*).

25 Moneyhon, Carl. "Conservation as Politics," in Merchant, Carolyn, ed. *Major Problems in American Environmental History*. Lexington, MA: D.C. Heath, 1993. p. 363.

26 Carson, Rachel. *Silent Spring*. New York: Houghton Mifflin, 1962.

27 Stegner, Wallace. *This Is Dinosaur: Echo Park Country and Its Magic Rivers*. Lanham, MD: Roberts Rinehart, (trade reprint) 1985.

28 Robinson, Forrest. "Clio Bereft of Calliope," in Robinson, Forrest G., ed. *The New Western History: The Territory Ahead*. Tucson: University of Arizona Press, 1997, pp. 61–98.

29 Ibid., p. 91.

30 Glotfelty, Cheryl, and Fromm, Harold, eds. *The Ecocriticism Reader*. Athens, GA: University of Georgia Press, 1996. p. xviii.

31 Ibid., p. xx.
32 Worster, Donald. *Nature's Economy.* New York: Cambridge University Press,1994. p. 355.
33 Limerick, Patricia Nelson. *The Legacy of Conquest: The Unbroken Past of the American West.* New York: W.W. Norton,1987, pp. 18–19.
34 Robinson, in Robinson 1997, p. 76.
35 Fromm, Harold. "From Transcendence to Obsolescence," in Glotfelty and Fromm 1996, p. 35.
36 Davis, Mike. *City of Quartz.* London: Vintage, 1990.
37 Davis, Mike. *Ecology of Fear.* London: Picador, 1999.
38 Davis 1990, p. 3.
39 Wrobel, David. *The End of American Exceptionalism: Frontier Anxiety from the Old West to the New Deal.* Lawrence, KS: University Press of Kansas, 1993, p. 5.
40 Guthrie, A.B. *The Big Sky.* New York: Houghton Mifflin, 1947, 1992.
41 McMurtry, Larry. *Buffalo Girls.* New York: Simon and Schuster, 1990.
42 Steinbeck, John. "The Leader of the People," *Norton Anthology of American Literature* (4th edition), Vol. 2. New York: W.W. Norton, 1994, p. 1735.
43 This tendency may be seen in works by Bierstadt, Moran, Church and Gifford, among others.
44 Revel, Jean-François. "Without Marx or Jesus: The New American Revolution Has Begun," in Lora, Ronald, ed. *America in the Sixties: Cultural Authorities in Transition.* New York: John Wiley and Sons, 1974, p. 421.
45 Fitzgerald, Frances. *Fire in the Lake.* Boston: Little, Brown, 1972, p. 7.
46 Turner 1996, p. 219.
47 See Hellman 1986, pp. 104–8.
48 Cimino, Michael. *The Deerhunter.* USA, 1978.
49 Hellman 1986, p. 178.
50 Ibid., p. 47.
51 Roper, John. *The American Presidents: Heroic Leadership from Kennedy to Clinton.* Edinburgh: Edinburgh University Press, 2000, p. 7.
52 Beidler, Philip. *American Literature and the Experience of Vietnam.* Athens, GA: University of Georgia Press, 1982, p. 11.
53 Herr, Michael. *Dispatches.* London: Picador, 1979, p. 55
54 Melling, Philip. *Vietnam in American Literature.* Boston: Twayne,1990, p. 119.
55 Lind, Michael. *Vietnam the Necessary War.* New York: The Free Press, 1999, p. 284.
56 Smith, Henry Nash. "Symbol and Idea in *Virgin Land,*" in Berkovich and Jehlen 1986, p. 28.
57 Owens, Barcley. *Cormac McCarthy's Western Novels.* Tucson: University of Arizona Press, 2000, p. 31, quoting Karnow, Stanley. *Vietnam: A History.* New York: Viking Press, 1983, p. 9.
58 Pratt, John Clark. "The Lost Frontier: American Myth in the Literature of the Vietnam War," in Mogen, D., Busby, M. and Bryant, P., eds. *The Frontier Experience and the American Dream: Essays on American Literature.* College Station, TX: Texas A & M University Press, 1989, p. 237 (quoting Hellman 1986, p. 110).
59 Coppola, Francis Ford. *Apocalypse Now.* USA, 1979.
60 Stone, Oliver. *Born on the Fourth of July.* USA, 1989.
61 Pratt, in Mogen et al. 1989, p. 238.
62 Hellman 1986, p. 120.

63 Ibid., p. 179.
64 Ibid., p. 157.
65 Slotkin, Richard. *Regeneration Through Violence*. Middletown, CT: Wesleyan University Press, 1973 (New York: Harper Perennial Edition, 1996), p. 308.
66 Yeats, William Butler. "The Second Coming," 1919.
67 Slotkin, Richard. *Gunfighter Nation: The Myth of the Frontier in Twentieth Century America*. Norman, OK: University of Oklahoma Press, 1998, p. 546.
68 McMahon, Robert J., ed. *Major Problems in the History of the Vietnam War*. Lexington, MA: D.C. Heath, 1995, p. 210.
69 Roper 2000, p. 137.
70 Worster, D. "Beyond the Agrarian Myth," in Limerick et al. 1991, pp. 15–16.
71 Reich, Charles. *The Greening of America*. New York: Random House, 1970, pp. 215–16.
72 Chatfield, Charles, and Debenedetti, Charles. "The Antiwar Movement and Public Opinion," in McMahon, Robert J., ed. *Major Problems in the History of the Vietnam War*. Lexington, MA: D.C. Heath,1995, pp. 507–8.
73 Newman, Lance. "Marxism and Ecocriticism," *ISLE*, Vol. 9, No. 2 (Summer 2002), p. 21.
74 Chomsky, Noam, Mitchell, Peter, and Schoeffel, John, eds. *Understanding Power: The Indispensable Chomsky*. London: Vintage, 2003, pp. 264–65.
75 Jameson, Frederic. *Postmodernism, or The Cultural Logic of Late Capitalism*. London: Verso, 1991, p. 353.
76 Herr 1979, p. 91.
77 Fitzgerald, Frances. *Fire in the Lake: The Vietnamese and the Americans in Vietnam*. Boston: Little, Brown, 1972, p. 424.
78 Lapham, Lewis H. "Mythography," *Harper's*, Vol. 304, No. 1821 (February 2002), p. 7.
79 Ibid., p. 8, pp. 57–65.
80 Kolodny, Annette. *The Land Before Her: Fantasy and Experience of the American Frontiers, 1630–1860*. Chapel Hill: University of North Carolina Press, 1984, p. 3.
81 Ibid., p. 4.
82 Baym, Nina. "Melodramas of Beset Manhood: How Theories of American Fiction Exclude Women Authors," *American Quarterly*, Vol. 33, No. 2 (Summer 1981), pp. 135–36.
83 Comer, Krista. *Landscapes of the New West: Gender and Geography in Contemporary Women's Writing*. Chapel Hill: University of North Carolina Press, 1999, p. 27.
84 Armitage, Susan, and Jameson, Elizabeth, eds. *The Women's West*. Norman: University of Oklahoma Press, 1987, p. 9.
85 Plumwood, Val. *Feminism and the Mastery of Nature*. London: Routledge, 2002, p. 21.
86 Fetterley, Judith. *The Resisting Reader: A Feminist Approach to American Fiction*. Bloomington: Indiana University Press, 1978, pp. xii–xiii.
87 Mack-Canty, Colleen. "Third-Wave Feminism and the Need to Reweave the Nature/Culture Duality," *NWSA Journal*, Vol. 16, No. 3 (Fall 2004). Also available online at http://www.gale.cengage.com/ExpandedAcademic/ page 10.

88 Fisher-Wirth, Anne. "Anasazi Cannibalism: Eating Eden," in Swift, John N., and Urgo, Joseph R., eds. *illa Cather and the American Southwest*. Lincoln: University of Nebraska Press, 2004, p. 29.
89 Stegner, Wallace. *A Shooting Star*. New York: Viking, 1961 (London: Penguin, 1996).
90 Smith 1950, p. 3.
91 Westling, Louise H. *The Green Breast of the New World: Landscape, Gender, and American Fiction*. Athens: University of Georgia Press, 1996, pp. 5–6.
92 Kolodny 1984, p. 4.
93 Manes, Christopher. "Nature and Silence," in Glotfelty, Cheryl, and Fromm, Harold, eds. *The Ecocriticism Reader*. Athens: University of Georgia Press, 1996, p. 23.
94 Stegner, Wallace. *Wolf Willow*. New York: Viking, 1962 (Penguin, 1990) p. 19.
95 Manes 1996, p. 24.
96 Holloway, David. *The Late Modernism of Cormac McCarthy*. Westport, Connecticut: Greenwood Press, 2002, p. 14.
97 Jarrett, Robert L. *Cormac McCarthy*. New York: Twayne, 1997, pp. vii–viii.
98 Holloway 2002, p. 1.
99 Jarrett 1997, p. 134.
100 Bell, Vereen. *The Achievement of Cormac McCarthy*. Baton Rouge: Louisiana State University Press, 1988, p. 133.
101 Phillips, Dana. "History and the Ugly Facts of *Blood Meridian*," in Lilley, James, ed. *Cormac McCarthy: New Directions*. Albuquerque: University of New Mexico Press, 2002, p. 32.
102 Ibid., p. 27.
103 *Angle of Repose*. New York: Doubleday, 1971 (London: Penguin, 1992) (hereafter *Angle*).
104 Comer 1999, pp. 41–42.
105 Stegner, Wallace. *Where the Bluebird Sings to the Lemonade Springs: Living and Writing in the West*. New York: Penguin, 1992, p. xv (hereafter *Bluebird*).
106 Comer 1999, p. 45.
107 *Bluebird*, p. xv.

2 Stegner's West

1 Jarrett, Robert L. "Reenactment, Commemoration, and Mythopoeia of Western History in McCarthy and Stegner's Fiction." (Unpublished essay presented at the Cormac McCarthy Society European Colloquy, University of Manchester, April 2002. Quoted by permission of the author.)
2 Tompkins, Jane. *West of Everything: The Inner Life of Westerns*. New York: Oxford University Press, 1992, p. 71.
3 Campbell, Neil. "Phases of Going: Owen Wister's Retreat from Hybridity in *The Virginian*," in Graulich, M., and Tatum, S., eds. *Reading The Virginian in the New West*. Lincoln: University of Nebraska Press, 2003, p. 214.
4 Comer, Krista. "Feminism, Western Writers, and New Western Regionalism," in *Updating the Literary West*, Fort Worth: Texas Christian University Press, 1997, p. 20.

5 Daniel, John. "Wallace Stegner's Hunger for Wholeness," in Meine, Curt, ed. *Wallace Stegner and the Continental Vision: Essays on Literature, History and Landscape*. Washington, DC: Island Press (The Center for Resource Economics), 1997, p. 42.

6 Benson, Jackson J. *Wallace Stegner: His Life and Work*. New York: Viking, 1996, p. 2.

7 Ibid., p. 3.

8 Benson, Jackson. *Wallace Stegner: A Study of the Short Fiction*. New York: Twayne, 1998, pp. xiii–xiv.

9 Stegner, Wallace. *The Sound of Mountain Water*. New York: Doubleday, 1969 (London: Penguin, 1997), pp. 170–85.

10 Cook-Lynn, Elizabeth. *Why I Can't Read Wallace Stegner and Other Essays: A Tribal Voice*. Madison: University of Wisconsin Press 1996, p. 32.

11 Ibid., pp. 38–39.

12 Benson 1996, p. 7.

13 Stegner, Wallace. *Crossing to Safety*. New York: Random House, 1987 (London: Penguin, 1988).

14 Isle, Walter. "History and Nature: Representations of the Great Plains in the Work of Sharon Butala and Wallace Stegner." *Great Plains Quarterly*, 19 (Spring 1999), p. 89.

15 Butala, Sharon. *The Perfection of the Morning*. Toronto: Harper Collins, 1994.

16 Stegner, Wallace. *Recapitulation*. New York: Doubleday, 1979 (University of Nebraska Press, 1986).

17 *Angle*, p. 367.

18 *Bluebird*, xvi.

19 Benson 1998, p. 10.

20 Comer 1999, p. 46.

21 Kolodny, Annette. *The Lay of the Land: Metaphor as Experience and History in American Life and Letters*. Chapel Hill: University of North Carolina Press, 1975, p. 147.

22 Kolodny 1984, p. 3.

23 Stegner, Wallace, *The Sound of Mountain Water*. New York: Doubleday, 1969 (London: Penguin, 1997), p. 187.

24 Kolodny 1975, p. 100.

25 Stegner, Wallace. *Marking the Sparrow's Fall: The Making of the American West*. New York: Henry Holt, 1998, p. 6.

26 Kolodny 1975, p. 147.

27 Comer 1999, p. 46.

28 Ibid., p. 46.

29 Graulich, Melody. "O Beautiful for Spacious Guys," in Mogen, D., Busby, M., and Bryant, P., eds. *The Frontier Experience and the American Dream: Essays on American Literature*, College Station: Texas A&M University Press, 1989, p. 187.

30 *Bluebird*, pp. 22–33.

31 Armitage, Susan. "Through Women's Eyes: A New View of the West," in Armitage, Susan, and Jameson, Elizabeth, eds. *The Women's West*. Norman: University of Oklahoma Press, 1987, p. 9.

32 Ronald, Ann. *Reader of the Purple Sage: Essays on Western Writers and Environmental Literature*. Reno: University of Nevada Press, 2003.

33 Etulain, Richard W. *Stegner: Conversations on History and Literature*. Salt Lake City: University of Utah Press, 1983, p. 42.

34 Ibid., p. 48.
35 Stegner, Wallace. *The Spectator Bird*. New York: Doubleday, 1976 (London: Penguin, 1990).
36 Graulich, Melody. "Ruminations on Stegner's Protective Impulse and the Art of Storytelling," in Meine 1997, p. 43.
37 Bredahl, A. Carl, Jr. *New Ground: Western American Narrative and the Literary Canon*. Chapel Hill: University of North Carolina Press, 1989, p. 5.
38 Slotkin, Richard. *The Fatal Environment: The Myth of the Frontier in the Age of Industrialization, 1800–1890*. New York: Atheneum, 1985 (Norman: University of Oklahoma Press, 1994), p. 5.
39 Sinclair, Upton. *The Jungle*. Champaign: University of Illinois Press, 1988.
40 Wrobel 1993, p. 13.
41 Comer 1999, p. 27.
42 Powell, J.W. *Report on the Lands of the Arid Regions*, Reports of the United States Geographical and Geological Survey of the Rocky Mountain Region. Washington, DC, 1878.
43 Etulain 1983, p. 90.
44 *Angle*, p. 104.
45 *Bluebird*, pp. xv–xxiii.
46 *Bluebird*, p. xv.
47 *Angle*, p. 60.
48 Ibid., p. 69.
49 Ibid., p. 72.
50 Ibid., p. 86.
51 Ibid., p. 93.
52 Ibid., p. 103.
53 Floyd, Janet. "A Sympathetic Misunderstanding? Mary Hallock Foote's Mining West," *Frontiers—A Journal of Women's Studies*, Vol. 22, No. 3 (2001), p. 150.
54 *Angle,* p. 367.
55 Ibid., p. 277.
56 Nelson, Nancy Owen. "The Critics," in Benson 1998, p. 131.
57 Berkovich and Jehlen 1986, p. 125.
58 Graulich, Melody. "Book Learning: *Angle of Repose* as Literary History," in Rankin, Charles E., ed. *Wallace Stegner, Man and Writer*. Albuquerque: University of New Mexico Press, 1996, pp. 240–41.
59 *Angle*, p. 424.
60 Fitzgerald, F. Scott. *The Great Gatsby*. New York: Scribner's, 1925 (1953), p. 21 (hereafter *Gatsby*).
61 Etulain 1983, pp. 73–74.
62 *A Shooting Star*, p. 336.
63 Ibid., pp. 161–62.
64 Etulain 1983, p. 74.
65 The Joe Allston stories comprise: "A Field Guide to the Western Birds," in *Collected Stories*. New York: Penguin, 1991; *All the Little Live Things*. New York: Penguin, 1991; and *The Spectator Bird*. New York: Penguin, 1990.
66 A short story titled "Indoor–Outdoor Living" which was the genesis of *All the Little Live Things* was written in the intervening years for *Pacifica* magazine, but is unavailable in print.
67 Etulain 1983, p. 76.

68 *All the Little Live Things*, p. 21.
69 Robinson, Forrest. "Fathers and Sons in Stegner's Ordered Dream of Man," *Arizona Quarterly*, Vol. 59, No. 3 (2003), p. 98.
70 *All the Little Live Things*, p. 338.
71 Ibid., p. 341.
72 *Bluebird*, p. 10.
73 Stegner, Wallace. *Discovery: The Search for Arabian Oil*. Beirut: Middle East Export Press, 1971.
74 Robinson 2003, p. 100.
75 Ibid., p. 101.
76 *All the Little Live Things*, p. 200.
77 *Collected Stories*, pp. 311–12.
78 *The Tempest*, V, 1,181.
79 *All the Little Live Things*, p. 65.
80 Ibid., pp. 344–45.
81 Stegner, Wallace. *The Spectator Bird*. New York: Doubleday, 1976 (London: Penguin, 1990), p. 37.
82 Ibid., pp. 38–39.
83 Marx, Leo. "Pastoralism in America," in Berkovich and Jehlen 1986, p. 59.
84 *Gatsby*, p. 182.
85 *The Spectator Bird*, p. 147.
86 Ibid., p. 182.
87 Westling 1996, p. 4.
88 Hepworth, James R. "Wallace Stegner's Practice of the Wild," in Meine 1997, p. 67.
89 *The Spectator Bird*, p. 213.
90 Kolodny 1984, p. 4.
91 *Blood Meridian*, p. 204.
92 Stegner, Wallace. *Crossing to Safety*. New York: Random House, 1987 (London: Penguin, 1988), p. 7.
93 Stegner, Wallace. *The Sound of Mountain Water*. New York: Doubleday, 1969, p. 195.
94 *Crossing to Safety*, p. 159.
95 Mansfield, Katherine. *Selected Stories*. Oxford: Oxford University Press, 1998.
96 Stegner, Wallace. *Second Growth*. New York: Doubleday, 1947 (Lincoln: University of Nebraska Press, 1985).
97 Bredahl 1989, p. 50.
98 Etulain, Richard W. *Re-imagining the Modern American West: A Century of Fiction, History, and Art*. Tucson: University of Arizona Press, 1996, p. 147.
99 Comer 1999, pp. 40–41.
100 *Bluebird*, p. 139.
101 Busby, Mark. "The Significance of the Frontier in Contemporary American Fiction," in Mogen et al. 1989, p. 103.
102 *The Sound of Mountain Water*, p. 187.
103 Ibid., p. 199.
104 Ibid., 194.
105 Guthrie 1947, p. 386.
106 *Bluebird*, pp. xv–xvi.
107 Ibid., pp. 47–48.
108 Ibid., p. 102.
109 Ibid., p. 57.

110 Ibid., p. 71.
111 Ibid., pp. xvi–xvii.
112 *Mountain*, p. 114.
113 Tuan, Yi-Fu. *Space and Place: The Perspective of Experience*. Minneapolis: University of Minnesota Press, 1997, p. 184.
114 *Marking the Sparrow's Fall*, p. 13.
115 Stegner, Wallace. *Beyond the Hundredth Meridian: John Wesley Powell and the Second Opening of the West*. Boston: Houghton Mifflin, 1954 (London: Penguin, 1992), p. 119.
116 Watkins, T.H. "Reluctant Tiger: Wallace Stegner Takes Up the Conservation Mantle," in Meine 1997, p. 146.
117 Ibid., p. 141.
118 Ibid., pp. 151–52.
119 Ibid., pp. 147–48.
120 *The Sound of Mountain Water*, p. 42.
121 Olsen, Brett J. "Wallace Stegner and the Environmental Ethic: Environmentalism as a Rejection of Western Myth," *Western American Literature*, Vol. 29, No. 2 (1994), p. 126.
122 Harvey, Mark W.T. "Wallace Stegner's Journey into Wilderness," *Literature and Belief*, Vol. 23, No. 1 (2003), p. 151.
123 Stegner, Wallace. "The Gift of Wilderness," in *One Way to Spell Man*, New York: Doubleday, 1982, p. 177.
124 Tyburski, Susan, J. "Wallace Stegner's Vision of Wilderness," *Western American Literature*, Vol. 18, No. 2 (1983), pp. 135–36.
125 Ibid., pp. 134–35, citing Eliade, Mirceau, *The Sacred and the Profane*, Harcourt Brace and World, New York, 1959 (1957)
126 Burke, Edmund. *A Philosophical Enquiry into the Origins of Our Ideas of the Sublime and Beautiful*. Oxford: Oxford University Press, 1990, p. 36.
127 Tyburski 1983, p. 138, citing Eliade, *The Sacred and Profane*.
128 Harvey 2003, p. 154.
129 Tyburski 1983, pp. 141–42.
130 *Wolf Willow*, p. 7.
131 Ibid., p. 281.
132 Momaday, Scott. "The American West and the Burden of Belief," in Ward, Geoffrey C., ed. *The West*. London: Weidenfeld & Nicholson, 1996, p. 377.
133 Emerson, Ralph Waldo. "Nature," *Norton Anthology of American Literature* (4th edition), Volume 1. New York: W.W. Norton, 1994.
134 Thoreau, Henry David. *Walden*. Ware, UK: Wordsworth American Classics, 1995.
135 Muir, John. *The Mountains of California*. New York: Penguin, 1985.
136 *The Sound of Mountain Water*, p. 146.
137 Etulain 1983, p. 177.
138 *Discovery!* p. xii.
139 Ibid., p. v.
140 *Wolf Willow*, p. 9.
141 Ibid., p. 19.
142 Ibid., p. 19.
143 Ibid., p. 22.
144 Ibid., p. 203.
145 Ibid., p. 273.
146 *The Gathering of Zion: The Story of the Mormon Trail*. New York: McGraw-Hill, 1964 (Lincoln: University of Nebraska Press, 1992).

147 Comer 1999, p. 11.
148 Buell, Lawrence. *The Environmental Imagination: Thoreau, Nature Writing and the Formation of American Culture.* Cambridge, MA: Harvard University Press, 1996, p. 7.
149 Stegner, Wallace. "Qualified Homage to Thoreau," in Henley, D., and Marsh, D., eds. *Heaven is Under Our Feet: A Book for Walden Woods.* Berkeley: University of California Press, 1991, p. 289.

3 McCarthy's Western Fictions

1 Bell 1988, p. 133.
2 Campbell 2000, p. 23.
3 Holloway 2002, pp. 19–27.
4 Campbell 2000, p. 6.
5 Ibid., p. 3.
6 Tompkins 1992, p. 4.
7 Spurgeon, Sara. *Exploding the Western: Myths of Empire on the Postmodern Frontier,* College Station: Texas A&M University Press, 2005, p. 17.
8 Fiedler, Leslie. *Love and Death in the American Novel.* Normal, IL: Dalkey Archive Editions, 1997, p. 142.
9 Tompkins 1992, p. 44.
10 Jarrett 1997, Ch. 4.
11 *Blood Meridian,* p. 3.
12 Jarrett 1997, p. 77.
13 Ibid., pp. 79–80.
14 Spurgeon 2005, p. 20.
15 Tompkins, 1992, p. 4.
16 Spurgeon 2005, p. 27.
17 *Blood Meridian,* p. 47.
18 Ibid., pp. 78–79.
19 Spurgeon 2005, p. 28.
20 Ibid.
21 *Blood Meridian,* p. 73.
22 Spurgeon 2005, p. 39.
23 Jarrett 1997, p. 99.
24 Holloway 2002, p. 78.
25 Lawrence, D.H., *Studies In Classic American Literature,* London: Penguin, 1977 (1923), p. 69.
26 Stegner, in Guthrie 1947, pp. xi(-)xii.
27 *Wolf Willow,* pp. 139–219.
28 Ruxton, George Frederick. *Wild Life in the Rocky Mountains.* New York: Macmillan, 1916, Chapter XVII, "Men and Manners." Available at http://www.xmission.com/~drudy/mtman/html/ruxton.html
29 Jarrett 1997, p. 105.
30 Ibid., p. 106.
31 Ibid., p. 107.
32 Tatum, Stephen. *Cormac McCarthy's All the Pretty Horses.* New York: Continuum Publishing Group, 2002, p. 23.
33 Moore, Michael. *Stupid White Men.* London: Penguin, 2002.
34 Holloway 2002, p. 29.
35 Chomsky, Noam. *Rethinking Camelot: JFK, the Vietnam War, and US Political Culture.* Cambridge, MA: Southend Press, 1993, p. 1.

36 Owens, Barcley. *Cormac McCarthy's Western Novels*. Tucson: University of Arizona Press, 2000, Chapter 2.
37 See Chomsky 1993, pp. 13–14.
38 Herr, Michael. *Dispatches*, London: Picador, 1998, p. 161.
39 Spurgeon 2005, p. 31.
40 Moos, Dan. "Lacking the Article Itself: Representation and History in Cormac McCarthy's *Blood Meridian*," *The Cormac McCarthy Journal*, No. 23 (Spring 2002), pp. 23–24.
41 Chomsky 1993, p. 103.
42 Roper, John. *The American Presidents: Heroic Leadership from Kennedy to Clinton*. Edinburgh: Edinburgh University Press, 2000, p. 63.
43 Ibid., p. 64.
44 Shaviro, Steven. "The Very Life of the Darkness," in Arnold, Edwin, and Luce, Diane, eds. *Perspectives on Cormac McCarthy*. Jackson: University Press of Mississippi, 1993, p. 146.
45 From "Sailing to Byzantium," by William Butler Yeats, from which the novel takes its title.
46 Browning, James. "Motel Fix: The Master of the Southwestern Gothic Novel Breaks His Friscalating Prose and Heads Indoors." Available at http://www.villagevoice.com/2005-07-05/books/motel-fix/
47 Messent, Peter. "No Way Back Forever," in Glenday, M.K., and Blazek, W., eds. *American Mythologies: Essays on Contemporary Literature*. Liverpool: University of Liverpool Press, 2005, pp. 129–30.
48 *Mountain*, pp. 561–62.
49 *No Country*, pp. 294–95.
50 *Gatsby*, p. 182.
51 Holloway 2002, p. 20.
52 Tannock, Stuart. "Nostalgia Critique," *Cultural Studies*, Vol. 9, No. 3. (1995), p. 454.
53 Ibid., p. 455.
54 Ibid., p. 459.
55 Ibid., p. 461.
56 Hickman, Trenton. "Against Nostalgia: Turning the Page of Cormac McCarthy's *Cities of the Plain*," *Western American Literature*, Vol. 42, No. 2 (2007), p. 145.
57 *Horses*, p. 5.
58 McCarthy, Cormac. *The Road*. London: Picador, 2006.
59 Hickman 2007, p. 146.
60 *Crossing*, p. 419.
61 Ibid., p. 420.
62 Holloway 2002, p. 1.
63 *No Country*, p. 304.
64 Daugherty, Leo. "*Blood Meridian* as Gnostic Tragedy," in Arnold, Edwin, and Luce, Diane, eds. *Perspectives on Cormac McCarthy*. Jackson: University Press of Mississippi, 1993, p. 162
65 Holloway 2002, pp. 62–63.
66 Ibid.
67 Westling 1996, p. 4.
68 Limerick 1988, p. 97.
69 Campbell 2000, p. 3.
70 Indeed, it might be added that this is the problem of all history, as suggested by Walter Benjamin's description of the Angel of History quoted by Benedict Anderson:

"His face is turned towards the past. Where we perceive a chain of events, he sees one single catastrophe which keeps piling wreckage upon wreckage and hurls it in front of his feet. The Angel would like to stay, awaken the dead, and make whole what has been smashed. But a storm is blowing from Paradise; it has got caught in his wings with such violence that the angel can no longer close them. This storm irresistibly propels him into the future to which his back is turned, while the pile of debris before him grows skyward. This storm is what we call progress."

But the Angel is immortal, and our faces are turned toward the obscurity ahead.

(Anderson, Benedict. *Imagined Communities*.
London: Verso, 1998, p. 162)

71 Comer 1999, p. 11.
72 *Horses*, p. 3.
73 McMurtry, Larry, *Horseman, Pass By*. London: Orion, 1997.
74 The resemblance to McMurtry's Lonnie in *Horseman, Pass By* is interesting. John Grady and Lonnie both live in vanishing worlds formerly presided over by now-dead grandfathers. These deaths turn both boys' worlds upside-down, cutting all links with the historic past. Lonnie also lived on the family ranch, which, with the death of the grandfather, is lost. Lonnie also lost his father in World War II, and his mother is dead.
75 *Horses*, p. 3.
76 Tatum 2002, p. 35.
77 Holloway 2002, p. 71.
78 *Horses*, p. 5.
79 Ibid., p. 6.
80 Campbell 2000, p. 26.
81 Holloway 2002, pp. 72–73.
82 Jarrett 1997, p. 98.
83 *Horses*, p. 21.
84 Jarrett 1997, p. 99.
85 Ibid.
86 *Cities*, p. 290.
87 *Horses*, p. 191.
88 Luce, Dianne. "'When You Wake': John Grady Cole's Heroism in *All the Pretty Horses*," in Hall, W., and Wallach, R., eds. *Sacred Violence: A Reader's Companion to Cormac McCarthy*. El Paso: Texas Western Press, 1995. p. 156.
89 *The Virginian*, p. 280.
90 Jarrett 1997, p. 101.
91 Tompkins 1992, pp. 39–40.
92 *Horses*, p. 28.
93 Ibid., p. 29.
94 McBride, Molly. "From Mutilation to Penetration: Cycles of Conquest in *Blood Meridian* and *All the Pretty Horses*," *Southwestern American Literature*, Vol. 25, No. 1 (Fall 1999), p. 29.
95 Silko, Leslie Marmon. *Ceremony*. New York: Penguin, 1977.
96 *Horses*, p. 17.
97 Ibid., pp. 25–26.
98 Tatum 2002, p. 37.
99 McMurtry, Larry. *Lonesome Dove*. London: Pan, 1990, p. 81.

100 Fehrenbach, T.R. *Lone Star: A History of Texas and the Texans*. New York: Collier, 1980, p. 31.
101 In *Recapitulation*.
102 As a footnote to this comparison, it is interesting to again consider the work of McMurtry, a student of Stegner who writes about the frontier world of McCarthy. At the conclusion of *Lonesome Dove* (1985) the mood is darkly elegiac. Woodrow Call, already in the 1870s an anachronism, returns from Montana, like Billy Parham carrying the bones of a dead "brother." He finds only a burnt-out saloon in his former home town. The saloon keeper has killed himself for love of a prostitute. Lonesome Dove, Call's last point of reference, is now gone, inhabited only by a mad Mexican cook and the memory of the Hat Creek outfit. The tenuous hold which Call had on a bit of the landscape is eradicated. McMurtry, though a historical novelist, is more like McCarthy than Stegner, and Call reveals parallels with both John Grady and Billy.
103 *Horses*, p. 138.
104 Jarrett 1997, p. 96.
105 *Horses*, p. 141.
106 Melville writes:

> Take five-and-twenty heaps of cinders dumped here and there in an outside city lot, imagine some of them magnified into mountains, and the vacant lot the sea, and you will have a fit idea of the general aspect of the Encantadas, or Enchanted Isles. A group rather of extinct volcanoes than of isles, looking much as the world at large might look after a penal conflagration...But the special curse, as one may call it, of the Encantadas...is that to them change never comes.
>
> (*The Encantadas or Enchanted Isles*,
> Sketch First: The Isles at Large)

107 While the concept of chivalry has been criticized as patriarchal, the original concept of courtly love, which is related to the cult of the Virgin Mary in medieval thought, emphasized selfless devotion of a knight to his lady, who was often higher than him in social status, and there was no obvious hope of fulfillment for the knight.
108 *Horses*, p. 140.
109 Kolodny 1975, p. 6.
110 Tatum 2002, p. 43.
111 *Horses*, p. 45.
112 Fehrenbach 1980, pp. 132–51.
113 Raban, Jonathan. *Badland*. London: Picador, 1996.
114 Fehrenbach 1980, pp. 279–324.
115 *Horses*, p. 97.
116 John Grady's father, who we know was a prisoner of the Japanese in the Second World War, would have seen much further depths revealed. In some sense John Grady may be aware of that and have the sense of equaling his father, or atoning for his sufferings.
117 Preston, Douglas. "Cannibals of the Canyon." *The New Yorker*, November 30, 1998.
118 *Gatsby*, p. 182.
119 Jameson, Frederic. *Postmodernism, or The Cultural Logic of Late Capitalism*. London: Verso, 1991, p. 18.
120 Ibid., p. 19.

121 Holloway 2002, pp. 77–78.
122 Marx, Leo, in Berkovich and Jehlen 1986, p. 59.
123 Quoted in Guillemin, George. "Sorrow, Allegory and Pastoralism in Cormac McCarthy's *Border Trilogy*," *Southern Quarterly*, Vol. 38, No. 3 (2000), p. 72.
124 Marx, in Berkovich and Jehlen 1986, p. 59.
125 McBride 1999, p. 26.
126 *Horses*, p. 168.
127 Chomsky, Noam, Mitchell, Peter, and Schoeffel, John, eds. *Understanding Power: The Indispensable Chomsky*. London: Vintage, 2003, pp. 146–48.
128 Luce, Dianne. "When You Wake," in Hall and Wallach 1995, p. 157.
129 *Horses*, p. 125.
130 Holloway 2002, p. 63.
131 Limerick 1988, p. 19
132 *Mountain*, pp. 561–62.
133 Fehrenbach 1980, pp. 569–92.
134 *Horses*, p. 238.
135 Campbell 2000, p. 26.
136 Tatum 2002, p. 65.
137 Luce, Dianne. "When You Wake," in Hall and Wallach 1995, p. 156.
138 See Ellis, Jay. "The Rape of Rawlins," *The Cormac McCarthy Journal*, Vol. 1, No. 1, The Cormac McCarthy Society, www.cormacmccarthy.com/journal.
139 McBride 1999, p. 29.
140 Rose, Gillian. *Feminism and Geography: The Limits of Geographical Knowledge* Cambridge: Polity Press, 1993, p. 94.
141 Ibid., p. 96.
142 Ibid., p. 105.
143 Slater, David. "Situating Geopolitical Representations: Inside/Outside and the Power of Imperial Interventions," in Massey, Doreen, Allen, John, and Sarre, Philip, eds. *Human Geography Today*. Cambridge: Polity Press, 1999, p. 71.
144 *Horses*, p. 45.
145 Ibid., p. 34.
146 McBride 1999, p. 28.
147 *Horses*, p. 278
148 Wegner, John. "'Mexico para los Mexicanos': Revolution, Mexico and McCarthy's Border Trilogy," *Southwestern American Literature*, Vol. 25, No. 1 (Fall 1999), p. 71.
149 Luce, Dianne. "When You Wake," in Hall and Wallach 1995, p. 157.
150 *Horses*, p. 93.
151 Luce, in Hall and Wallach 1995, p. 157
152 Ibid., p. 160.
153 McBride 1999, pp. 29–30.
154 Rose, Gillian. *Feminism and Geography: The Limits of Geographical Knowledge*. Cambridge: Polity Press, 1993, pp. 97–98.
155 Kolodny 1984, p. 9.
156 Westling 1996, pp. 4–5.
157 Browning, James. "Motel Fix: The Master of the Southwestern Gothic Novel Breaks His Friscalating Prose and Heads Indoors," available at http://www.villagevoice.com/2005-07-05/books/motel-fix/

158 Sullivan, Nell. "Boys Will Be Boys and Girls Will Be Gone: The Circuit of Male Desire in Cormac McCarthy's *Border Trilogy*." *Southern Quarterly*, Vol. 38, No. 3 (Spring 2000), p. 171.
159 *Crossing*, p. 352.
160 Sullivan 2000, pp. 167–68.
161 Ibid., p. 171.
162 Ibid., p. 183.
163 Ibid., p. 168.
164 Rose 1993, p. 6.
165 Baym, Nina. "Melodramas of Beset Manhood: How Theories of American Fiction Exclude Women Authors," *American Quarterly*, Vol. 33, No. 2 (Summer, 1981), p. 133.
166 *Crossing*, p. 330.
167 Sullivan 2000, p. 169.
168 *Crossing*, p. 377.
169 Ibid. p. 220.
170 Proulx, Annie. *Close Range: Wyoming Stories*. London: Fourth Estate, 1999.
171 *Cities*, p. 5.
172 Ibid., p. 9.
173 Ibid., p. 10.
174 Ibid., p. 50.
175 Ibid., p. 119.
176 *Horses*, p. 17.
177 Ibid., p. 282.
178 *Horses*, p. 302.
179 *Blood Meridian*, p. 198.
180 Ibid., p. 198.
181 *Horses*, p. 128 (my translation).
182 *Crossing*, p. 59.
183 Ibid., p. 68.
184 Bailey, Charles. "The Last Stage of the Hero's Evolution: Cormac McCarthy's *Cities of the Plain*," *Southwestern American Literature*, Vol. 25, No. 1 (1999), pp. 74–82.
185 Sullivan 2000, p. 169.
186 *Crossing*, p. 4.
187 Tompkins 1992.
188 *Cities*, p. 238.
189 Ibid., p. 239.
190 Cavazza, Jose L. "La ultima novela del norteamericano, `Ciudades de la llanura', exuda un estado tenso de exilio interior." *La Capital*, Suplemento Cultural, Rosario, Argentina (April, 2000); my translation.
191 Tompkins 1992, p. 144.
192 Williams, Don. "All the Pretty Colors of Cormac McCarthy: Has the Master of the Macabre Gone Soft?" *Chattahoochee Review*, 13 (Summer 1993).
193 *Crossing*, p. 63.
194 Tompkins 1992, p. 71.
195 Pitts, Jonathan. "Writing on *Blood Meridian* as a Devisionary Western," *Western American Literature*. Vol. 33, No. 1 (Spring 1998), pp. 9–10.
196 Ibid., p. 17.
197 Ibid.
198 *Blood Meridian*, p. 113.

199 Holloway, David. "Modernism, Nature and Utopia: Another Look at 'Optical Democracy' in Cormac McCarthy's Western Quartet," *Southern Quarterly*, Vol. 38, No. 3 (Spring 2000), p. 192.
200 Hyde, Anne, F. "Cultural Filters: the Significance of Perception," in Milner, Clyde A., ed. *A New Significance: Re-envisioning the History of the American West*. New York: Oxford University Press, 1996, p. 181.
201 *The Crossing*, pp. 184–85.

Conclusion: Across a Great Divide

1 *The Road*, p. 24.
2 Ibid., p. 28.
3 Kerouac, Jack. *On the Road*. New York: Viking, 1957.
4 From "Truckin'" by The Grateful Dead.
5 Robinson, Forrest G., "We Should Talk: Western History and Western Literature in Dialogue," *American Literary History*, Vol. 16, No. 1 (2004), p. 133.
6 *Horses*, p. 302.
7 Nelson, Nancy Owen, in Benson 1998, p. 131.
8 Reisner 2001, p. 485.
9 Olsen 1994, p. 125.
10 Cronon, William, ed. *Uncommon Ground: Rethinking the Human Place in Nature*. New York: Norton, 1996, p. 75.
11 Ibid., p. 80.
12 Ibid., p. 81.
13 Olsen 1994, p. 135.
14 Hitt, Christopher. "Towards an Ecological Sublime." *New Literary History*. Vol. 30 (1999), p. 603, citing Cronon, William. "The Trouble with Wilderness: or, Getting Back to the Wrong Nature", in Cronon 1996, pp. 69–90.
15 Butala 1994, p. 55.
16 Evernden, Neil. *The Social Creation of Nature*. Baltimore: Johns Hopkins University Press, 1992, p. 117.
17 Stegner, Wallace. "The Gift of Wilderness," in *One Way to Spell Man*. New York: Doubleday, 1982, pp. 175–76.
18 Hyde, Anne, F. "Cultural Filters: The Significance of Perception," in Milner, Clyde A., ed. *A New Significance: Re-envisioning the History of the American West*. New York: Oxford University Press, 1996, p. 175.
19 Cronon, William. "A Place for Stories: Nature, History, and Narrative," *Journal of American History* (March 1992), p. 1369.
20 Holloway 2002, p. 135.
21 Jarrett 1997, p. 138.
22 Ibid., p. 139.
23 *Blood Meridian*, p. 15.
24 Ibid., p. 4.
25 Ibid., p. 19.
26 Ibid., p. 42.
27 Ibid., p. 113.
28 Ibid., p. 315.
29 Ibid., p. 46. In astrological terms, the Anareta is the planet in one's horoscope which portends death.
30 Ibid., p. 285.
31 *Horses*, p. 299.

32 *Blood Meridian*, p. 249.
33 Shaviro, Steven. "'The Very Life of the Darkness': A Reading of *Blood Meridian*," in Arnold, Edwin, and Luce, Diane, eds. *Perspectives on Cormac McCarthy*. Jackson: University Press of Mississippi, 1993, p. 147.
34 *Blood Meridian*, p. 78.
35 **North Labrador**
      A land of leaning ice
      Hugged by plaster grey arches of sky,
      Flings itself silently
      Into eternity
      "Has no one come here to win you,
      Or left you with the faintest blush
      Upon your glittering breasts?
      Have you no memories, O Darkly Bright?"
      Cold hushed, there is only the shifting of moments
      That journey toward no Spring—
      No birth, no death, no time nor sun
      In answer.
                          Hart Crane (1899–1932)

36 *Horses*, p. 5.
37 *Blood Meridian*, pp. 52–53.
38 *The Virginian*, p. ix, introduction.
39 Ibid., p. 8.
40 *Cities*, p. 291.
41 Arnold, Edwin. "McCarthy and the Sacred," in Lilley, James, ed. *Cormac McCarthy: New Directions*. Albuquerque: University of New Mexico Press, 2002, p. 234.
42 Baym, Nina. "Melodramas of Beset Manhood: How Theories of American Fiction Exclude Women Authors," *American Quarterly*, Vol. 33, No. 2 (Summer 1981), pp. 123–39, p. 134.

Bibliography

Primary sources

McCarthy, Cormac. *Blood Meridian or The Evening Redness in the West*. New York: Alfred A. Knopf, 1985 (London: Picador, 1989).
—— *All the Pretty Horses*. New York: Alfred A. Knopf, 1992 (London: Picador, 1993).
—— *The Crossing*. New York: Alfred A. Knopf, 1994.
—— *Cities of the Plain*. New York: Alfred A. Knopf, 1998.
—— *No Country for Old Men*. New York: Alfred A. Knopf, 2005.
—— *The Road*. London: Picador, 2006.
Stegner, Wallace. *Remembering Laughter*. New York: Little, Brown, 1937 (London: Penguin, 1996).
—— *The Big Rock Candy Mountain*. New York: Doubleday, 1943 (London: Penguin, 1991).
—— *Second Growth*. New York: Doubleday, 1947 (Lincoln: University of Nebraska Press, 1985).
—— *The Preacher and the Slave*. New York: Doubleday, 1950 (reprinted as *Joe Hill*, London: Penguin 1990).
—— *Beyond the Hundredth Meridian: John Wesley Powell and the Second Opening of the West*. Boston: Houghton Mifflin, 1954 (London: Penguin, 1992).
—— *A Shooting Star*. New York: Viking, 1961 (London: Penguin, 1996).
—— *Wolf Willow*. New York: Viking, 1962 (London: Penguin, 1990).
—— *The Gathering of Zion: The Story of the Mormon Trail*. New York: McGraw-Hill, 1964 (Lincoln: University of Nebraska Press, 1992).
—— *All the Little Live Things*. New York: Viking, 1967 (London: Penguin, 1991).
—— *The Sound of Mountain Water*. New York: Doubleday, 1969 (London: Penguin, 1997).
—— *Angle of Repose*. New York: Doubleday, 1971 (London: Penguin, 1992).
—— *Discovery: The Search for Arabian Oil*. Beirut: Middle East Export Press, 1971.
—— *The Spectator Bird*. New York: Doubleday, 1976 (London: Penguin, 1990).

—— *Recapitulation*. New York: Doubleday, 1979 (Lincoln: University of Nebraska Press, 1986).

—— "The Gift of Wilderness," in *One Way to Spell Man*. New York: Doubleday, 1982.

—— *Crossing to Safety*. New York: Random House, 1987 (London: Penguin, 1988).

—— *Collected Stories*. New York: Random House, 1990 (London: Penguin, 1991).

—— *Where the Bluebird Sings to the Lemonade Springs: Living and Writing in the West*. New York: Penguin, 1992.

—— *Marking the Sparrow's Fall: the Making of the American West*. New York: Henry Holt, 1998.

Secondary sources: literature

Cather, Willa. *O Pioneers!* New York: Dover, 1993.

—— *My Antonia*. New York: Dover, 1994.

—— *Death Comes for the Archbishop*. London: Virago, 1997.

Cooper, James Fenimore. *The Last of the Mohicans*. Oxford: Oxford University Press, 1994.

Crèvecoeur, J. Hector St. John de. *Letters from an American Farmer*. New York: Penguin, 1986.

Didion, Joan. *Play It As It Lays*. New York: Farrar, Straus and Giroux, 1970.

Emerson, Ralph Waldo. "Nature," in *Norton Anthology of American Literature* (4th edition), Volume 1. New York: Norton, 1994.

Fitzgerald, F. Scott. *The Great Gatsby*. New York: Scribner's, 1925 (1953).

Guthrie, A.B. *The Big Sky*. New York: Houghton Mifflin, 1947 (1992).

Hawthorne, Nathaniel, *The Scarlet Letter*, in *Norton Anthology of American Literature* (4th edition), Volume 1. New York: Norton, 1994.

James, Henry. *The Bostonians*. Oxford: Oxford University Press, 1984.

McCarthy, Cormac. *The Orchard Keeper*. New York: Random House, 1965 (London: Picador, 1994).

—— *Outer Dark*. New York: Random House, 1968 (London: Picador, 1994).

—— *Child of God*. New York: Random House, 1973 (London: Picador, 1989).

—— *Suttree*. New York: Random House, 1979 (London: Picador, 1989).

—— *The Stonemason*. London: Picador, 1997.

—— *The Sunset Limited*. New York: Vintage, 2006.

McMurtry, Larry. *Buffalo Girls*. New York: Simon and Schuster, 1990.

—— *Lonesome Dove*. London: Pan, 1990.

—— *Streets of Laredo*. New York: Simon and Schuster, 1993.

—— *Horseman, Pass By*. London: Orion, 1997.

Mansfield, Katherine. *Selected Stories*. Oxford: Oxford University Press, 1998.

Melville, Herman. *Moby Dick*. New York: Norton Critical Editions, 1967.

Naipaul, V.S. *A Way in the World*. London, Heinemann, 1994.

Perkins, Charlotte Gilman. "The Yellow Wallpaper," in *Norton Anthology of American Literature* (4th edition), Volume 2. New York: Norton, 1994.

Proulx, Annie. *Accordion Crimes.* London, Fourth Estate, 1997.
—— *Close Range: Wyoming Stories.* London: Fourth Estate, 1999.
Silko, Leslie Marmon. *Ceremony.* New York: Penguin, 1977.
Smiley, Jane. *A Thousand Acres.* New York: Harper Collins, 1991.
Steinbeck, John. "The Leader of the People," in *Norton Anthology of American Literature* (4th edition), Volume 2. New York: Norton, 1994.
—— *The Grapes of Wrath.* London: Minerva, 1996 (1939).
Stewart, George R. *Earth Abides.* New York: Ballantine, 1983.
Thoreau, Henry David. *Walden.* Ware, UK: Wordsworth American Classics, 1995.
Twain, Mark. *Roughing It.* New York: Penguin, 1985.
—— *Huckleberry Finn.* Ware, UK: Wordsworth Editions, 1992.
Virgil. *The Eclogues and the Georgics,* translated by C. Day Lewis. Oxford: Oxford University Press, 1983.
Wister, Owen. *The Virginian.* New York: Macmillan, 1902.

Criticism and theory

Allmendinger, Blake. *Ten Most Wanted: The New Western Literature.* New York: Routledge, 1998.
Armitage, Susan, and Jameson, Elizabeth, eds. *The Women's West.* Norman: University of Oklahoma Press, 1987.
Arnold, Edwin, and Luce, Diane. "McCarthy's Moral Parables," *Southern Quarterly,* Vol. 30, No. 4 (Summer, 1992), pp. 31–50.
—— eds. *Perspectives on Cormac McCarthy.* Jackson: University Press of Mississippi, 1993.
Arthur, Anthony. *Critical Essays on Wallace Stegner.* Boston: G.K. Hall, 1982.
Bailey, Charles. "The Last Stage of the Hero's Evolution: Cormac McCarthy's *Cities of the Plain,*" *Southwestern American Literature,* Vol. 25, No. 1 (1999), pp. 74–82.
Banting, Pamela, ed. *Fresh Tracks: Writing the Western Landscape.* Victoria, British Columbia: Polestar Books, 1998.
Baym, Nina. "Melodramas of Beset Manhood: How Theories of American Fiction Exclude Women Authors," *American Quarterly,* Vol. 33, No. 2 (Summer, 1981), pp. 123–39.
—— "Region and Environment in American Literature," *New England Quarterly,* Vol. 77, No. 2 (2004), pp. 300–8.
—— "Old West, New West, Postwest, Real West," *American Literary History,* Vol. 18, No. 4 (Winter, 2006), pp. 814–28.
Beidler, Philip. *American Literature and the Experience of Vietnam.* Athens: University of Georgia Press, 1982.
Bell, Ian F.A., and Adams, D.K., eds. *American Literary Landscapes: The Fiction and the Fact.* New York: Vision Press Critical Studies Series, 1989.
Bell, Vereen. *The Achievement of Cormac McCarthy.* Baton Rouge: Louisiana State University Press, 1988.
—— "Between the Wish and the Thing the World Lies Waiting," *Southern Review,* Vol. 28, No. 4 (1992), pp. 920–27.

Benson, Jackson J. *Wallace Stegner: His Life and Work*. New York: Viking, 1996.

—— *Wallace Stegner: A Study of the Short Fiction*. New York: Twayne, 1998.

—— *Down by the Lemonade Springs: Essays on Wallace Stegner*. Reno and Las Vegas: University of Nevada Press, 2001.

Berkovich, Sacvan, and Jehlen, Myra, eds. *Ideology and Classic American Literature*. New York: Cambridge University Press, 1986.

Berry, Wendell. "Wallace Stegner and the Great Community," *South Dakota Review*, Vol. 23, No. 4 (1985), pp. 10–18.

Bradbury, Malcolm. *The Modern American Novel*. Oxford: Oxford University Press, 1983.

Bredahl, A. Carl, Jr. *New Ground: Western American Narrative and the Literary Canon*. Chapel Hill: University of North Carolina Press, 1989.

Brewton, Vince. "The Changing Landscape of Violence in Cormac McCarthy's Early Novels and the Border Trilogy," *Southern Literary Journal*, Vol. 37, No. 1 (2004), pp. 121–43.

Browning, James. "Motel Fix: The Master of the Southwestern Gothic Novel Breaks his Friscalating Prose and Heads Indoors," *Village Voice*, July 5, 2005; available at http://www.villagevoice.com/2005-07-05/books/motel-fix/

Burrows, J.R. "The Pastoral Convention in the California Novels of Wallace Stegner," unpublished thesis, 1988.

—— "Wallace Stegner's Version of Pastoral," *Western American Literature*, Vol. 25, No. 1 (May, 1990), pp. 15–25.

Busby, Mark. "Texas and the Great Southwest," in Crow, Charles L., ed. *A Companion to the Regional Literatures of America*. Malden, MA: Blackwell, 2003.

Campbell, Neil. *The Cultures of the New American West*. Edinburgh: Edinburgh University Press, 2000.

—— "Phases of Going: Owen Wister's Retreat from Hybridity in *The Virginian*," in Graulich, M., and Tatum, S., eds. *Reading The Virginian in the New West*. Lincoln: University of Nebraska Press, 2003.

Cavazza, Jose L. "La ultima novela del norteamericano, 'Ciudades de la llanura', exuda un estado tenso de exilio interior," *La Capital*, Suplemento Cultural, Rosario, Argentina (April, 2000).

Cheuse, Alan. "A Note on Landscape in *All the Pretty Horses*," *Southern Quarterly*, Vol. 30, No. 4 (Summer, 1992), pp. 140–42.

Cohen, Michael P. *The Pathless Way: John Muir and American Wilderness*. Madison: University of Wisconsin Press, 1984.

Comer, Krista. *Landscapes of the New West: Gender and Geography in Contemporary Women's Writing*. Chapel Hill: University of North Carolina Press, 1999.

Cook-Lynn, Elizabeth. *Why I Can't Read Wallace Stegner and Other Essays: A Tribal Voice*. Madison: University of Wisconsin Press 1996.

Cracroft, Richard H. "I Have Never Recovered from the Country: The American West of Wallace Stegner," in Crow, Charles L., ed. *A Companion to the Regional Literatures of America*, Malden, MA: Blackwell, 2003.

Cronon, William, ed. *Uncommon Ground: Rethinking the Human Place in Nature*. New York: Norton, 1996.

Crow, Charles L., ed. *A Companion to the Regional Literatures of America.* Malden, MA: Blackwell, 2003.

Cutchins, Dennis. "All the Pretty Horses: Cormac McCarthy's Reading of *For Whom the Bell Tolls*," *Western American Literature*, Vol. 41, No. 3 (Fall, 2006), pp. 267–99.

Daiches, David. *Willa Cather: A Critical Introduction.* Ithaca, NY: Cornell University Press, 1951.

Daugherty, Leo. "*Blood Meridian* as Gnostic Tragedy," *Southern Quarterly*, Vol. 30, No. 4 (Summer, 1992), pp. 122–33.

Ellis, Jay. "The Rape of Rawlins," *The Cormac McCarthy Journal*, Vol. 1, No. 1 (2001); available at www.cormacmccarthy.com/journal

Empson, William. *Some Versions of Pastoral.* London: Penguin, 1995 (1935).

Etulain, Richard W. *Stegner: Conversations on History and Literature.* Salt Lake City: University of Utah Press, 1983 (Reno: University of Nevada Press, 1996).

—— *Re-imagining the Modern American West: A Century of Fiction, History, and Art.* Tucson: University of Arizona Press, 1996.

Fender, Stephen. *American Literature in Context, 1620–1830.* London: Methuen, 1983.

Fetterley, Judith. *The Resisting Reader: A Feminist Approach to American Fiction.* Bloomington: Indiana University Press, 1978.

Fiedler, Leslie. "Mythicizing the Unspeakable," *Journal of American Folklore*, Vol. 103, No. 410 (1990), pp. 390–99.

—— *Love and Death in the American Novel.* Normal, IL: Dalkey Archive Editions, 1997.

Fisher-Wirth, Anne. "Anasazi Cannibalism: Eating Eden," in Swift, John N., and Urgo, Joseph R., eds. *Willa Cather and the American Southwest.* Lincoln: University of Nebraska Press, 2004.

Floyd, Janet. "A Sympathetic Misunderstanding? Mary Hallock Foote's Mining West," *Frontiers—A Journal of Women's Studies*, Vol. 22, No. 3 (September, 2001), pp. 148–67.

Frohock, W.M. *The Novel of Violence in America.* London: Arthur Barker, 1959.

Giles, Paul. "Transnationalism and Classic American Literature," *PMLA: Publications of the Modern Language Association of America*, Vol. 118, No. 1 (January, 2003), pp. 62–77.

Glotfelty, Cheryl, and Fromm, Harold, eds. *The Ecocriticism Reader.* Athens: University of Georgia Press, 1996.

Grammer, John M. "Pastoral and History in Cormac McCarthy's South," *Southern Quarterly*, Vol. 30, No. 4 (Summer, 1992), pp. 19–30.

Graulich, Melody. "The Guides to Conduct that a Tradition Offers: Wallace Stegner's *Angle of Repose*," *South Dakota Review*, Vol. 23, No. 4 (Winter, 1985), pp. 87–106.

Graulich, Melody, and Tatum, Stephen, eds. *New Essays on Owen Wister's The Virginian.* Lincoln: University of Nebraska Press, 2002.

Guillemin, Georg. *The Pastoral Vision of Cormac McCarthy.* College Station: Texas A&M Press, 2004.

Hall, Wade, and Wallach, Rick, eds. *Sacred Violence: A Reader's Companion to Cormac McCarthy.* El Paso: Texas Western Press, 1995.

Harvey, Mark. "Wallace Stegner's Journey into Wilderness," *Literature and Belief*, Vol. 23, No. 1 (2003), pp. 147–61.

Heyne, Eric, ed. *Desert, Garden, Margin, Range: Literature on the American Frontier.* New York: Twayne, 1992.

Hickman, Trenton. "Against Nostalgia: Turning the Page of Cormac McCarthy's *Cities of the Plain*," *Western American Literature*, Vol. 42, No. 2 (2007), pp. 142–63.

Hitt, Christopher. "Towards an Ecological Sublime," *New Literary History*, Vol. 30 (1999), pp. 603–23.

Holloway, David. "Modernism, Nature and Utopia: Another Look at 'Optical Democracy' in Cormac McCarthy's Western Quartet," *Southern Quarterly*, Vol. 38, No. 3 (Spring, 2000), pp. 186–205.

—— *The Late Modernism of Cormac McCarthy.* Westport, CT: Greenwood Press, 2002.

Houston, James D. "Wallace Stegner: Universal Truths Rooted in a Region," *South Dakota Review*, Vol. 23, No. 4 (1985), pp. 6–8.

Isle, Walter. "History and Nature: Representations of the Great Plains in the Work of Sharon Butala and Wallace Stegner," *Great Plains Quarterly*, Vol. 19 (Spring, 1999), pp. 89–95.

Jarrett, Robert L. *Cormac McCarthy.* New York: Twayne, 1997.

—— "Reenactment, Commemoration, and Mythopoeia of Western History in McCarthy and Stegner's Fiction," unpublished essay presented at the Cormac McCarthy Society European Colloquy, University of Manchester, April 2002.

Johnson, Michael L. *New Westers: The West in Contemporary American Culture.* Lawrence, KS: University Press of Kansas, 1996.

Karrell, Linda. "The Burden of Letters: Willa Cather, Wallace Stegner, and the Literary Tradition of the American West," *The Mower's Tree: The Newsletter of the Cather Colloquium*, Fall/Winter (2004), pp. 8–10, 15.

—— "The Postmodern Author on Stage: Fair Use and Wallace Stegner,"*American Drama*, Vol. 14, No. 2 (Summer, 2005), pp. 70–89.

Kolodny, Annette. *The Lay of the Land: Metaphor as Experience and History in American Life and Letters.* Chapel Hill: University of North Carolina Press, 1975.

—— *The Land Before Her: Fantasy and Experience of the American Frontiers, 1630–1860.* Chapel Hill: University of North Carolina Press, 1984.

—— "Letting Go Our Grand Obsessions: Notes Toward a New Literary History of the American Frontiers," *American Literature*, Vol. 64, No. 1 (1992), pp. 1–18.

Kowaleski, Michael, ed. *Reading the West: New Essays on the Literature of the American West.* New York: Cambridge University Press, 1996.

—— "Contemporary Regionalism," in Crow, Charles L., ed. *A Companion to the Regional Literatures of America.* Malden, MA: Blackwell, 2003.

Lawrence, D.H. *Studies In Classic American Literature.* London: Penguin, 1977 (1923).

Lewis, R.W.B. *The American Adam.* Chicago: University of Chicago Press, 1959.

Lilley, James, ed. *Cormac McCarthy: New Directions.* Albuquerque: University of New Mexico Press, 2002.

McBride, Molly. "From Mutilation to Penetration: Cycles of Conquest in *Blood Meridian* and *All the Pretty Horses*," *Southwestern American Literature*, Vol. 25, No. 1 (Fall, 1999), pp. 24–35.

Manes, Christopher. "Nature and Silence," in Glotfelty, Cheryl, and Fromm, Harold, eds. *The Ecocriticism Reader.* Athens: University of Georgia Press, 1996.

Marx, Leo. *The Machine in the Garden.* New York: Oxford University Press, 1964.

Matthiessen, F.O. *American Renaissance: Art and Expression in the Age of Emerson and Whitman.* New York: Oxford University Press, 1941, 1968.

Meine, Curt, ed. *Wallace Stegner and the Continental Vision: Essays on Literature, History and Landscape.* Washington, DC: Island Press (The Center for Resource Economics), 1997.

Melling, Philip. *Vietnam in American Literature.* Boston: Twayne, 1990.

Messent, Peter. "No Way Back Forever," in Glenday, M.K., and Blazek, W., eds. *American Mythologies: Essays on Contemporary Literature.* Liverpool: University of Liverpool Press, 2005.

Milton, John R. *The Novel of the American West.* Lincoln: University of Nebraska Press, 1980.

—— "Conversation with Wallace Stegner," *South Dakota Review*, Vol. 26, No.4 (1988), pp. 45–57.

Mogen, D., Busby, M. and Bryant, P., eds. *The Frontier Experience and the American Dream: Essays on American Literature.* College Station: Texas A&M University Press, 1989.

Moos, Dan. "Lacking the Article Itself: Representation and History in Cormac McCarthy's *Blood Meridian*," *The Cormac McCarthy Journal*, No. 2 (Spring, 2002); available at www.cormacmccarthy.com/journal

Morris, Gregory L., ed. *Talking Up a Storm: Voices of the New West.* Lincoln: University of Nebraska Press, 1994.

Nash, Roderick. *Wilderness and the American Mind.* New Haven: Yale University Press, 1967, 1982.

Occhino, Janet. "Inside Out: The West of Wallace Stegner's *Angle of Repose*: The American West Re-imagined," *ANQ*, Vol. 9, No. 3 (Summer, 1996), pp. 30–39.

Olsen, Brett J. "Wallace Stegner and the Environmental Ethic: Environmentalism as a Rejection of Western Myth," *Western American Literature*, Vol. 29, No. 2 (1994), pp. 123–42.

Owens, Barcley. *Cormac McCarthy's Western Novels.* Tucson: University of Arizona Press, 2000.

Pilkington, Tom. "Fate and Free Will on the American Frontier: Cormac McCarthy's Western Fiction," *Western American Literature*, Vol. 27, No. 4 (Winter, 1993), pp. 311–22.

Pitts, Jonathan. "Writing on *Blood Meridian* as a Devisionary Western," *Western American Literature*, Vol. 33, No. 1 (Spring, 1998), pp. 7–25.

Prown, J.D., Anderson, N.K., Cronon, W., Dippie, B.W., Sandweiss, M.A., Schoelwer, S.P., and Lamar, H.R. *Discovered Lands, Invented Pasts: Transforming Visions of the American West.* New Haven: Yale University Press, 1992.

Rankin, Charles E., ed. *Wallace Stegner, Man and Writer.* Albuquerque: University of New Mexico Press, 1996.

Reisling, Russell. *The Unusable Past.* New York: Methuen, 1986.

Ridge, Martin. "Frederick Jackson Turner and His Ghost: The Writing of Western History," *Proceedings of the American Antiquarian Society*, Vol. 4 (1991), pp. 65–76.

Robinson, Forrest G. "Fathers and Sons in Stegner's Ordered Dream of Man," *Arizona Quarterly*, Vol. 59, No. 3 (2003), pp. 97–114.

—— "We Should Talk: Western History and Western Literature in Dialogue," *American Literary History*, Vol. 16, No. 1 (2004), pp. 132–43.

Robinson, Forrest G., and Robinson, Margaret G. *Wallace Stegner.* Boston: Twayne, 1977.

Ronald, Ann. *Reader of the Purple Sage: Essays on Western Writers and Environmental Literature.* Reno: University of Nevada Press, 2003.

Roth, John K., ed. *American Diversity, American Identity,* New York: Henry Holt, 1995.

Rothfork, John. "Cormac McCarthy as Pragmatist," *Critique: Studies in Contemporary Fiction*, Vol. 47, No. 2 (Winter, 2006), pp. 201–14.

Rowe, John Carlos. "Nineteenth-Century United States Literary Culture and Transnationality," *PMLA*, Vol. 118, No. 1 (2003), pp. 37–68.

Sepich, John Emil. "Historical Sources in *Blood Meridian*," *Southern Quarterly*, Vol. 30, No. 4 (Summer, 1992), pp. 93–110.

—— *Notes on Blood Meridian.* Louisville, KY: Bellarmine College Press, 1993.

Shaviro, Steven. "A Reading of *Blood Meridian*," *Southern Quarterly*, Vol. 30, No. 4 (Summer, 1992), pp. 111–21.

Slotkin, Richard. *Regeneration Through Violence.* Middletown, CT: Wesleyan University Press, 1973 (New York: Harper Perennial Editions, 1996).

—— *The Fatal Environment: The Myth of the Frontier in the Age of Industrialization, 1800–1890.* New York: Atheneum, 1985 (Norman: University of Oklahoma Press, 1994).

—— *Gunfighter Nation: The Myth of the Frontier in Twentieth Century America.* Norman: University of Oklahoma Press 1998.

Smith, Henry Nash. *Virgin Land: The American West as Symbol and Myth.* Cambridge, MA: Harvard University Press, 1950, 1978.

Spurgeon, Sara L. "Pledged in Blood": Truth and Redemption in Cormac McCarthy's *All the Pretty Horses*, *Western American Literature*, Vol. 34, No. 1 (Spring, 1999), pp. 35–44.

—— *Exploding the Westerm: Myths of Empire on the Postmodern Frontier,* College Station: Texas A&M University Press, 2005.

Stegner, Mary, and Stegner, Page, eds. *The Geography of Hope: A Tribute to Wallace Stegner.* San Francisco: Sierra Club Books, 1996.

Sullivan, Nell. "Boys Will Be Boys and Girls Will Be Gone": The Circuit of Male Desire in Cormac McCarthy's *Border Trilogy*," *Southern Quarterly*, Vol. 38, No. 3 (Spring, 2000), pp. 167–85.

Swift, John N., and Urgo, Joseph R., eds. *Willa Cather and the American Southwest.* Lincoln: University of Nebraska Press, 2004.

Tatum, Stephen. "The Solace of Animal Faces," *Arizona Quarterly*, Vol. 50, No. 4 (Winter, 1994), pp. 113–56.

—— "Topographies of Transition in Western American Literature," *Western American Literature*, Vol. 32, No. 4 (Winter, 1998), pp. 310–53.

―――― *Cormac McCarthy's All the Pretty Horses*. New York: Continuum Publishing Group, 2002.

―――― "Postfrontier Horizons," *MFS: Modern Fiction Studies*, Vol. 50, No. 2 (Summer, 2004), pp. 460–68.

―――― "Spectral Beauty and Forensic Aesthetics in the West," *Western American Literature*, Vol. 41, No. 2 (Summer, 2006), pp. 123–45.

Thacker, Robert. "Erasing the Forty-Ninth Parallel: Nationalism, Prairie Criticism, and the Case of Wallace Stegner," *Essays on Canadian Writing*, Vol. 61 (Spring, 1997), pp. 179–202.

Thomas, John L. *A Country in the Mind: Wallace Stegner, Bernard DeVoto, History and the American Land*. New York: Routledge, 2000.

Tompkins, Jane. *West of Everything: The Inner Life of Westerns*. New York: Oxford University Press, 1992.

Trombley, James Alexander. "A Simultaneous and Joined Identity: The Ecocommunitarian Ideal in Wallace Stegner's American West," *Cercles*, Vol. 13 (2005), pp. 25–33.

Tyburski, Susan J. "Wallace Stegner's Vision of Wilderness," *Western American Literature*, Vol. 18, No. 2 (1983), pp. 133–48.

Vitalis, Robert. "Wallace Stegner's Arabian Discovery: The Imperial Entailments of a Continental Vision," working paper 8, The Cold War as Global Conflict, International Center for Advanced Studies, New York University, September 2003.

Wallace, Garry. "Meeting McCarthy," *Southern Quarterly*, Vol. 30, No. 4 (Summer, 1992), pp. 134–39.

Wallach, Rick, ed. *Myth, Legend, Dust: Critical Responses to Cormac McCarthy*. Manchester: Manchester University Press, 2000.

Watkins, T.H. "Bearing Witness for the Land: The Conservation Career of Wallace Stegner," *South Dakota Review*, Vol. 23, No. 4 (1985), pp. 42–57.

Wegner, John. "'Mexico para los Mexicanos': Revolution, Mexico and McCarthy's Border Trilogy," *Southwestern American Literature*, Vol. 25, No. 1 (Fall, 1999), pp. 63–73.

Western Literature Association. *Updating the Literary West*. Fort Worth: Texas Christian University Press, 1997.

Westling, Louise H. *The Green Breast of the New World: Landscape, Gender, and American Fiction*. Athens: University of Georgia Press, 1996.

Williams, David L. "Prairies and Plains: The Levelling of Difference in Stegner's Wolf Willow," *American Review of Canadian Studies*, Vol. 33, No. 4 (Winter, 2003), pp. 607–16.

Williams, Don. "All the Pretty Colors of Cormac McCarthy: Has the Master of the Macabre Gone Soft?" *Chattahoochee Review*, Vol. 13 (Summer, 1993), pp. 1–7.

Woodward, Richard B. "Cormac McCarthy's Venomous Fiction," *New York Times*, April 19, 1992.

Wriglesworth, Chad. "Stegner's Wolf Willow," *The Explicator*, Vol. 62, No. 1 (Fall, 2003), pp. 42–44.

Wrobel, David. *The End of American Exceptionalism: Frontier Anxiety from the Old West to the New Deal*. Lawrence: University Press of Kansas, 1993.

Young, Thomas D., Jr. "The Imprisonment of Sensibility: *Suttree*," *Southern Quarterly*, Vol. 30, No. 4 (Summer, 1992), pp. 72–92.

History, Politics

Allen, John Logan. *Lewis and Clark and the Image of the American Northwest*. New York: Dover, 1975.

Ambrose, Stephen E. *Undaunted Courage: Meriwether Lewis, Thomas Jefferson and the Opening of the American West*. New York: Simon and Schuster, 1996.

Bakeless, John. *America as Seen by Its First Explorers: The Eyes of Discovery*. New York: Dover, 1950, 1989.

Bibby, Michael *The Vietnam War and Postmodernity*. Amherst: University of Massachusetts Press, 1999.

Brown, Dee. *Bury My Heart at Wounded Knee*. London: Vintage, 1970, 1991.

Buzzanco, Robert. *Vietnam and the Transformation of American Life*. Oxford: Blackwell, 1999

Chomsky, Noam. *Rethinking Camelot: JFK, the Vietnam War, and US Political Culture*. Cambridge, MA: Southend Press, 1993.

Chomsky, Noam, Mitchell, Peter, and Schoeffel, John, eds. *Understanding Power: The Indispensable Chomsky*. London: Vintage, 2003.

Cronon, William, Miles, George, and Gitlin, Jay, eds. *Under an Open Sky: Rethinking America's Western Past*. New York: Norton, 1992.

DeVoto, Bernard, ed. *The Journals of Lewis and Clark*. New York: Houghton Mifflin, 1953, 1997.

Fehrenbach, T.R. *Lone Star: A History of Texas and the Texans*. New York: Collier, 1980.

Fitzgerald, Frances. *Fire in the Lake: The Vietnamese and the Americans in Vietnam*. Boston: Little, Brown, 1972.

Fussell, Edwin. *Frontier: American Literature and the American West*. Princeton: Princeton University Press, 1965.

Hellman, John. *American Myth and the Legacy of Vietnam*. New York: Columbia University Press, 1986.

Herr, Michael. *Dispatches*. London: Picador, 1998.

Jefferson, Thomas. *Notes on the State of Virginia*, in *Norton Anthology of American Literature* (4th edition), Volume 1. New York: Norton, 1994.

Kaiko, Takeshi. *Into a Black Sun*. Glasgow: William Collins and Sons, 1990.

Karnow, Stanley. *Vietnam: A History*. New York: Viking, 1983.

Kutchen, Larry F. "The Neo-Turnerian Frontier," *Early American Literature*, Vol. 40, No. 1 (2005), pp. 163–71.

Lapham, Lewis H. "Mythography," *Harper's*, Vol. 304, No. 1821 (February, 2002).

Limerick, Patricia Nelson. *The Legacy of Conquest: The Unbroken Past of the American West*. New York: Norton, 1987.

Limerick, P.N., Milner, C.A., and Rankin, C.E. *Trails: Toward a New Western History*. Lawrence: University Press of Kansas, 1991.

Lind, Michael. *Vietnam the Necessary War*. New York: The Free Press, 1999.

Lora, Ronald. *America in the Sixties: Cultural Authorities in Transition*. New York: John Wiley and Sons, 1974.

McMahon, Robert J., ed. *Major Problems in the History of the Vietnam War*. Lexington, MA: D.C. Heath, 1995.

Merchant, Carolyn, ed. *Major Problems in American Environmental History*. Lexington, MA: D.C. Heath, 1993.

Milner, Clyde A., ed. *A New Significance: Re-envisioning the History of the American West*. New York: Oxford University Press, 1996.

Milner, C.A., O'Connor, C.A., and Sandweiss, M.A., eds. *Oxford History of the American West*. New York: Oxford University Press, 1994.

Milner, C.A., Butler, A.M., and Lewis, D.R., eds. *Major Problems in the History of the American West*. Boston: Houghton Mifflin, 1997.

Nicholl, Charles. *The Creature in the Map: Sir Walter Raleigh's Quest for El Dorado*. London: Vintage, 1996.

Nordhoff, Charles. *Nordhoff's West Coast: California, Oregon and Hawaii*. London: KPI, 1987 (facsimile reprint of 1874 edition).

Noy, Gary, ed. *Distant Horizons: Documents from the Nineteenth Century American West*. Lincoln: University of Nebraska Press, 1999.

Paul, Rodman W., ed. *A Victorian Gentlewoman in the Far West: The Reminiscences of Mary Hallock Foote*. San Marino, CA: Henry E. Huntington Library and Art Gallery, 1972.

Powell, J.W. *Report on the Lands of the Arid Regions*, Reports of the United States Geographical and Geological Survey of the Rocky Mountain Region. Washington, DC, 1878.

Raban, Jonathan. *Badland*. London: Picador, 1996.

Robinson, Forrest G., ed. *The New Western History: The Territory Ahead*. Tucson: University of Arizona Press, 1997.

Roper, John. *The American Presidents: Heroic Leadership from Kennedy to Clinton*. Edinburgh: Edinburgh University Press, 2000.

Rothman, Hal K. *Reopening the American West*. Tucson: University of Arizona Press, 1998.

Ruxton, George Frederick. *Wild Life in the Rocky Mountains*. New York: Macmillan, 1916; available at http://www.xmission.com/~drudy/mtman/html/ruxton.html

Stewart, George R. *Names on the Land: A Historical Account of Place-Naming in the United States*. Boston: Houghton Mifflin, 1967.

Trollope, Frances. *Domestic Manners of the Americans*. London: Century, 1984.

Turner, Frederick Jackson. *Re-reading Frederick Jackson Turner*. New Haven: Yale University Press, 1994.

—— *The Frontier in American History*. New York: Dover, 1996 (facsimile reprint of Henry Holt 1920 edition).

Walsh, Margaret. *The American West: Visions and Revisions*. Cambridge: Cambridge University Press, 2005

Ward, Geoffrey C., ed. *The West*. London: Weidenfeld & Nicholson, 1996.

White, Richard and Limerick, P.N. *The Frontier in American Culture: Essays by Richard White and Patricia Nelson Limerick*, edited by James R. Grossman. Berkeley: University of California Press, 1994.

Worster, Donald. *Under Western Skies: Nature and History in the American West*. New York: Oxford University Press, 1992.

Cultural Studies

Anderson, Benedict. *Imagined Communities*. London: Verso, 1983, 1998.

Baudrillard, Jean. *America*. London: Verso, 1988.

Bhaba, Homi. *Nation and Narration*. London: Routledge, 1990.

Branch, Michael. "You Say You Want a Revolution: Environmental Reform in the Literature of the 1860s and 1960s," *Viet Nam Generation: A Journal of Recent History and Contemporary Issues*, Vol. 5, Nos 1–4 (March, 1994), pp. 1–4.

Castaneda, A., Armitage, P., Hart, K., and Weathermon, S.H. *Gender on the Borderlands: The Frontiers Reader*. Lincoln and London: University of Nebraska Press, 2007.

Collard, A., and Contrucci, J. *Rape of the Wild: Man's Violence against Animals and the Earth*. London: Women's Press, 1988.

Davis, Mike. *City of Quartz*. London: Vintage, 1990.

—— *Ecology of Fear*. London: Picador, 1999.

De Beauvoir, Simone. *The Second Sex*, translated by H.M. Parshley. London: Picador, 1988.

Dudley, Edward, and Novak, Maximillian, eds. *The Wild Man Within*. Pittsburg: University of Pittsburg Press, 1972.

Fitzgerald, Frances. *Cities on a Hill*. New York: Simon and Schuster, 1986.

Harrison, Robert Pogue. *Forests: The Shadow of Civilization*. Chicago: University of Chicago Press, 1992.

Hutcheon, Linda. *A Poetics of Postmodernism*. London: Routledge, 1988.

—— *The Politics of Postmodernism* (2nd edition). London: Routledge, 2002.

Jameson, Frederic. *Postmodernism, or The Cultural Logic of Late Capitalism*. London: Verso, 1991.

Jarvis, Brian. *Postmodern Cartographies: The Geographical Imagination in Contemporary American Culture*. London: Pluto Press, 1998.

Kapell, Matthew. "Civilization and its Discontents: American Monomythic Structure as Historical Simulacrum," *Popular Culture Review*, Vol. 13, No. 2 (2002), pp. 129–35.

Knobloch, Frieda. *The Culture of Wilderness: Agriculture as Colonization in the American West*. Chapel Hill: University of North Carolina Press, 1996.

Mack-Canty, Colleen. "Third-Wave Feminism and the Need to Reweave the Nature/Culture Duality," *NWSA Journal*, Vol. 16, No. 3 (Fall, 2004), pp. 154–79.

Miller, John. *Egotopia: Narcissism and the New American Landscape*. Tuscaloosa: University of Alabama Press, 1997.

Moore, Michael. *Stupid White Men*. London: Penguin, 2002.

Oelschlaeger, Max. *The Idea of Wilderness*. New Haven: Yale University Press, 1991.

Pearce, Roy Harvey. *Savagism and Civilization*. Los Angeles: University of California Press, 1953, 1988.

Phillips, Dana. *The Truth of Ecology: Nature, Culture, and Literature in America*. New York: Oxford University Press, 2003.

Soja, Edward. *Postmodern Geographies: The Reassertion of Space in Critical Social Theory*. London: Verso, 1989.

Tannock, Stuart. "Nostalgia Critique," *Cultural Studies*, Vol. 9, No. 3. (1995), pp. 453–64.

Wright, Will. *The Wild West: The Mythical Cowboy and Social Theory*. London: Sage, 2001.

Landscape, Environmentalism, Geography and Nature

Abbey, Edward. *Desert Solitaire*. New York: Touchstone, 1990.

Austin, Mary. *The Land of Little Rain*. New York: Dover, 1996.

Bissell, Tom. "Eternal Winter: Lessons of the Aral Sea Disaster," *Harper's*, Vol. 304, No. 1823 (April, 2002).

Buell, Lawrence. *The Environmental Imagination: Thoreau, Nature Writing and the Formation of American Culture*. Cambridge, MA: Harvard University Press, 1996.

Butala, Sharon. *The Perfection of the Morning*. Toronto: Harper Collins, 1994.

Carson, Rachel. *Silent Spring*. New York: Houghton Mifflin, 1962.

Conzen, Michael P., ed. *The Making of the American Landscape*. London: Harper Collins, 1994.

Coupe, Laurence, ed. *The Green Studies Reader: from Romanticism to Eco-criticism*. London: Routledge, 2000.

Cronon, William, ed. "A Place for Stories: Nature, History, and Narrative," *Journal of American History*, Vol. 78 (March, 1992), pp. 1347–76.

—— *Uncommon Ground: Rethinking the Human Place in Nature*. New York: Norton, 1996.

Finkhouse, John, and Crawford, Mark, eds. *A River Too Far: The Past and Future of the Arid West*. Reno: Nevada Humanities Committee, University of Nevada Press, 1991.

Henley, D., and Marsh, D., eds. *Heaven is Under Our Feet: A Book for Walden Woods*. Berkeley: University of California Press, 1991.

Jackson, John Brinckerhoff. *Landscape in Sight: Looking at America*. New Haven: Yale University Press, 1997.

Massey, Doreen. *Space, Place and Gender*. Cambridge: Polity Press, 1994.

Massey, Doreen, Allen, John, and Sarre, Philip, *Human Geography Today*. Cambridge: Polity Press, 1999.

Mies, Maria, and Shiva, Vandana. *Ecofeminism*, Halifax, NS: Fernwood Publications, 1993.

Mitchell, W.J.T., ed. *Landscape and Power*. Chicago: University of Chicago Press, 1994.

Molyneaux, Brian Leigh. *The Sacred Earth*. London: Duncan Baird, 1995.

Muir, John. *The Mountains of California*. New York: Penguin, 1985.

Plumwood, Val. *Feminism and the Mastery of Nature*. London: Routledge, 2002.

Reisner, Marc. *Cadillac Desert: The American West and its Disappearing Water*. London: Pimlico, 2001.

Rose, Gillian. *Feminism and Geography: The Limits of Geographical Knowledge*. Cambridge: Polity Press, 1993.

Schama, Simon. *Landscape and Memory*. London: Harper Collins, 1995.

Thompson, George F., ed. *Landscape in America*. Austin: University of Texas Press, 1995.

Tuan, Yi-Fu. *Space and Place: The Perspective of Experience*. Minneapolis: University of Minnesota Press, 1997.

Wilton, Andrew, and Barringer, Tim. *American Sublime: Landscape Painting in the United States 1820 – 1880*. London: Tate Publishing, 2002.

Worster, Donald. *Nature's Economy* (2nd edition). New York: Cambridge University Press, 1994.

Mythology, Religion, Psychology and Philosophy

Burke, Edmund. *A Philosophical Enquiry into the Origins of Our Ideas of the Sublime and Beautiful.* Oxford: Oxford University Press, 1990.

Campbell, Joseph. *The Hero with a Thousand Faces.* Princeton: Princeton University Press, 1973.

Eliade, Mirceau. *The Sacred and the Profane.* New York: Harcourt Brace and World, 1959.

Jung, Carl G. *Man and His Symbols.* London: Aldus Books, 1979.

McLeish, Kenneth. *Myth.* London: Bloomsbury, 1996.

Uhlinger, Dean Lee. *Desert Light: Myths and Visions of the Great Southwest.* San Francisco: Chronicle Books, 1993.

Index